The Bookshop, the Draper, the Candlestick Maker

Annie Gray

The Bookshop, the Draper, the Candlestick Maker

A history of the high street

Profile Books

First published in Great Britain in 2024 by
Profile Books Ltd
29 Cloth Fair
London
EC1A 7JQ

www.profilebooks.com

1 3 5 7 9 10 8 6 4 2

Designed and set by EM&EN
Printed and bound in Great Britain by Clays Ltd, Elcograf S.p.A.

A CIP catalogue record for this book is available from the British Library.

ISBN 978 1 80081 2246
eISBN 978 1 80081 2260

FSC
www.fsc.org
MIX
Paper | Supporting
responsible forestry
FSC® C018072

For Matt, finally, one just for you

Contents

Introduction

On average, I walk along my local high street once a week. I live in a city, but a small one. The high street here would struggle to hold a visitor for more than half an hour (unless, like me, you are easily distracted by a good bookshop). I can buy most of what I need on a weekly basis, even without going to the city centre supermarket. We have a couple of packaging-free shops, a scattering of pharmacies, some health shops, a butcher, and various café-bakeries catering for both the flat-white-and-sour-dough-croissant brigade and the builders'-tea-and-white-sliced lovers. There's a bike shop which also sells toys, models, fabric and paint; a cookware and obscure cleaning products empo-rium with a sideline in wallpaper; a gardening/pet shop; and a sports shop which also has uniforms for the local schools. Theres's the usual array of small clothing chains, some pubs and a lot – really, quite a lot – of charity shops.

I'm a regular at only about four of these shops, plus the twice-weekly market. Some I regard with mild horror (shout out to the stinky sandwich shop and the remaindered book-shop which pumps out bubbles and has a window full of plastic tat). In the interests of full disclosure, I admit that I am not a fan of shopping for pleasure, and the idea of a Saturday morn-ing spent in the pursuit of a new outfit makes me want to run and hide.

And yet, I love my high street. I love looking in the window of the shoe shop at high heels I'd never be seen dead in; I always sniff the air as I go past the chocolate shop; and I like making faces back at the kids in the barbers as their parents tell them to sit still while they have their hair cut. In fact, I love all high streets. I find them endlessly fascinating. The need – or sometimes simple desire – to buy something specific might draw me in, but once I'm there the experience goes way beyond mere shopping.

What defines a high street? The *Oxford English Dictionary* calls it simply 'the main shopping street of a town or city', which is short, but to the point. Or how about 'the most important and liveliest shopping and commercial street of a town, or of a city district'? Other definitions add important nuances, mainly around what it is not: the high street is not privately owned (i.e. it is not a shopping mall – though a mall may appear on it); it is not suburban; and, while a lot of villages have a road called high street, it is not rural. High streets implicitly occur only in places of a certain size, though this is rarely defined, and changes depending on the era, as one century's metropolis is another's forgotten backwater.[1]

It's certainly not just about the shopping. Shops are the focus here because they are often what we mean when we talk about the high street, and because they are the key factor when we define it. But while you cannot (perhaps) have a high street without shops, they are also a background for so much more. High streets are the focal point of a town, and by extension, the communities which live in them. They are the location both residents and visitors will head to as a place of first resort, whether they seek things to buy, places to eat and drink, or ways to enjoy themselves. The high street might include services, from banks to insurance brokers, along with street performers, people shouting about politics and religion, parades and charity 'chuggers' or poppy sellers, depending on the time of year.

The high street does not have to involve spending. You might be there to look at the Christmas lights, or to gain inspiration for a new outfit. You might meet friends at a local landmark, feel inclined to put flowers on a memorial, or simply sit for a while reading a book. As well as benches, streetlights, troughs full of flowers (and not infrequently signs asking people not to nick the fuchsias) and public loos, there's also likely to be a cab rank, post boxes, and a telephone box containing a defibrillator (or unwanted books).

In larger towns, the type I'm talking about in this book, the high street is often more than just one street. The exact area might be ill-defined, encompassing several main streets and the areas between them – and the main locus might move over time.

I'm sure you can think of high streets you love and high streets you're less keen on. The modern-day cry is that the high street is dying, that the commercial and service function of such streets is increasingly gone, driven to the brink by the rise of out-of-town shopping centres, supermarkets, and the internet. In the past couple of decades thousands of independent stores have been lost, and several thousand more chain outlets have disappeared, though some brand names survive in a hollowed-out form online. But 'bricks and mortar' retail isn't alone in amassing bankruptcies or buyouts. Online retailers also go bust, and turnover within the sector is high, no matter how or where products are sold.

We talk of decline, of failure, and of empty shops and desolate shopping streets, and in some towns and high streets there's an undeniable sense of shabbiness. Areas with high levels of deprivation (and low levels of tourism) inevitably have more forlorn high streets – though it's important not to assume they aren't still meeting the needs of the local population just because they don't have anywhere with stripped-back walls and overpriced coffee. Every town is different: every high street is as well. Ninety-eight per cent of the British public say they'd care at least a bit if their local high street disappeared; the fact that we are even asking this question shows how bad the outlook seems to be.[2]

The high street definitely isn't what it used to be. But should we really couch this in terms of failure? Would we not be better off, perhaps, talking simply of change? Certainly, twenty or thirty years ago high streets were busier, with more desirable shops, and plenty of them. Most of us will have warm fuzzy feelings over particular stores which defined our teenage years, glossing over terrible changing-rooms or the fact that pick 'n' mix wasn't actually that great. We can all see the changes wrought by the last few decades, and we are all aware of the discourse surrounding the modern high street.

There have always been debates, though, and many of them aren't new. Throughout history we've argued over luxury and necessity, over the morality of spending, and over the way in which shopping encourages us all to be rapacious, wasteful and rude – or not. We've struggled to square the enjoyment of personal service with the desire for speed and ease. And we've argued over small shops versus big shops, chains versus independents, and what, exactly, should be the rules governing shopkeepers and shoppers alike.

Meanwhile the role of women has been continually contentious, with shop assistants in the past often assumed to be selling their bodies as well as their wares, and female shoppers portrayed as spendthrift and feckless, especially when they did not – or more usually could not – earn for themselves the money they were so happy to spend.

We haven't resolved any of these questions, though we may have added a few more. Whichever era you fetch up in, you'll find yourself considering capitalism and consumerism, along with the balance of power between producers, consumers and retailers.

This book comes out of my interest in food, specifically the procurement of it. An awful lot of shopping is for food, and historically a significant part of our weekly budget was spent on it – around a third of household income for the majority of people in the late nineteenth century, dropping to around a fifth in the 1950s.[3] Although the earliest shops were as likely to be jewellers or swordsmiths as bakers or butchers, food was – and is – crucial to the high street, whether in the form of shops, restaurants, pubs or street vendors.

For a long time, writing about the high street centred on the idea of a 'revolution', both in consumerism and retail practice. Questions over when this 'revolution' took place have dominated academic discourse, and have seeped into popular mentality, giving rise to a vague feeling that it all started quite suddenly in the middle of the nineteenth century. But apparent markers of modernity such as fixed shops, the encouragement of browsing, shopping for pleasure and cash sales came in gradually and co-existed with earlier practice for decades, if not centuries. Likewise, it's important not to see the modern high street as some sort of culmination of centuries of forward development. What we have now – like at any other time – is simply an evolutionary point. Older forms of accessing goods – via markets, pedlars, barter with neighbours or friends, or, indeed, by making them ourselves – have not been eclipsed by shops because they are somehow more modern or 'better'. A new way of doing something does not necessarily push out an old one, and the path to where we are today is not a linear one.

I've chosen to concentrate on certain key shops, and specifically the products found in them, which are (mostly) still a part of the high street today. In each main chapter we'll start with a shopping list, and an idea of the shopper behind it. Over the course of the book, we'll visit grocers and bookshops, toyshops and clothing stores, shoe shops and pharmacies, among others. There were many other types of shop, some of which were present for hundreds of years, others of which lasted only a short time, to which I've devoted less space. You'll find only passing mention of tobacconists, saddlers, bookmakers, music dealers and whitesmiths (a type of metal worker), for example. I've also chosen not to cover services, like banks or barbers, and you'll only see the occasional reference to sellers which were always on the periphery of the high street, such as pawnbrokers and second-hand clothing dealers.

I won't be taking you physically far away from the high street at all, though you will find yourself reading about the market, for its relationship with the high street is long and significant. And, of course, we'll stop to eat. You'll also be invited to walk down some high streets, at various points in time, to see what it all looks like on the ground.

We're going to concentrate on the period between 1650 and 1965. While shopping for pleasure certainly existed prior to then, the mid-seventeenth century is generally acknowledged to be the earliest time we can properly identify a high street in the larger towns and cities of the UK. This is when we see clusters of fixed shops in one location, and a sense that those shops may be pleasurable as well as practical.[4] It's a time of seismic change in Britain, when revolution, civil war and the short-lived English Republic all impacted upon people's beliefs and behaviours. Since nothing exists in a vacuum, and the gradual nature of change is one of the key themes of this book, we'll start by looking at what came before. Likewise, although the main part of the book stops just before most of us can really remember what the high street looked like, all the elements of the modern high street are present by then, so the last chapter really just brings the story up to date.

It's impossible not to view the past through the present and make comparisons. Sometimes it is in the physicality of shopping – exchanges are a bit like malls, and bazaars are a bit like department stores. Sometimes it's in the way in which people talk about the high street: a sense of 'use it or lose it', or debates over ethics or morals which lead some people to get disproportionately angry, whether that's about temperance hotels or vegan cafés. It's not wrong to compare, and to use our own experiences to make sense of the past. But we shouldn't take it too far, and we should remember that within the parameters of each era the high street always reflected the needs and desires of the people who used it.

It's time, now, to leave the modern era behind, and to go back to where it all started. Let's head, not exactly to the high street, but to the market, the church, and the centre of a typical British town.

Chapter One

Up to the 1650s

I saw in this crowd as you shall hear later.
Bakers and brewers and butchers a-many,
Woollen-websters and weavers of linen,
Tailors and tinkers, toll-takers in markets,
Masons and miners and men of all crafts.
Of all kinds of labourers there stood forth some;
Ditchers and diggers that do their work ill
And spend all the day singing 'Dieu vous sauve, dame Emme!'
Cooks and their knaves cried 'Pies, hot pies!
Good pork and good goose! Come, dine! Come, dine!'[1]

– William Langland, *Piers Plowman* (1360s–1380s)

When William Langland wrote his allegorical poem *Piers Plowman* in the late fourteenth century, he included people and crafts his reader would know. Makers and vendors of food, drink and cloth jostled in his dreamscape with the people who would buy their wares. They formed a crowd in the marketplace, surrounded by cookshops and taverns crying for custom. The scene was busy, noisy and full of smells. It was, in short, a pretty typical, albeit fictional, market day in a medieval town.

For most of history, shopping has been focused on the market, and what we'd now call the high street developed around the market area. Until at least the eighteenth century – and in many cases well beyond – acquiring everyday goods meant going to the market. Even the term for buying food and other basic items reflected this: not shopping, but marketing. To get there, you might walk down a Market Street or a Broad Street. But there were also High Streets. The term was in use by Anglo-Saxon times, and simply meant the main road. Sometimes it was literally high, raised above other roads into the town by dint of repeated resurfacing or being shored up against flooding.

God versus goods

Until the thirteenth century, you'd probably have found the market in the churchyard. Religion was an integral part of medieval life, and the central focus of any town was its church, along with civic buildings such as guildhalls (the guild in this case being the town corporation or council, and the term guildhall simply meaning town hall). It made sense to locate the market at this easily identifiable point. Then came the Black Death pandemic of 1348–52, which caused a population drop of 30–40 per cent. In its wake, more of those left moved into towns. By the end of the century twenty-seven towns had a population of more than 2,500, and town authorities found themselves having to rethink the way urban space was organised to cope with population pressure. Market day could bring hundreds of extra bodies into a town, with all the potential for disruption and annoyance to permanent residents that implied – along, of course, with the opportunity to sell stuff to visitors who were there for that exact purpose.

New, planned marketplaces were the answer. They were regulated by town law, with the town authorities, or sometimes the local aristocrat or other owning body, profiting from rents and other fees, such as fines for breaking the many rules that were imposed, but frequently ignored. The right to hold a market was a coveted one, denoting a change in status as the town was recognised as a local hub by Royal Charter (hence the phrase charter market). Markets quickly became a focal point, not just for retail, but also for food and drink, plus other activities such as public performance, protest and the enacting of punishments. Visiting the marketplace, you might listen to a public proclamation or pause to wonder what the unfortunate person in the stocks had done. Perhaps you'd have your pocket picked while trying to fathom how a conjuror was making a ball jump from one cup to another.

The church was still important though. Many of these medieval marketplaces were sited with the church at one end or very close, retaining the link between feeding body and soul, and reminding you that earthly goods were as nothing compared to what lay beyond. Even when they moved away from the churchyard, they retained the market cross, or one was newly constructed. In Malmesbury, Wiltshire, the market cross was explicitly erected so that 'persons which resort hither in

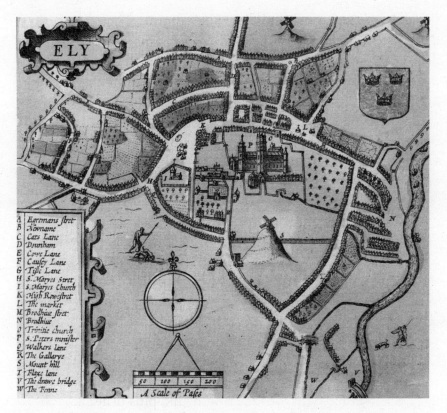

A Egremans ſtreet
B Nowname
C Cats Lane
D Downham
E Cowe Lane
F Cauſey Lane
G Tiple Lane
H S. Maryes Stret
I S. Maryes Church
K High Rowe ſtret
L The market
M Brodhiue ſtret
N Brodhiue
O Trinitie church
P S. Peters mniſter
Q Walkers lane
R The Gallarye
S Mount hill
T Flaxe lane
V Tho drawe bridge
W The Fenne

A Scale of Paſes

Fig. 1.1. Ely, Cambridgeshire, in 1611. *L* is the market complete with cross and scattered infill buildings, and the street leading from *L* to *K* is the high street.

market ouvert might think upon their dear Saviour which died for them upon the Crosse, of which this fair Market Crosse is a sign and symbol; to the end that rogues and cozeners may look upon it and cease them of their guile'.[2] It was hardly subtle. However, as uplifting as linking Jesus and the renouncing of dodgy dealings sounded in practice, in reality the crosses quickly became a focus for materiality, in the form of mainly female butter sellers who came in from the surrounding farms for the day. The plinths upon which the crosses stood were useful for laying out wares, and they were an obvious focal

Fig. 1.2. Malmesbury Market Cross in 1845. Erected around 1490, with lavish sculptures of saints and a carving of the crucifixion. This picture was published about fifty years after a significant renovation project. The cross remains in situ.

point for finding a product which benefited from early buying, before the sun got up, the dust rose, and you risked ending up with rancid, gritty butter. Eventually, in some towns, the cross became known as the butter cross, sometimes now with a roof added to provide shelter. Surviving examples include those in Oakham, Canterbury and Barnard Castle.

Retail was surrounded with suspicion. It was very tightly regulated, the three major crimes being engrossing, forestalling and regrating. Engrossing and forestalling referred to the practice of buying goods wholesale, or before they reached the market, thereby denying the individual consumer the chance to buy them direct from the seller. Regrating was the inevitable result, whereby the offender was found to be selling goods on at a profit. There was a great deal of colourful language aimed in the direction of the evil middlemen, and the dislike ran very deep and continued for a very long time. One bill of 1593 declared on-sellers of yarn to be 'wanting the fear of God, and caring only for their own private gain'.[3] All of this was predicated on the idea that market traders were also producers: that markets were the means by which small-scale farmers and artisans might sell a little of their surplus produce, or the fruits of their hard labour, to an innocent populace that must be protected from unscrupulous individuals who sought only to make money from other people's hard work. A vague belief that households should be mainly self-sufficient, only buying what they could not produce, also underlay this, along with moral concerns over luxury and consumption, and a sense that financial profit was wrong.

As refreshing as this view might sound today, as we confront nightmare tales of long supply chains and worker exploitation, it was unrealistic even then; rose-tinting the past before it had even really become the past. It ignored the idea that producers might be better off producing, allowing others with more time, inclination and aptitude to act as a bridge between them and the end consumer. It also side-stepped the fact that very few households really were self-sufficient, and that most didn't want to be. Whether you made your own clothes or used a tailor, you still needed to buy cloth and trimmings. And while some grew vegetables or farmed livestock, if you lived in a town, you probably didn't.

Town or country, buying pork or butchering your own pig, you'd doubtless want to enliven plain, home-grown meals. Imported foodstuffs included spices such as pepper, which was readily available and eagerly consumed, not just by the rich, but also by the middle tier of society – merchants and master craftsmen as opposed to nobles. By the sixteenth century even the upper working classes had the occasional bit of disposable income, working hard to have some extra money precisely to spend on something they didn't or couldn't produce themselves. Buying such goods was fun. They made food taste better and clothes look nicer and made life, in general, more comfortable. Plus, bought goods were expensive and a marker of status, and status has always been a reason to splash the cash.

The fair

In any case, the wholesale trade was not only well established, but even had its own network of markets, or, more properly, fairs. Most regions had one (or more). They were huge events, taking place over several days, and bringing in buyers and sellers from across the country and beyond. For the rich, whether private individuals, or institutions such as religious houses or university colleges, they were important for bulk-buying for the year ahead. Meanwhile merchants with an eye to the dark practice of regrating would also attend, in search of stock to sell on to a wealthy clientele. Expensive, one-off purchases could be made, for the variety of goods on offer was enormous, far beyond the simple market in terms of both quantity and quality. Fairs attracted massive crowds with people travelling for days or weeks to attend, and, while selling was their main function, you'd also expect to enjoy a lot of drinking, eating and general carousing.

Some fairs took place within the city boundaries, spilling out from market squares to invade the whole town. In York, the regulations for the Monday after Ascension Day fair listed the area designated for each type of trader, including: 'Cloth from Leeds, Halifax, Wakefield, Bradford and those parts in the street from the Common Hall up towards Stayngate [Stone-gate]. Cloth from Kendal, Ripon, Knaresborough . . . in the street from Common Hall to Conynstrete [Coney Street]. All goldsmiths, jewellers, vestmentmakers, silkwomen, mercers, grocers and hardwaremen in Petergate . . . all pewters, founders and metallers in Colliergate. All ironmongers and all other ironware in Fossgate. All hatmakers, saddlers, glovers, coopers, turners . . . in Walmgate.' It went on, adding cartwrights, ale sellers, salt merchants, bedsellers, mattress makers, tanners and shoemakers, among others, to the list, and stating firmly that the poulterers must not 'keep their stuff in houses or hostelries, upon pain of forfeiture'.[4] The sense of incipient unruliness lurks just below the surface throughout.

Unsurprisingly, it was easier to hold your fair outside the urban area, in a set location whose spillover potential and mischief-making could include neighbouring fields, rather than the dwellings of the townspeople. Around Stourbridge Common in Cambridgeshire, which by the late medieval period hosted the largest fair in Europe, farmers had to agree to harvest any crops before August 24th or they would simply be trampled beneath the press of feet, hooves and claws.[5] It must have taken the best part of a year for the ground to fully recover – though at least the level of effluent would have provided for free manure.

Fairs were a big part of medieval and Tudor life, but by the seventeenth century, with middlemen more established, and trading conditions in towns changing, they were slowly declining, the stallholders changing from mainly traders to mainly entertainers. Most died out, though some, such as the Nottingham Fair, survived, or were re-established, and exist purely as funfairs today. Some became associated briefly with specific goods – Nottingham has been known as the Goose Fair since at least the 1540s. (If you want modern proof that the spirit of the fair's medieval iteration still lurks beneath, look out for the pulled sugar lollipop known as cock-on-a-stick.)

The market

Back to the everyday, and in the town itself, a royal charter would allow for at least one all-purpose market on one day a week. The ideal was that market traders lived in the surrounds of the town, or had workshops within it, and sold their wares from strictly temporary premises. However, while some sellers were small-scale, selling a few excess eggs or some vegetables only at one local market, others were already more focused on selling, and traded at several different markets across the week. Although food was the biggest element, you could buy almost anything: cloth and shoes, ironmongery and household wares, consumables such as candles – imagine it and someone would try and sell you it. There was also a flourishing trade in used goods and in mending items past their best.

As towns grew, so too did their markets, and zoning became vital, both for the consumer, so that they could easily locate the goods they were after, and the practical functioning of the town. Some trades were particularly smelly, such as fish selling; others were messy, such as butchery. Leatherwork combined both stench and mess, as tanners relied on urine and excrement to tan their hides and were the cause of endless complaints from anyone unlucky enough to be even a vague neighbour. Civic authorities did their best to curb the worst excesses. In Coventry butchers were bound to bury bloody waste outside the city limits while avoiding 'filthy operations', such as singeing stubble off carcasses, within the market area.[6] Markets could be just as hard to contain as fairs, especially as the population grew and the number of traders increased, in recognition of which authorities followed the example set by fairs and laid out where exactly each trader should set up, as well as exhorting them to behave responsibly. In larger towns, the main market might also be supplemented by auxiliary affairs, specialising in certain goods – think corn, hay, wood and flowers.

London, of course, was the best example of this, as it was by far the biggest city in the country even then. Its markets constantly overflowed from the streets and squares intended to contain them, leading to tension with residents and other road users. One edict laid out that 'all manner of victuals that are sold by persons in Chepe [Cheapside], upon Cornhill and else-where in the city, such as bread, cheese, poultry, fruit, hides and skins, onions and garlic, and all other small victuals, for sale as well by denizens as by strangers, shall stand midway between the kennels [gutters] of the streets, so as to be a nuisance to no-one, under pain of forfeiture of the article'.[7] If you were a Londoner, you could find fish and meat at Stocks Market; flowers and vegetables on Cheapside, along with poultry and dairy; more meat, this time from out-of-town sellers, on Newgate Street, and many more.

Visitors were awed at the sheer level of produce which poured into the city, with one commenting that 'it is extraordinary to see the great quantity and quality of the meat – beef and mutton – that comes every day from the slaughterhouses in this city, let alone the meat that is sold at a special market [Leadenhall] every Wednesday for meat brought in from outside the city'.[8] The names of many streets across Britain still reflect their medieval purpose, and even in the much rebuilt City of London you can still walk along Bread Street, Milk Street and Poultry Street. The latter was at one stage known as the even more graphic Scalding Lane (from the habit of scalding poultry with boiling water to slightly melt the fat and enable easier plucking). Smaller towns may have fewer such evocatively named streets, but you don't have to look far to find a Butter-market, Cornmarket or Shambles. The latter, of which the most famous example is in York, was a meat-selling area, the term coming from the Old English for table or counter, in this case used for butchery.

By the end of the sixteenth century around 800 towns had a marketplace, and acted, therefore, as local shopping hubs.[9] But don't imagine that the unruliness, mess and annoyance was really confined to only one day a week. While they might have been conceived of as open spaces, with strictly temporary stalls, marketplace stallholders were busy circumventing the rules pretty much as soon as they were in place.[10] Even if a stallholder planned to open only once a week, there were very good reasons to prefer a more permanent selling place than just a table and – if you were lucky – a basic roof under which to find shelter.

Leading the way were butchers who really liked the idea of a permanent shambles, constructed to enable easy sluicing down and access for live animals. In this they were fully supported by landowners, who saw the construction of more permanent structures as a way of increasing rents. If you'd wandered through a market from the fourteenth century onwards, the chances are you'd find a butchers' shambles occupying one end, now with wooden houses. The usual construction had two storeys and secure doors with shuttered hatches and a table for cutting outside on the street. Other traders followed. The attraction was obvious: a fixed premises meant you could lock stock up and keep it on site, rather than having to lug it from a workshop or abattoir. It also meant you could build something which gave a level of protection from the elements for you, your customers and your stock. Infilling of market squares became rife. Opening on more than just market day quickly followed.

It wasn't just traders and private landowners who saw the usefulness of permanent structures (and the potential profits which could be derived via extended opening and higher rates). Civic authorities also got in on the act. Not content with roofed butter crosses, now some towns built larger shelters for temporary stalls. Some were effectively open-sided barns; others had upper storeys housing guildhalls or courts, or incorporated ground-floor fixed shops.[11] In many towns, the church also built rows of shops on their land (after all, why should the town and local aristocrat get all the glory and rental income?). York has a good example in the shape of Lady Row: one of the earliest surviving examples of a jettied building. Today five tiny shops huddle together under a protruding first floor and long, single roof which parallels the street. As built, there were eleven bays, with the bottom rooms almost certainly occupied by workshops.[12]

None of this was exactly radical. The market may have been the main way in which people shopped, but there were fixed, permanent shops and other facilities surrounding every marketplace. Small, one-room lock-ups within larger buildings had been a feature of towns since the Roman era, usually housing businesses that needed fire, which was not a great idea in an open market made largely from wood; understandably they were often banned. Examples included glassblowing and metalwork, but also one of the other big draws of the high street, the making and vending of cooked food. You could expect any established marketplace to be surrounded by alehouses and taverns (often in cellars), along with bakers and cookshops selling pies and baked goods for take-away and immediate consumption.

Some, possibly most, of these early shops were so in both senses of the word – they sold stuff, but they were also workshops. People were supposed to make things in a workshop and sell them at the market, but they weren't exactly going to turn would-be customers away if they turned up at the shop. Thus, in fixed premises slightly away from the market you could find furniture makers, ironmongers, shoemakers, potters, chandlers (candlemakers), saddlers, buckle makers, wiredrawers, cutlers, hosiers (for hose, long trousers not coming in for a few more centuries), button makers and more. Again, London's makers

Fig. 1.3. Lady Row (Our Lady's Row), Goodramgate, York, built 1316–17, much altered since. This picture was taken *c.*1893.

and sellers led the way in turning workshops into selling shops and moving the focus for buying away from the market. One visitor in 1500 declared that 'in a single street called "the street" leading to St Paul's there are fifty-two goldsmith's shops, so rich and full of silver vessels, great and small, that in all the shops in Milan, Rome, Venice and Florence together it seems to me you would not find so many of such magnificence as you would find in London'.[13] These weren't just workshops with a selling bench, but properly set-up shops in the full sense of the word.[14]

It was clear that some sellers were not even pretending to be makers, and the vitriol directed against regraters in general became increasingly focused on shopkeepers. One of Elizabeth I's Privy Councillors fulminated against them in 1577, declaring them 'not worthy of the name of merchants, but of hucksters, of chapmen of choice, who retailing small wares, are not able to better their own estate but with falsehood, lying and perjury'.[15] He was fighting a war which was already lost. By 1600, Norwich, a town of around 12,000 people, already had 111 tailors, 60 grocers, 51 shoemakers, 36 butchers, 18 mercers (silks) and drapers (cloth), 13 barbers, 10 haberdashers, 8 cutlers, 7 apothecaries, 5 fishmongers, 4 goldsmiths, 3 stationers and 2 ironmongers – plus the thriving market.

The shops

What form did these shops and other premises take? They were as varied then as they are now. Many were still the single room lock-up style units you'd have been familiar with at any point over the last few centuries. Some were inserted into (or tacked on to) the ground floors of dwellings built at right angles to the street, on long, narrow plots which might well not have changed since the Romans, or perhaps the Vikings, if they'd settled where you lived. Others were inserts within civic buildings. You might find one room, or more, and those which had infilled the market in particular often had two floors, with the upper floor used for storage – or living space. Still more might be in converted undercrofts or cellars. Then there were selling spaces that were effectively showrooms in merchants' own private houses, accessible only to the wealthy, who might dine or drink with the merchant as part of closing the deal. The rise of such merchants, buying directly from continental suppliers and selling on to the rich, was another reason for the decline of the medieval fairs. Now the aspiring aristocrat could deal with a convenient merchant at any point in the year, no longer having to wait for an annual shindig, or risk rubbing shoulders with the hoi polloi who'd come to drink and not buy serious things for serious money.

Fig. 1.4. 26 Market Place, Lavenham. Built *c.* 1500 as a domestic house, with a shop occupying the front room of the ground floor. The stall boards visible here may originally have been on the inside, forming a counter, moved outside at an unknown date. The building was later converted into a pub and later still (*c.* 1855) a chapel. It is now a National Trust tea rooms.

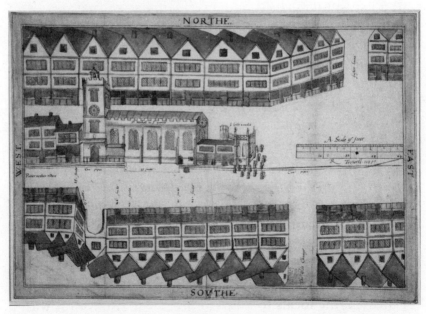

Fig. 1.5. Cheapside, London, 1538. Every house has a bulk (wooden stall) added to the lower storey, with open windows for selling. There are even bulks up against the church, while the buildings to the right may have started as temporary stalls. The ornate structure to the far right of the church is a water conduit, surrounded by jugs.

Very occasionally, small clusters of shops were built which were truly splendid, designed to enable walking, browsing and socialising, as was the case in Chester. The Chester Rows were built somewhere between the thirteenth and fourteenth centuries and consisted not only of vaulted cellars and ground-floor units, but also of a second storey with a covered walkway forming a gallery containing even more shops.

Given the variety of shops, it's not surprising that the experience of visiting them differed greatly as well. Most were tiny, certainly not intended for a would-be customer to enter. In Lavenham, Suffolk, there was a shop measuring 3.65m by 2.4m (roughly 12ft by 8ft, or around the size of a very short parking space). The units on London's Cheapside were about the same size, though the coveted corner sites could be significantly smaller – down to 1.2m (4ft) square (equivalent to the space taken up by four washing machines).[16] You'd interact with the shopkeeper through the window, which was unglazed, large, and protected at night with sturdy shutters. Larger shops did encourage people to enter, especially where security was a concern, or if you were wealthy and might need to be cosseted a bit, for example in a goldsmiths or spice merchant.

Markets were generally only allowed to trade during daylight hours, another example of the level of distrust surrounding the selling of goods. Light meant visibility – markets tended to be cramped and murky even during the day – which apparently encouraged honesty. Some towns restricted shops to similar hours (or tried to). In general, however, they were open for as long as there was trade. In larger towns, that meant being open for much of the day, making the most of passing trade, as well as encouraging locals to make a special trip, safe in the knowledge that the shop would be open.

The seld

Along with markets and shops on open streets came another experiment in providing a venue for people to trade. First established in the twelfth century but lasting until the sixteenth, meet the seld. Selds were privately owned, and therefore not open to the level of public exhibition and freedom associated with the main high street and market experience. The name was sometimes used to describe long, narrow lines of market stalls, but quickly came to mean a permanent hall containing tens of small booths, each leased to a different trader. They tended to be located behind the main street frontage, found by heading down a narrow alleyway from the shopping area, and while louvres in the roof let in air and some light, they were almost certainly as gloomy inside as any market. However, they were not really intended for the casual wanderer, instead aiming squarely at those in search of something specific. Most specialised in one type of product and therefore occupied a space somewhere between a wholesaler at a fair and a large market trader. In Winchester you could find different selds for wool and linen traders, while in Middlewich, Cheshire, a seld was set aside for traders coming from beyond the immediate region. London had selds for glovers, girdlemakers and leather tanners. Unlike markets, selds weren't primarily about food, though some had cellars, containing the inevitable taverns; they were also open every day.[17]

Selds thrived for around 250 years. However, the underlying idea did not go away. They provided lots of choice to the shopper, and lots of shoppers for the merchants, conveniently grouped under one, permanent, roof; we'll see several different iterations as we travel through the centuries.

The philosophy of shopping

By the early sixteenth century, ideas about shopping were changing. Towns just kept on growing, through both population increase and migration. More permanent residents in a town meant a greater need for vendors to open throughout the week, not just on market day, and not just from a stall. The strict system of controls over selling was crumbling. The medieval guild system, which had governed entry to professions including any form of craft, baking and butchery, was breaking down, and over the next couple of centuries the surviving guilds would become charitable and educational organisations, rather than governing bodies for their respective trades.

Another mark of the changes in society was the end of the sumptuary laws, which had previously laid down who could buy what according to class, therefore restricting the number of potential customers for a wide range of goods. Examples of sumptuary laws include rulings on who could eat turkey and swan (and how many of each), as well as who had the right to wear silk, fur and velvet. They were widely flouted. One London servant, arrested in 1565, was accused of wearing 'a very monstrous and outrageous great pair of hose' (of which sadly no pictorial evidence survives).[18] By the late sixteenth century sumptuary laws were used more explicitly as a stimulus to internal trade: one Act of 1571 stated that all men over the age of six should wear a wool bonnet (cap) on a Sunday. The laws were finally repealed in England in 1604 (it took until 1701 in Scotland). Subsequent attempts to occasionally reintroduce them were more of a thinly disguised way of raising tax, while demonstrating an outward desire to help British industry. Steep fines were levied for flouters, but the rich, eager to be buried in imported silk rather than British wool, were happy to pay.

Underlying the sumptuary laws was a continued moral unease over the consumption of luxury goods, along with the knowledge that luxury often meant imported, and imported meant money leaving the country. But the population who could afford such goods was growing, and the number of potential imports was increasing too. Trade with the Americas was booming, both through Spain and, by the early seventeenth century, directly through the establishment of British colonies. Trade routes to the East had also improved, so there were just more foreign goods around.[19] It became increasingly difficult to disapprove wholly of regrating as a sign of moral depravity, since an Indian calico maker was hardly in a position to journey to Britain to sell his or her cloth, and a trapper just back from Newfoundland didn't necessarily have the skills to sell his own furs directly to the end wearer. Of course, you might still disapprove of the idea of buying the calico in the first place, when a nice Irish linen would do the same thing – except linen wasn't cotton, and calicos were printed, and really much prettier and lighter – and don't you want your wife/daughter/sister/lover to look her finest? They were just one of a burgeoning range of new and interesting things to buy.

If you weren't swayed by a cotton calico, you might still find your head (and purse) turned by tobacco. Tobacco was introduced in the late sixteenth century and quickly became highly desirable, and with it all the accoutrements of smoking, the most obvious of which were pipes. Clay pipes are perhaps the first example of disposable consumer goods: while they were intended for multiple uses, the brittle clay meant they broke easily, and seventeenth- and eighteenth-century archaeological digs turn up a multitude of clay pipe stems (which were also used as wig curlers).

Then there was wallpaper, which was enthusiastically seized upon as a way of redecorating in fantastical ways at a relatively reasonable cost. The earliest wallpapers date to the start of the sixteenth century, but it was in the seventeenth century that they became more popular, a rise which was based on its affordability to middle-class consumers.[20] And, of course, there was food, an area of significant change. By 1600 the slow spread of ingredients from the New World via Spain and Portugal to England meant that culinary delights such as the sweet potato, the standard potato and the Jerusalem artichoke were either reaching, or on the cusp of reaching, British kitchens (all of these were referred to as potato, which is challenging when deciphering contemporary recipes). Other New World imports included turkey and squashes, both of which were rapidly naturalised.

By the mid-seventeenth century, chocolate, tea and coffee were creeping into the diet of the rich, along with pineapples, chillies, tomatoes, plus a lot of new brassicas from Italy. Sugar was planted in Cyprus, Madeira and then the West Indies, and you might also enjoy the increasing availability of previously very expensive spices from Indonesia. Much of this was driven by western European countries including Spain, Portugal and, slightly later, Britain, pursuing aggressive policies of colonialisation and exploitation of foreign lands and workers, an approach which would sadly become the norm by the end of the seventeenth century. This included the introduction of slavery to the New World, which was partly driven by European demand for ever cheaper tobacco and sugar.

All of this led, slowly, to an attitude change. Internal trade, shopping for luxuries, and a focus on selling rather than making and selling were very slowly recast as good, not bad. As we grapple with the environmental and social impact of consumerism today, a lot of these arguments still resonate. Views differ as to how much is too much, to what extent a love of luxury goods is morally wrong, and how to balance the needs of producers with the desires of consumers in an inequitable world. By the end of the seventeenth century some commentators were openly arguing that any economic activity was publicly valuable, setting themselves against the majority who continued to rail against conspicuous consumption, the cash economy and the growth of shopping both as a trade and a leisure activity.

Most notably, in 1714 Bernard Mandeville published *The Fable of the Bees*, subtitled *Private Vices, Publick Benefits*. His arguments went well beyond justifying shopping for pleasure and fed into enlightenment debates over economic theory and the nature of virtue. By pointing out that 'Fickleness in diet, furniture and dress' was, while nominally a vice, also 'the very wheel that turned the trade', he articulated the idea that spending money – buying stuff – was beneficial. He applauded the desire to show off and spend money: 'if none were to drink Wine but such only as stand in need of it, nor any Body more than his Health requir'd, that Multitude of Wine-Merchants, Vintners, Coopers, &c. that make such a considerable Show in this flourishing City, would be in a miserable Condition. The same may be said not only of Card and Dice-makers, that are the immediate Ministers to a Legion of Vices; but of Mercers, Upholsterers, Tailors, and many others, that would be starv'd in half a Year's time, if Pride and Luxury were at once to be banished the Nation.'[21]

He was, at this point, a voice in the wilderness, at least in print, and the debate continued well into the eighteenth century, largely carried out in much-plagiarised polemical rants, plays and occasionally well-reasoned books. If you wished to engage with the debates and read the outpourings of words, you could indulge yourself by buying a range of pamphlets from a bookseller – who was quite possibly no longer printing his or her own books, but simply binding the loose pages and selling the results, making them part of the very nexus of simple retailers that some of the works they were selling criticised so much. But then, as now, most people just got on with it, making peace with any ethical concerns they might have, according to their desire to engage – or not – with the wider context of their actions.

The war of words didn't really matter. Angry as some writers became, the fixed shop was a *fait accompli* by the time the debates around consumption and easy access to goods beyond the necessitous heated up. Food shopping remained overwhelmingly market-based, but cloth and other less ephemeral items were now much less so. By 1600 even small towns had permanent traders – Wem in Shropshire counted a grocer, five mercers, a draper, a chandler and eight chapmen (a general trader at the bottom of the hierarchy of shopping specialisms). They may well have been trading from very basic premises, but the fact that the probate records of the time listed them at their address by their trade suggests that they kept stock and sold merchandise from that location.[22] Inventory data, which is very rich for the seventeenth century, shows that many shopkeepers kept a great deal of stock. It was one of the reasons they moved towards having a fixed shop in the first place – and increasingly town authorities saw this as potentially beneficial. The medieval trope of the cunning profiteer buying up everything and hoarding it until prices went up was now replaced by the (sort of) public-spirited food trader maintaining enough stores to feed a population in time of trouble. This was, after all, still a time when the plague swept over towns relatively regularly, necessitating lockdowns and curfews, and there was always a perceived risk of starvation if supply lines were too last-minute.

Still, the act of selling goods without making them, and buying out of desire rather than necessity, wasn't afforded acceptance straight away. Moral tensions over wastefulness and luxury lurked in the background, bubbling through into popular discourse before disappearing for a while but never truly dying. A deep-seated distrust of shopkeepers, and fear of being ripped off, underlay much of the discourse on the development of retail. But it was complicated; too much concentration on the debates around consumption ignores the wider context of the high street, which, by the middle of the seventeenth century, was recognisably a place for far more than just shopping.

Leisure is central to modern definitions of the high street. Yes, there are shops, but we also head there to walk (or jog), to browse, meet friends, and eat, drink and generally make merry. By the seventeenth century some towns – the larger, wealthier ones – inarguably had areas based around retail, but which were used more broadly for leisure. The concept was fraught with class tension: to have leisure time implied wealth, which led back to arguments about frittering away time and money. Worse still, it turned out even the less well-off quite enjoyed spending time around the developing high street, especially since there wasn't actually a need to spend money. How dare they stroll the shops when they should have been working to generate wealth for their employers?! There were opportunities to be had in catering to this nascent leisure market, enticing people who weren't looking to spend money into doing just that. The offerings on our high streets have always been solutions to the challenges posed at each specific time. Let's look at one of the most salient early examples of this: the exchanges of seventeenth-century London.

The exchanges

Visit the Royal Exchange today, and you'll find yourself in a mid-Victorian building, full of high-end shops and a lot of eating places. It's the third iteration of the building, and the only one of four British exchanges to survive. The Royal Exchange was the first to be built, in the 1570s. Its roots lay partly in the selds of the previous centuries, as well as in medieval market halls lined with stalls (or indeed the Roman Forums whose colonnades were filled with trestles and traders). Closer

Fig. 1.6. The Royal Exchange, London, *c.*1680. This is the second iteration of the Royal Exchange, after the first was destroyed in the 1666 Great Fire of London. It was again destroyed by fire in 1838, and rebuilt six years later. Extensively renovated in 2001, the building still houses luxury shops and restuarants.

to home lay London's Westminster Hall, home to two of the law courts, which was both a public building and a shopping site, as retailers set up fairly basic – but permanent – booths along the sides. The stalls took advantage of a captive clientele of lawyers, being mainly stationers and booksellers, plus quick-selling – and easily locked away at night – portable wares. Thomas Gresham, who masterminded the Royal Exchange, took this idea and added in inspiration from the Antwerp Bourse, a grandiose building that provided a practical space for merchants to meet, with cover, privacy and safety guaranteed, as well as being

a statement of wealth and intent. Gresham was a canny operator who managed to get the London Aldermen on board to buy
the land, while he employed an architect and covered (most of)
the building costs.

The result was something quite new. Unlike the selds,
hidden behind the main streets and aimed mainly at other
merchants, this was resplendent, with grand archways at the
entrance, and a tall bell tower marking out the location. The
only other buildings as tall were the spires of the various
churches, also furnished with bells, making the exchange into
an unsubtle declaration that trade might just be as important
as religion. On the ground floor, which was all black and white
marble flooring and private rooms for conducting business,
the merchants gathered. Above them, on a linked series of first-
floor galleries, were shops. Visiting, you might also have heard
the galleries called walks, promenades or malls. The number of
shops fluctuated between 100 and 160, suggesting strongly that
they were more akin to wooden booths than entirely permanent structures, and that flexibility was built into the concept
from the very start. It was, importantly, and unlike the streets
surrounding it, privately owned, and as tightly regulated as any
medieval market. The merchants came straight away, enjoying
the shelter, the prestige, and the fact that they now had a central hub for receiving post, hearing the latest news, putting up
notices and networking.

Initially the shopkeepers were less keen. Gresham, a man
of useful connections, invited the Queen to come and visit,
faking the level of completion and enticing would-be traders in
with cut-price rents to make the whole thing buzz. It was an
excellent move – she promptly added the Royal to the name,
and that touch of glamour turned its fortunes around. By
1600 it was well away, mentioned in tourist guides as one of
the must-see places of London, and attracting a wealthy (or at
least well-dressed and therefore able to pass as wealthy) crowd

of men and women who came to browse, to promenade and to people-watch. Not only could you ogle the merchants below, but also fellow shoppers. If you were there on a Sunday afternoon you might even happen upon musicians playing from a specially constructed gallery. In 1667 one admirer described it as 'a great storehouse whence the nobility and gentry of England were furnished with most of those costly things wherewith they did adorn either their closets or themselves. Here, if anywhere, might a man have seen the glory of the world in a moment.'[23]

Inevitably, it attracted competition, and so to the next iteration, the New Exchange, slightly less successful, but still very much part of the shopping experience for wealthy Londoners or visitors for about 100 years. Again, it was built by one leading noble, armed only with enormous wealth, the backing of King James I and VI and a 60-metre (200ft) length of the Strand. Unlike the Royal Exchange, it was purely geared towards shopping for pleasure. This time around there were no merchants, just shops. Again, it struggled at first, with complaints that the units were too small, that there wasn't enough suitable housing around for potential shopkeepers to live, work and store stock in, and that there wasn't enough trade. Jingoistic attempts to call it 'Britain's Bourse' (the builders still lusting after the prestige of Antwerp's iteration) fell flat. However, as the West End developed around the middle of the century, eventually eclipsing the City as a place for genteel shopping, things improved. By the 1670s the complaints were more around lack of suitable parking for coaches than a dearth of choice within the exchange itself.

The New Exchange, like the Royal Exchange, was on private land and had rules. They were designed to keep the venues upmarket, both in appearance and reality. Thus, opening hours were set (6am–9pm in summer, 7am–7pm in winter) and regulated by the bell. At closing time, tenants agreed to clean down and sweep up, disposing of any rubbish properly. They also agreed not to 'throw or pour out into the walk or range or out at any of the windows any piss or other noisesome thing'. To aid in this, urinals were provided, venting, of course, straight into the Thames behind. Transgressions merited a fine, or, if you were a servant, a beating. A room was provided for meting out physical punishment, along with public stocks to dissuade beggars and other unwanted hangers-on.[24]

The exchanges were built in response to an existing desire to shop for fun and use shopping excursions as a form of leisure. They in turn helped to develop these habits, which were not confined to London, but were, inevitably, more obvious in towns with a sizable middle and upper-class population. No other town tried to emulate the exchanges, probably because they took a huge amount of investment, and needed a large audience. Two more city-based exchanges were built, the Middle Exchange and the Exeter Exchange, but neither was that successful. Both concentrated exclusively on retail, with no other function. By the time they opened, the existing exchanges were running into issues. Both the Royal and the New had, from their early days, attracted lots of what the owners and users regarded as unsavoury elements. Beggars, pickpockets, prostitutes and pedlars clustered around the entrances. No food sellers were allowed to trade within, apart from confectioners, who sold expensive sugarwork to the rich and weren't in any way messy or noisy, so it was a big draw for street food traders such as orange sellers and piemen. Then there were 'servants and apprentices' who played ball games in the street, breaking windows and generally enjoying the atmosphere in their own, less rarefied, way. As shopping provision developed, the geographical centre shifted west again, now to St James's, leaving the exchanges stranded. The Middle lasted twenty-two years before its demolition in 1694, while the Exeter eventually found a new purpose as the home of a wildly popular menagerie. The New Exchange was torn down for housing in 1737. The Royal

Fig. 1.7. The New Exchange, 1772. Both shopping (or possibly merely 'tumbling') and flirting are in evidence here, as well as the gender assumptions of the time. The gentlemen lounge around the leather-clad volumes of the bookstall, while the ladies attend closely to a display of fabric.

survived, partly due to its location in the City, and partly as it had other functions to draw people in and provide both a reason for being, and an audience for its shops.

A key reason for their decline was an association with prostitution, which fed into a more generalised tension over women, shops and public leisure activities. Inside the Royal Exchange, around 45 per cent of the shops were run, and owned, by women, compared to a measly 6 per cent of women shopkeepers in towns in general. If you were a woman, this was another reason to patronise these shops, where you might be able to discuss the intricacies of the latest fashions or the feel of a fabric with someone who knew what it would be like to wear. The presence of so many women of a lower status, dressed to impress, and surrounded by the clean, upmarket surrounds of the galleries, made more than a few male eyes bulge. The relentlessly sex-obsessed Edward (Ned) Ward, in his slightly later satirical work *The London Spy*, described the New Exchange's shop-women as having 'as much mind to dispose of themselves as the commodities they dealt in'.[25] This was, obviously, unfair, but he wasn't the only one to harbour such suspicions (or hopes). Satire of the time made much of the link between female consumption and perceived female idleness, wasting time on shopping for pleasure or – horror – spending time with friends. A terrible worry was the easy availability of so many pretty things to all these unsupervised wealthy wives: 'The merchants should keep their wives from visiting the upper rooms too often, lest they tire their purses by attiring themselves . . . There's many Gentle-women come hither, that, to help their faces and complexion, break their husbands' backs.'[26] The reduction of women to sheep-like consumers, and to men as disadvantaged providers, was to prove a rich source of criticism – and an increasingly boring stereotype – for a long time to come.

The high street

Outside the exchanges, women working in shops were very visible, partly due to their novelty. London's Cheapside, by now no longer just full of goldsmiths, became known for tradesmen's wives sitting outside the shops, specifically to engage and (apparently) beguile passing men. One would-be customer commented that 'in truth a fine-face lady in a wainscot-carved seat is a worthy ornament to a tradesman's shop, and an attractive [one], I'll warrant. Her husband shall find it in the custom of his ware, I'll assure him.'[27] The practice doesn't seem to have spread more widely, but the chance to engage in banter with attractive, yet conveniently unavailable women does seem to have acted as an enticement to some. Not that all the women were unavailable. Sex workers saw the opportunities afforded by the draw of the shops, and the smaller alleys on the edges of main shopping districts gained nicknames such as Popkirtle Lane (a kirtle was the standard women's garment of the time) and Gropecunt Lane, another indication of the importance of auxiliary trades and activities to the apparently main business of shopping.

By the 1650s, then, high streets in the modern sense were becoming a feature of many towns and cities. They were already subject to debates about morality, access and expected behaviour. They weren't extensive, and smaller towns especially had few specialist outlets. Many shopkeepers operated part-time. But that was not entirely the point. The idea of shopping for pleasure was established, with the arguments around whether it was good or bad pushed into irrelevance by the simple fact of the number of people doing it – or wanting to do it.

Let's go, therefore, to the high street. Let's walk along the road, and see what shops are really there. Make a note of your shopping list, retrieve your basket from its hook. Got a carriage? So much the better, though you may struggle to get it down the narrow streets. You won't need any coin unless you plan to pay an account, and paper notes don't exist yet. Dress well though, for your creditworthiness (and therefore ability to procure what you want) will be judged on what you wear. And keep your wits about you, for shopping is rarely straightforward. Ready? Off we go.

Coney Street, York, 1728

Welcome to York, a bustling port and major social centre for the north of England. You've possibly come for the assizes, or perhaps the races, which are a huge draw: within the last few years race days have become incredibly crowded, with anything up to 150 coaches crowding on to the course.

Trade is not what it was, though, as the river is silting up and the port of Hull taking over. The Royal Garrison has left, and attempts to find a new way to elevate the city have drawn a blank. In 1632 the council petitioned the government for a new university to be sited in the town, complaining that 'we the inhabitants of the northern parts of this kingdom find our share in this common want and calamity to be very great, insomuch that we have been looked upon as a rude and barbarous people, in respect of those parts which by reason on their vicinity to the universities, have more fully partaked of their light and influence'.[28] It didn't work and now the focus has shifted to making York a destination town.

York is already a regional hub, but it's felt that city investment in things like a coffee roastery, assembly rooms and a new mayoral residence will encourage visitors to spend more time here. Local lawyer Francis Drake is working on a comprehensive guide to the city. He says much of its income comes from the elites who have found that life in York is cheaper than living on their country estates, with a wider choice of goods in the shops, better educational opportunities (especially for women) and lots to do. There are weekly assemblies including a 'musik assembly', theatre shows and a company of 'strollers' (players) who are (he says) the best in the country. Apparently 'the politeness of the gentlemen, the richness of the dress, and

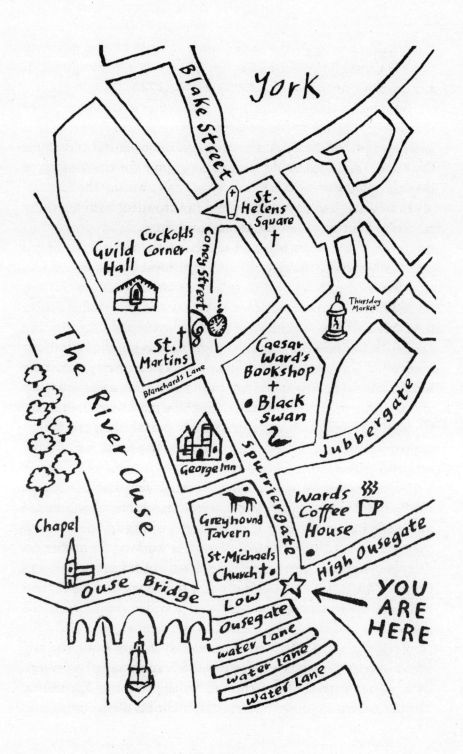

remarkable beauty of the ladies, and, of late, the magnificence of the rooms they meet in, cannot be equalled, throughout, in any part of Europe'.

But there's lots here for those with lesser means too. Coney (or Conyng) Street is the main shopping street (Drake calls it 'the best built in the city'). The name comes from the Old Norse for King. You're probably staying on it, for the main inns are there.

Our walk today will start on Spurriergate, where you're currently standing. Low Ousegate is to your left, sloping down to the muddy river bank and the Ouse Bridge, currently the only bridge across the river. With five arches it's quite an attraction, built in 1566 and housing a chapel to the south. Such is its renown that you can buy a small, spiced cake named after it, shaped (if you squint) a bit like the central arch. Writer Daniel Defoe says the bridge is 'vastly strong and . . . without exception, the greatest in England', and compares it to the Rialto. He's generally quite complimentary about the city, and although he moans about the assemblies, which he thinks are 'a plan laid for the ruin of the nation's morals', he admits that 'no city in England is better furnished with provisions of every kind, nor so cheap, in proportion to the goodness of things'.[29]

Look to your right, and on the corner with High Ousegate you'll find Ward's Coffee House, which in December will house a show featuring 'the new art of dexterity of hand and the Royal Sword Dance'. (Defoe would doubtless hate it.) Opposite, as you take your first steps on to Spurriergate itself, is St Michael's Church, with its graveyard tucked in next to it. Head past and continue up the narrow street, which runs parallel with the river.

Both sides are lined with buildings, mostly from the last two centuries. Some have two storeys, but many have three, generally jettied with timber frames and sharply pointed rooflines. The occasional modern, flat-fronted brick building stands out.

These are mainly private houses, for the street is a mixture of residential and commercial use. There are several townhouses with gardens leading down to the river, some of which belong to merchants taking advantage of the easy unloading opportunities directly into their private cellars below. There's money about – Spurriergate will be the site of York's first private bank in 1734.[30] To your left, five or so houses on, you'll find the Greyhound tavern, with its long, narrow bar heading back from the road. Almost opposite is the entrance to Jubbergate, which leads (tortuously) to the Thursday Marketplace and its ornate covered cross. Passing it, you are now on Coney Street proper.

You can't escape the river. Glance towards it down Blanshard's Lane, one of a series of tiny alleys – also known as water lanes – which snake off to the river. They are lined with dark, cramped housing: single-roomed dwellings for the poor, and provide access for the nightsoilmen to collect the human waste from the city privies and cart it down to the river for disposal. The locals use the river for swimming, as well as using the water to wash and cook with, even though at low tide the smell of mud carries a distinctive tang from all the excrement. The shouts and thuds of barges unloading at the wharves get louder as you suddenly glimpse the crowded riverfront.

This part of the street is dominated by the Black Swan inn on your right. It's one of two coaching inns, so watch out for the clatter of hooves and wheels as the stagecoaches run past you. There are departures from the Black Swan to a number of cities, including London, where 'if god permits' you can reach another Black Swan in Holborn in just four days. As one of York's principal streets, the road is paved, with wooden bollards to demarcate the sidewalks, but they aren't much of a barrier, and the paving doesn't extend to the side streets. It's dusty in summer, muddy in winter. And despite the children collecting dog and horse shit for the tanneries, it's hard to avoid stepping in it.

Many of the buildings here house shops. Some house more than one – Caesar Ward's bookshop is over the Black Swan. Most of the ground floors have something in the way of a shop, often in wooden lean-tos attached to the fronts, and you'll see carved wooden signs hanging in the doorways, giving an indication of what they might sell. There's a watchmaker at the sign of the Golden Cup, and an ivory worker at the Crown and Pearl. The open windows are more like hatches, really, and can be shut up at night. They are lined with goods, and while there are doorways, and some people do go in and out, most of the selling is done through the window. In some places there are boards sticking out on to the street acting like tables for display or the examination of goods. This is also where people stand haggling with the shop assistants, so you'll need to duck and weave a bit to get through. Don't gawp too much, as it's busy.

Just beyond the Black Swan, down a short passage, are the judges' lodgings. The houses on this side used to have gardens behind them, but they are rapidly being filled with more buildings as demand in the city is high. Look up at the first floors of the houses here – the wealth of the city is very apparent in the ornate plasterwork visible through the windows. On your left you might glimpse the arms of the Vintners' company worked into the wall in one house, along with mermaids, roses and pomegranates.

As you reach the halfway point three buildings on, you might want to take a moment. On your left is York's most famous inn, the George. It's a glorious building, with three storeys and a low attic. The architecture, which includes gables and bays, as well as jetties to support the upper floors, is of the last century and it has the most exuberant frontage on the street. York's plasterers and stucco workers had quite the reputation a few decades ago, and the whole thing is a riot of applied decoration, finished off with a lurid door almost certainly acquired from the Augustinian friary that used to take up most of Old Coney Street (now called Lendal). Over this is a bay window holding the music room – as you approach you'll hear the strains of violins. Expect a waft of coffee and tobacco smoke, for Kidd's Coffee House is just next door.

You may be struck by how dilapidated some of the buildings are, despite the efforts to promote the city as modern and genteel. On the other side of the George there's a building held up with scaffolding, while down a bit and on the right there's a short row of timber-framed buildings in varied states of repair. The first two have more of those ornate plasterwork ceilings visible through the first-floor bays, and the shops below them have windows with displays of linens and gloves and ribbons hanging from the upper shutter. But next to them is a Tudor semi-ruin. Perhaps it strikes you that this would be an ideal location for a new street, allowing access to Davygate – but it won't happen for another seventeen years.

There's another water lane on your left, by St Martin's Church. If you venture down, you'll find a small row of medieval houses in the churchyard, before the view opens up across the river. On the opposite bank, the town is less developed, and there are orchards and gardens just a little way up, a bucolic contrast to your current surroundings. Seagulls fly overhead, and the mudflats are very exposed, the smell growing stronger as the wake from the ferry leaving Lendal tower slaps against the bank. Go back up to Coney Street, check the time on the clock, which sticks out from the church. It was paid for by the parishioners and put up in 1668. The locals are very proud of it. On the right now is the Leopard, a rather downmarket tavern, with an alleyway leading behind it to the former warm water baths (the cold baths are on Stonegate). Do you venture in? The building is a rather fashionable one, erected in 1691 in the latest style and looking vaguely like a very small Hampton Court. However, demand was less than was hoped, and the bagnio, as it's known, is now a brothel, so it depends exactly what you've come here for.

You might well spot men – and women – with inky fingers hurrying about here. York is an important printing centre, and though many of the presses are off near the Minster, there are several on Coney Street as well. In 1734 one of the two rival newspapers in the city, the *York Courant*, will move to Coney Street, setting up its presses in the former bagnio.

As you near the end of the street, it opens up, though only slightly. St Helen's Square is not what you'd necessarily call a square, being small, triangular, and largely filled with a walled mound housing St Helen's graveyard. Drake is sniffy about it, calling it 'very inconvenient for the passing of coaches or carriages into Blake Street'. He does have a point, for the bodies can mount up, and now that Blake Street is about to get a new assembly rooms the council is grappling with how to make the square a little more salubrious.

They've already started improving it, you note now. On your left as you reach the square is the as-yet-unroofed Mansion House, the new town residence for the Mayors of York. It's replacing the former St Christopher's Chapel, itself long since converted into a house. The new construction is intended to allow the Lord Mayor to '[keep] up the grandeur and dignity of the city, by making public entertainments at his house'. The Mayors are almost all shopkeepers (and the occasional lawyer) and lack the necessary premises of their own. When finished, it will have a large ballroom, dining room, cellars and kitchens, and it backs on to the Guildhall, alongside which is the last of the three water lanes – Common Hall Lane (Common Hall is another name for the Guildhall). Despite the lack of roof, Mansion House was used last year as a venue to celebrate George II's coronation. The area outside it is known as Cuckold's Corner, and while Blake prudishly says he cannot think why it is called that, at night it very much lives up to its name. It won't be

Fig. 1.8. Coney Street from St Helen's Square, York, *c.*1800. We've just walked from the other end of the street, finishing here, outside Mansion House (now, a few decades on, fully complete and neatly paved). Looking back down the street you can see the clock of St Martin's, with The George just beyond it. If you were to walk down the alleyway to your right, you'd find the Guildhall and, beyond that, the still bustling, and still smelly, river Ouse.

paved until 1777 and a few years later the square will be opened up with the demolition of a row of houses.

Try to avoid the mud as you skirt the square: it's worth lingering, for here you'll find more shops – look out for the stay-maker, the draper and the two milliners, though, in all fairness, the perfumier might be more of a priority right now.[31]

Chapter Two

1650–1750

Their shops are dens, the buyer is their prey.[1]

- John Dryden, *The Medal* (1682)

Shopping list: *Currants, tobacco, lace and some shoe buckles*

For this chapter's shopping excursion, you are comfortably wealthy: quite probably a member of that most English of classes, the squire-archy (gentry). Your shopping list is a mixture of the practical and the pleasurable, but just the notion of buying it all from shops, rather than the market, means you have aspiration, to say the least. You employ quite a few servants, but everything here is relatively costly, at least if it is good quality, so you're wise to procure it all yourself, rather than leaving it to a cook or maid. Plus, there are personal items which you need to choose to match your wardrobe. Let's assume this is the relaxed kind of shopping, stocking up the pantry and buying in anticipation of a need, rather than a rushed trip for provisions before an important dinner party. Take your time: enjoy yourself.

We're starting out in the mid-seventeenth century. Britain was a republic from 1649 until 1660, and it was a time of political tension and frequent unrest. There were wars at sea and on land, first with the Dutch, and then with the French and the Spanish, and so many changes of monarch between 1660 and 1715 that the whole idea of dynastic succession started to look decidedly shaky. There were only twenty-eight years when the king or queen on the throne didn't have a rival king foment-ing rebellion from abroad. Still, all that war led to innovation – including the Bank of England, the stock market and, in 1720, the first stock market crash, in the form of the South Sea Bubble. It was an era where the rich wore fine silk and swords, fashionably red heels (on both men and women) and resplendently curled wigs. The poor, meanwhile, sunk their woes with gin, culminating in the gin act of 1751, an early attempt at prohibition, which went about as well as the more famous American iteration of the 1920s. The 1660s are also notable for the Great Fire of London, the last great outbreak of the bubonic plague (again, in London, though other towns did, believe it or not, exist) and the development of the party political system.

The British population was slowly growing. The biggest cities (after London) were Norwich, Bristol, York and Newcastle, plus Edinburgh, Glasgow and Aberdeen. Population estimates are notoriously unreliable, but it's thought that around 17 per cent of the population lived in towns of more than 5,000 inhabitants. With the possible exception of the wealthier elements of London society, the shopping focus of the late-seventeenth-century town remained the market. Particularly useful for fresh food, and indeed the only place to buy fruit and vegetables, as well as most dairy products, market stalls supplied the main wants of most households. In the countryside you'd also, of course, be growing your own. If you were wealthy enough to have a landed estate, you'd manage part of it so that it would supply the kitchens with game: poorer people kept a pig. Few, if any, households were self-sufficient, and even the largest of estates regularly ordered goods from local suppliers as well as the more prestigious shops of London. You'd only see a duke at the market if he owned the land it was built on, but for someone in his retinue the weekly trudge to the market was non-negotiable.

Even if you had servants, everyday shopping – marketing – wasn't necessarily something to delegate. Grumbles about increased retail activity and declining oversight from guilds or town councils fed into worries that laxer regulations would enable more potential crooks to operate, and that honest traders would suffer. One pamphlet of 1681 stated plainly that 'there is a very great complaint in most of the market towns in this kingdom, of the great decay in trade, both by many working, and especially by all ancient shopkeeping tradesmen, as the woollen draper, the linen draper, the mercer, the grocer and others'. The author went on, 'the grounds of this grievance is, because many do believe, that all men promiscuously ought to have liberty to set up any trade for a livelihood, and especially the shopkeeping trade'.[2] The usual arguments about on-selling followed, now with added bite, for the concern over middlemen here wasn't just that they hoiked the prices, but that 'they have usurped the sole power of selling . . . both for what price, and for what time, and to whom they please'. There was a real fear that dodgy shopkeepers could undercut good ones, stealing their custom and forcing them out of business. Even then, the problem of monopolies, and the effect of middlemen setting unrealistic prices that forced producers into poverty, while giving traders a fat profit, was recognised.[3]

Various helpful solutions were proposed. Some were those of the past, with the onus very much on the government – sumptuary laws, re-establishing the guild system, setting up more markets. The government did try to curb imports with heavy taxes, though the inevitable result of this was to create trade wars, which meant British exports suffered as well.[4] More widely, though, the agency of the individual was recognised, with an acknowledgement that persuading people to do the right thing at an individual level was also important. Many of the suggestions of our 1681 pamphleteer were aimed at the poor, who presumably weren't supposed to want nice things (though also would not have been reading these helpful ideas, literacy rates being low). It was, therefore, fine to accuse workers of 'strange idleness and stubbornness', and then propose they swap linen for flannel, 'because they may wear it a month without washing'. The gentry got away with being scolded for preferring French wine over English cider and allowing their younger sons to enter trade rather than join the army to die gloriously of disease near a battlefield in northern France.[5]

How much of the rhetoric around shopping was widely read is difficult to tell. But the ideas that underpinned it, combined with the underlying reality of purchasing goods, spread into more general literature. This includes a growing number of recipe books and household manuals, the authors of which were unsurprisingly concerned less with the morals of marketing, and more with daily practicalities, including how to thwart a would-be cheat. Hannah Glasse, one of the bestselling authors of the era, advised the worried shopper to insist on tasting butter taken from the middle of the block, never accepting a sample ready-prepared. With meat, the secret was to feel it at the bone, and then smell your fingers to know if it was off.[6] Marketing was fraught with peril, especially as regards food, since getting it wrong was both expensive and potentially injurious to health. Shops might be unregulated, but they were also permanent, and one of the keys to good service was a good and personal relationship with the shopkeeper.

Towns were at their busiest on market day, and if you lived at a distance, you probably only made the trip once a week. As you emerged from the shade and clatter of the market and skirted the stalls which spilled out from the main square, you'd have encountered your first shops. There were butchers, and bakers, and other makers, many of which we think of as conceptually integral to the high street, but which were (and are) physically located on the periphery of it. That's not to say the purchase of a bun or a flitch of bacon didn't bring pleasure, and certainly it involved careful selection, but you'd hardly spend large amounts of leisure time staring at the quartern loaves stacked on the shelf outside the bakery.

However, there's more. It's (very vaguely) estimated that there were around 50,000 shopkeepers in 1688, rising to 142,000 by 1750.[7] Large towns now had extensive provision. By the late seventeenth century Norwich had added vintners, gunsmiths, tobacconists, confectioners and upholsterers to its already impressive list. Around 25 per cent of towns had a bookseller, wine merchant and clockmaker, with 10 per cent managing silversmiths, confectioners and furniture workers.[8] The difference between good shopping provision and more mediocre was judged by the level of specialism – travel writer Celia Fiennes commented on Newcastle that 'their shops are good and of distinct trades, not selling many things in one shop as is the custom in most country towns and cities'.[9]

Locating the high street

The shops were found in or around the market square. Daniel Defoe, in his lengthy guide to shopkeeping, *The Complete English Tradesman* (1726), stated quite simply that in the country all shopkeepers should aim to be around the marketplace.[10] Even by the 1740s, when shops (now including greengrocers and cheesemongers) were more established and markets conversely less of a magnet, Worcester grocer Thomas Dickenson's trade rose by 70 per cent on market days.[11]

Back in the 1680s, grocer's apprentice William Stout recorded the unending work of preparing for the increased sales on market day. Later, as a shopkeeper in his own right, having found a shop 'in the best of the marketplace', it was on market days that he employed his sister Elin as an extra pair of hands, where she was 'as ready in serving retail customers as a young apprentice could have done'.[12]

Inevitably, it was different in London (although individual marketplaces did still attract retailers and leisure facilities – think of Covent Garden, surrounded by theatres, shops and coffee houses). London was huge, and at the forefront of fashion. When parliament was sitting, its all-male denizens congregated on the capital, bringing their families. The period during which parliament sat became known as 'the season' by the early eighteenth century, for it was then that parties were held, matches were made, and all the rituals of upper-class sociability performed. Inevitably, these rituals meant looking and playing the part – thus shopping for food, clothes, tableware, furniture and all the minutiae required to put on a good show. All around St James's Street specialist shops multiplied. They weren't dependent on market days to bring in shoppers, and so would-be shopkeepers looked for different criteria. Location was key in a different way, for such shops were often still zoned, much as traders were in the markets. Defoe said that 'many trades have their peculiar streets, and proper places for the sale of their goods, where people expect to find such goods, they go thither for them'.

Conversely, the mixed-use high street was perhaps slower to develop in London precisely because there were so many shops. Breaking away from the crowd was risky: 'what retail trade would a milliner have among the fishmongers' shops on Fishstreet-hill; or a toyman about Queenhithe? When a shop is ill-chosen, the tradesman starves, he is out of the way, and business will not follow him that runs away from it.'[13] Visitors seeking some items in London today will still find such clusters of shops. The jewellers' shopfronts and workshops that line the streets around Hatton Garden are hardly on the scale of the seventeenth century, but reflect the movement of the goldsmiths and gem workers from Cheapside to Clerkenwell as the City, and its shops, evolved.

Every high street was different. However, wherever you were, you could expect certain broad similarities. Your high street would rarely be paved, unless you were in a very large town with budget to spare. In York you can still walk along a street called Pavement, which was called Marketshire until the fourteenth century, with the change of name probably due to its being paved very early.[14] On one or both sides of the road you'd usually find a raised sidewalk, possibly with some token wooden bollards, intended for pedestrians, upon which traffic was not supposed to impinge. Shops themselves, too, were regulated so that they didn't project into the space intended for foot traffic, though the jettied stories above meant that nominally clear streets still weren't exactly a haven of light and openness.

Seeing the sky was made even more challenging by the increasing proliferation of shop signs. They started as painted wooden boards, which according to one visitor had the effect of making Cheapside 'like the Medici gallery', but were later joined by wrought-iron signs as well. They remained limited in most places until the 1680s, but as shops increased in number, all competing for custom, and desirous of being seen, the signs got bigger and bolder. They were vital for locating retailers, especially when describing how to find them, for house numbers weren't introduced until the early eighteenth century, and were slow to catch on.

At first – in the mid- to late seventeenth century – the signs were easy to work out, for the pictures on them usually related to what was being sold. A staymaker might advertise with a silhouette of a pair of stays; an ironworker with a kettle (at this stage meaning a double-handled cooking pot rather than the vaguely Victorian copper number beloved of certain modern tea shops). Bakers used wheatsheaves or, in the case of one shop in Bury St Edmunds, a baker's peel. You could spot a tobacconist by the sign of a black boy (sometimes wearing tobacco leaves for good and entirely false measure), and a draper by the sign of the golden fleece. However, it quickly got confusing. What about when several shops occupied the same, crammed-in premises, with others operating on upper floors? Or when shopkeepers succeeded each other, not always selling the same thing, but wanting to maintain a sign which people already knew? Take the case of James Maddox, a coffin maker, who moved to the site of a former grocer's. Naturally he wanted a coffin on his sign, but people were used to the previous one. His solution? To trade at the sign of the sugarloaf (the sign of the grocer) and three coffins. Joseph Addison moaned that it wasn't fair on the customer: 'What can be more inconsistent than to see a bawd at the sign of the Angel, or a tailor at the Lion? A cook should not live at the Boot, not a shoemaker at the Roasted Pig; and yet, for want of regulation, I have seen a goat set up before a perfumer, and the French King's Head at a sword-cutter's.'[15] To the modern eye, it's natural to assume that many of these signs meant taverns, for something like the crown and pearl certainly sounds like a pub – but most of them were just signs, with motifs piled upon motif.

It was all very confusing, and the street addresses got ever longer as a result. Here's Ann Askew, a London shoemaker in 1735: 'at the Boot, next door to the Three Tuns and Rummer, in Gracechurch Street'. (Addison would have approved). On the other hand, compare the addresses of the tooth operators (pullers), Samuel Darkin the elder and younger. The elder was next door to the Cow and Hare, which gave no indication at all of his trade, while his (presumably) son operated 'at the sign of the Bleeder and Star, the corner of Adam & Eve Alley in Church Lane, Whitechapel', which is quite horrifically evocative. Worse still, he added on his adverts: 'Beware of imposters. My name is on the sign.' The mind boggles.[16]

These details come from trade cards, which many traders issued as shops swelled in number from the 1670s. Most that survive are from London, where competition was at its fiercest, and street layouts most confusing. They were effectively small flyers advertising a shop and carrying directions or a picture to help find them. Early cards were simple, perhaps a picture of the sign and an idea of the product plus a small 'puff' as the typically breathy and rather inflated advertising blurbs came to be known. Cutler Thomas Hollis stated he traded from the

Ann Askew, Shoemaker,

At the *Boot*, next Door to the *Three Tuns* and *Rummer* in *Grace-Church-Street*.

SELLS all Sorts of Men's Shoes, Boots, and Slippers: Likewise, Women's fine Shoes, Clogs, and Slippers ready made Wholesale and Retail at reasonable Rates.

N. B. Likewise, Merchants Trading to the Plantations, may be furnish'd with all Sorts of Shoes.

Fig. 2.1. Trade card of Ann Askew, a London shoemaker, 1735. The picture may well represent her shop sign.

Little Minories, gave a large picture of the Crossed Swords he traded under, a smaller pictures of knives in a block, with his wares listed as 'canes, elephant teeth, English and German steel, city and country knives, scissors, shears, razors, pen knives, hones, steel boxes and tongs, shoe buckles, pairing knives, smoothing irons, bell metal buttons and such like ware at reasonable prices'. Seventy years later, in an indication of how much consumer goods were proliferating, fellow cutler John Brailsford's trade card pictured all of these and more, for he also sold cork screens, spurs, tobacco, dog collars, pocket books, brushes, curling tongs, ink stands, and 'all sorts of Birmingham and Sheffield ware [silver plated goods]'.[17]

Brailsford was typical of the type of shopkeeper found in many towns: nominally a specialist, but actually quite a lot

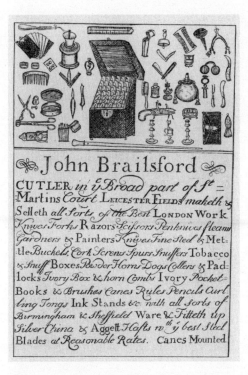

Fig. 2.2. Trade card of John Brailsford, London, *c.*1750. Although nominally a cutler, Brailsford's card shows the rapid expansion in consumer goods in the mid-eighteenth century. The less literate (or clear-visioned) are supplied with a handy pictorial depiction of what they will find on offer to buy or order.

broader. One of the major complaints about the increasing number of shops was that not everyone had served a proper apprenticeship, paying to serve out a (usually) seven-year period learning the trade, before being able to set up in their own right. But an apprenticeship didn't guarantee success. Grocer William Stout had many boys pass through his shop, some of whom went on to run their own shops, while others left to pursue different trades. One, John Baynes, went from his own shop to marriage into a ship-building family in Sunderland, then started building houses, and ended up with a street named for him although 'he grew very fat and corpulent and died in about the fortieth year of his age'.[18] Some, including Stout's nephew, went bust.

In short, your high street was in flux both physically and in terms of people and types of shop. Certainly, some shops were passed from father to son, or husband to wife, but there was constant movement. Walking down the high street meant taking in changes, observing the signs as they increased in number, and fathoming out which traders to patronise. Meanwhile, as the focus of the town started to shift away from the market, the shopping area became the place to find some of the activities previously associated with the market. Putting on a bear-baiting show? Take your bears for a walk down the high street and drum up some trade. The same goes for your fighting cocks. Cock-fighting was still popular, as a brief vogue for building new cockpits as part of improving town facilities showed. Manchester's cockpit on Deansgate – then, as now, a major shopping street – was part of an extensive complex that included pens and feeding rooms for the cocks, the public arena, an assembly rooms, a bowling green and a tavern.[19]

Another reminder that the high street has always been about more than shopping comes in the form of Solomon Eccles, a notorious provider of local colour to the community of shoppers and lawyers who frequented the shopping booths lining Westminster Hall. Pepys mentioned seeing him in July 1667: '. . . a man, a Quaker, came naked through the Hall, only very civilly tied about the privates to avoid scandal, and with a chafing-dish of fire and brimstone burning upon his head . . . crying, "Repent! repent!"' Daniel Defoe called him 'famous' and was at pains to point out he wasn't 'infected in the head', merely a religious ranter left over from the Interregnum. If a naked enthusiast didn't quite do it for you, you could always pop outside to admire the rotting heads of Oliver Cromwell and his generals on stakes.[20] Other towns presumably had their own versions of Eccles: they certainly had their own displays of live or dead criminals to impose order on the town.

This is all very well, but your purpose here is not merely to gawp like an innocent abroad. Let's return to your shopping list. Practicalities first.

Currants are a key ingredient in many cakes, biscuits and puddings, far more common in recipes than raisins. They're good with rabbits and fish as well, and often used in sauces. Definitely one for the dry larder. By the early 1700s about 40 per cent of towns had a grocer or tea-dealer, and it was the mark of an up-and-coming town – so head for the sign of the sugarloaf (or even sugarloaves if your grocer is particularly aspirational).

The grocer

The origins of the grocery trade go back to 1345 and the founding of the Company of Grossers. The Company was a rebranding of the London Pepperers' Guild and the grossers – or grocers by the mid-fifteenth century – were associated with the spice trade from the very start.[21] The exact nature of what they sold was never really defined. Spices, certainly, and other imported foodstuffs, including sugar, which had counted as a spice when first introduced as it was so expensive. However, the Company also included apothecaries for a while. Some shopkeepers traded nominally as one thing – ironmongers, mercers and drapers – but were also grocers. Ralph Edge, an ironmonger in 1680s Tarporley (Cheshire), stocked fifteen different types of cloth, ready-made haberdashery such as caps and stockings, thimbles, tobacco boxes, glasses, knives, knitting needles, curtain rings, bibles, candles, soap, oil for lamps, spices, seeds and dried fruit.[22] Over in Rochdale, Lawrence Newall's mercer's shop inventory listed long pepper, bayberries [probably barberries] and sugar loaves along with the expected woollen cloth and thread. It was common for village shops to stock a wide range of goods – but many of the shops in towns were also very varied.

Grocers, like all shops on the high street, opened roughly in line with established custom based on markets – daybreak to when stock ran out – which in practice meant that they were fully open from 9am until 9 or 10pm. Most shopkeepers lived above their retail premises, both by custom and by preference. It wasn't unknown for people to wake them up in the middle of the night and demand to be served.[23] Wealthier shopkeepers sometimes lived away from the shop, a trend which increased in the eighteenth century. Their apprentices still lived in, as much for security as anything else.

Village shopkeeper and enjoyably bacchanalian Thomas Turner recorded an incident when he got up to answer the door to one of his drinking companions from the night before, a Mrs Porter 'who pretended she wanted some cream of tartar'. Given that he'd left the group at 3am, 'very far from sober', and it was only three hours later, he probably should have been wiser, for the cream of tartar was only an excuse. In Mrs Porter burst, accompanied by her husband and another couple, all decidedly inebriated. They threatened to break down his bedroom door, then got him out of bed half naked, and 'instead of my upper clothes, they gave me time to put on my wife's petticoats; and in this manner made me dance, without shoes and stockings, until they had emptied the bottle of wine, and also a bottle of my beer'. The party eventually broke up at 3pm, by which time Turner (somewhat hypocritically) suggested, they were 'ashamed of their stupid enterprise and drunken perambulation'.[24]

As in earlier periods, many early shops were decidedly impermanent looking. It was very common for them to occupy a wooden lean-to, built on to the side of an existing wooden or brick structure, sometimes as an extension to the more solid structure behind and sometimes as an independent space. These were known as bulks and would survive until the nineteenth century in some places, though town improvement schemes swept most away in the late eighteenth century.[25] If a street needed widening, for example to allow two carriages to pass, they were easily jettisoned. They were cold in winter, hot in summer, frequently leaked, and were not at all vermin-proof. If your grocer was doing well, he would rapidly upgrade to something less draughty and more secure.

In London the Great Fire of 1666 destroyed many of the shops in the City, and the regulations that were issued in its wake give a glimpse into the way in which shops worked, whether they were bulks or those which operated from a front room or ground floor. Shopkeepers were instructed not to allow their projecting counters, called shop or stall boards, to extend more than 11 inches (30 cm) into the street. These boards extended from the shop window, which was the key to the building being a shop. 'Open the window' meant opening the shop, and, outside London and a few other places that had elite shops, it remained unusual for customers to enter the shop itself. As was the case earlier in the century, the norm was for the window to have shutters, hinged horizontally in the middle, which opened up and down. The upper shutter not only offered shelter but also the chance to hang goods to catch the eye of passers-by. It was less important, perhaps, in the grocery trade, but for haberdashers it provided the chance to hang up gloves and caps, for bakers it was jumbles (sweet boiled and baked pastries, knotted a bit like pretzels) on sticks, and for shoemakers it was boots and shoes and the occasional bright buckle. The lower shutter acted as the shop board, extending out into the street to form a counter for the inspection of goods. Shop inventories refer to 'grills' and 'lattices' which might double as protection from light-fingered passers-by, as well as being another way to make a shop look attractive as they were festooned with goods. Of course, the open window meant that the shopkeeper froze in winter, and it was not unusual to find bedraggled apprentices miserably huddled in their clothing trying to keep warm.

Within the shop, you'd probably find a man. Women served in shops, and indeed ran them, but don't tend to show up in the official figures because so many were wives, sisters and daughters, erased from the official record thanks to the pres-

Fig. 2.3. Trade card of William Overley, a London joiner, 1720s. The shop, inserted into (or on to) an existing building, is typical of the era. You can even see the shopkeeper waiting hopefully at his window to catch any passing trade.

ence of a male head of the household. Estimates based on trade directories are unreliable because they tended to list only the bigger businesses, but even these records suggest that by the early eighteenth century around 10–15 per cent of shops were run by women, predominantly in the millinery and haberdashery trades. There are some well-known female grocers – Mary Tuke's 1720s shop in York is lauded as the birthplace of the city's chocolate industry, and a few decades later Mancunian ex-housekeeper Elizabeth Raffald wrote a bestselling cookery book while running her shop (she also dealt with a feckless husband, ran a servants' registry and was an all-round powerhouse). But women couldn't officially serve as apprentices, and unless they were careful when they married, their husbands would take over ownership of any shop they had. William Stout recorded a case where he helped set a local woman, Elin Godsalve, up in business while her husband was in prison. Upon the latter's return, he fell back into 'expensive living', trashed her reputation as a reliable shopkeeper and then disappeared, leaving her with new-born twins and ruinous debt.[26]

Whether serving you at the window or from within the shop, your grocer's produce would be stored mainly in boxes and barrels, from which he could take a sample and spread it out to show you. You could buy some things pre-packed, which was a job for the apprentices. Here's William Stout again, looking back at his training in 1683: 'I was mostly employed in the shop in the weekdays, in making up goods for the market day, as sugar, tobacco, nails and other goods, and particularly prunes, which we made up in the summer time about one hundred weight weekly.'[27] Inventories contain references to various types of paper used for packing up the most commonly requested things, but it wasn't always virgin. Paper was still made using rags and was a finite resource, so was reused many times. As with today's packaging-free shops, you could also bring your own containers.

Early modern grocers sold a very wide variety of things. This might well include the next item on your shopping list, tobacco. Specialist snuff men and tobacconists had started to appear in larger towns, but tobacco was also a real staple of the grocery trade, and very profitable, forming around a third of sales in some cases.[28] Like many grocery wares, it was imported from the Americas via ports including Liverpool and Bristol. Developing the all-important personal relationship with your grocer could be a challenge at times, for shopkeepers bought directly from merchants and via wholesalers and travelled across the country to inspect, collect and bring back their stock. They were sometimes absent for weeks at a time. Additionally, London was universally seen as a place to simultaneously envy and compare one's own town to and necessitated an obligatory annual visit. This was a chance not only to negotiate for stock, but also to gain ideas from the latest trends to hit the capital.

By the early eighteenth century, improvements in the road network meant that goods could easily be transported across the country. As business models between wholesalers and individual stockists developed, and the range of goods grew, both grocers and cloth dealers started to subcontract negotiations to representatives based in London or other major hubs. On the other hand, some experimented with more direct methods, precisely to cut out the middleman. William Stout commissioned a merchant on board a ship bound for Barbados to return with sugar, ginger and cotton, though the results were unsatisfactory, and he decided not to do it again. Although their heyday was passing, the big fairs were still good for obtaining some foreign-made goods, as well as for catching up with other shopkeepers.

No customer standing at a grocer's window could be unaware of the wider world. You'd see sugar from the West Indies, produced under hideously exploitative conditions, which rarely intruded upon the customer's consciousness – yet. There would be spices from the New World – chillies in particular were becoming popular, often listed as chyan (cayenne) – and the Old. Nutmeg and mace were ubiquitous in late-seventeenth-century recipes and came from Indonesia, where the Dutch were behaving as badly as the British in expanding their nascent empire. Rice was shipped from Europe and the Americas. Blocks of chocolate – roasted beans ground into a rough, slightly gritty paste and moulded in small cakes – were processed either in the ports or before shipping. Apparently, chocolate from Bristol sometimes tasted of fish, a result of the beans being stored next to salted or dried fish in the ship's hold. Towards the end of the seventeenth century, some of these goods decreased in price in line with British exploitation of what they regarded as virgin territory in the Caribbean, along with success in fighting off the French and Spanish in India and South America. Your grocer might well decide to expand.

In 1697 William Stout sold his shop and all its fittings to his newly qualified apprentice. This included 'boxes, chests, scales, weights and all the other movable goods in the shop'. There were also drawers, commissioned from a local joiner.[29] By 1700 the inventories of grocers reflected the increase in available goods, and the eagerness of people to buy them. Sixty per cent of shop inventories at the turn of the century in Kent have drawers listed, indicating a slow move towards bigger shops into which customers might enter.

There were pitfalls in carrying a wide range of goods, though. William Stout's decidedly disappointing nephew found this out when playing a (he thought) hilarious prank on a 'lad' who stopped by and 'begged' a ready-filled clay pipe. The nephew added a few grains of gunpowder to the pipe (ho ho) but failed to then close the relevant drawer properly. The lad lit his pipe, which spluttered and exploded in a suitably comedic way – until a spark leapt into the open drawer, igniting the gunpowder stored within and blowing the shop up. Nobody died, though nephew, lad and an unfortunate maid were 'sorely scorched', and the back door was split apart.[30] The nephew ultimately ended up bankrupt and embroiled in a family feud because of his idiocy, and was saved from utter ignominy only by Stout being rather more charitable than most of us would probably manage.

Another feature of shops, not just grocers, was the payment ledger. Market shopping was all based on the principle of haggling, and the same system applied in shops. Few things had fixed prices yet, though the ready-packed prunes and nails

THE WEST PROSPECT OF THE CHURCH OF S. ETHELBURGH.

To Sir Robert Godschall Kn.
Alderman of the Ward of Bishopsgate.
London.

Fig. 2.4. Bishopgate, London, 1736. The church is that of
St Ethelburga-the-Virgin, which still exisits. The street is a lovely
mixture of window-selling, people in shops, and a few glazed fronts.
The butcher's shop has a cutting table on the street, while the
bookseller or printer has pages pinned to the door surround.
The bollards afford a limited protection to people walking
along the street.

were almost there. By the early eighteenth century newspapers carried adverts stating goods were 'to be had for ready
money'. This started with the grocers, and applied initially to
things such as tea, sold wholesale via public auctions, which
meant that anyone who wished could ascertain the price their

shopkeeper probably paid for things. In 1711 Norwich grocer John Hoyle, branching out into dairy goods, advertised 'good Cheshire cheese at three pence halfpenny a pound, Warwickshire at three pence farthing'.[31] But this was slow to take off, and generally you'd agree a price after a bit of back and forth.

Not that many customers carried money. If you were a new customer, you'd have to prove you were creditworthy and pay up straight away, but most debts went down in the ledger, to be settled at a later date. There was a lack of small coin in the late seventeenth century, and the little that was in circulation was often heavily debased. It was such a big problem that among the many itinerant traders attracted to high streets were those who bought counterfeit coins with the street cry of 'Brass money! Broken or whole!'[32]

Some shops devised an alternative to the official coinage, and issued private coins, known now as trade tokens. They were stamped with the name of the shop and the denomination and circulated widely within the catchment area. However, the main solution, once your shopkeeper trusted you, was to offer credit. In theory customers made regular small payments, and regular small purchases, and the two sort of balanced out. In practice, while most people did pay – eventually – almost every shop carried a level of bad debt. As long as the shopkeeper had enough money to pay his or her own accounts, some debt didn't matter, except when they died, and it proved impossible for their dependants to reclaim the debts (after a year you couldn't pursue people in court any more). Getting the balance right was hard. In 1750 around 50 per cent of grocers' sales were paid via credit and it was even more standard in the clothing and fabric trades.[33]

There was, therefore, a lot of goodwill involved in shopping, hence the necessity of good relationships. You trusted the grocer not to rip you off or sell you dodgy stock, and they trusted that you would pay them back. Maintaining relationships was a huge part of shopkeeping, and shopkeepers were never off duty. If not buying stock or serving in the shop, they might be schmoozing particularly important customers, or simply being cordial to more everyday clients. March 1664 found Roger Lowe, a grocer in Ashton-in-Makerfield, complaining in his diary that 'this night I was invited to go to Gawther Taylor's to drink Braggod for wife bought her commodities of me and she said if I would not come, then farewell; so I was constrained to go, but I stayed but for a short time'.[34] (Braggod was a mead/beer mash up, often rather potent.) It wasn't always unwelcome, but it did mean that at times the line between shopping and socialising was so blurred as to be invisible.

You've agreed a good price, and have your raisins and tobacco safely stashed about your person. If you are a woman, you might have to head home now, or at least head for somewhere much quieter. Public toilets won't appear for another 200 years or so. Relieving oneself in the street is against town regulations, though it must be admitted that some men don't seem that concerned, especially if they've had a few. One 1712 review of the Guy of Warwick on London's Milk Street stated waspishly, 'the beer right good, but the sots pissing against the wall, offensive to opposite females, who cannot endure those things in their sight'.[35]

It's dinnertime anyway, at least for fashionable people like you. Writing in 1736, Francis Drake is at pains to point out that in York, the wealthy dine at 12pm, just like people in London. He is slightly behind the times: for the very wealthy the dining hour is more like 2pm. Dinner is the main meal of the day, and it's something you might want to sit down for. Again, gender will dictate your next move. Women, you'll have to head home if you are in any way respectable. Men, you have more choices. Look for the sign of the pie crust or dagger and roast meat and enter, quite possibly via some basement steps, into the fug of a chophouse.

The chophouse

If you were out and about and wanted food, you had two main options. One was to find a street vendor; the other was to seek out a precursor to the modern restaurant. Cookshop was a generic term, in use by the 1540s, for a wide range of fixed premises, selling food both to eat in and to take away. The grander cookshops provided quite extensive catering services and were very well established. For a long time, they had been controlled by the Guild of Cooks and Pastelers (pastry-cooks), but by the late seventeenth century there was a new type of cookshop in town, known sometimes as a chophouse, and sometimes as an 'ordinary', after the fixed-price menu which they offered around mid-day.[36]

Chophouses were cheap and cheerful eating places, their menus basic and centred on meat. They were ideal for the busy man-about-town, and deliberately cultivated an image of comfortable masculinity, Englishness and solidity. The concept was summed up by a letter in *The Spectator*, in which the author complained that his wife was addicted to fashion, and 'all the goods in my house have been changed three times in seven years'. He could cope with the constant replacing of furniture, china and the new fancy fire grate which gave out no heat, but not the fashionable food, for 'I have a plain stomach, and have a constant loathing of whatever comes to my own table, for which reason I dine at the chophouse three days a week'.[37]

Inside, you'd rarely find female customers, but you might well find a woman in charge of the room or serving the food. One 1737 guide to polite manners explained that when playing cards, 'if anyone has forgot or failed to put in, we are not to rudely call out, like the mistress of a mutton chop-house, when a customer's going away, has the gentleman paid?'[38] Some chophouses specialised, others were more like the one Henri Misson visited in 1719: 'generally four spits, one over another, carry round each five or six pieces of butcher's meat, beef, mutton, veal, pork, and lamb; you have what quantity you please cut off, fat, lean, much or little done; with this, a little salt and mustard upon the side of a plate, a bottle of beer, and a roll; and there is your whole feast'.[39] You'd also get broth made from the drippings and bones, so it was effectively a two-course meal for as little as a groat (fourpence – to put this into context, it cost sixpence to get a ferry from Westminster to London Bridge, or tuppence for half a pint of gin).[40] But there were chophouses to suit all budgets. Samuel Pepys normally paid 12–18d (pence) for his meals at an ordinary, but also patronised a more basic cookshop with an 8d menu.[41]

Had your fill? It's back to the shops. The crowds are more raucous after dinner – and although most of the manual workers are still at work, there are lots of gentlemen returning to their offices or determinedly spending the afternoon going from tavern to tavern in search of entertainment.

You need lace, which means a cloth merchant. Mercers are traditionally found at the sign of the golden ball, generally combined with something else. You may find the golden ball and blue anchor, or golden ball and rose and crown. Then again, you might also find one under the sign of the pagoda, the cacti or various Indian kings, queens and other exotic-looking figures, all vaguely indicating imported cloth via any symbol which looked a bit non-European.[42]

The mercer

Drapers and mercers were the mainstays of the high street. Clothing was a necessity, and that meant cloth. Cloth merchants were among the first to move beyond the market, embracing the chance to expand and store stock, and welcome customers to spend time inside their shops. Choosing cloth meant browsing, not just visually, but physically, feeling samples and hefting them to check on their weight and drape. Along with tailors, they were invariably the most plentiful type of shop on the high street as it expanded, reflecting the wide range of people they served as well as the varied nature and price of fabric. By 1750 Manchester had fifty-two of them, compared to eleven cabinet makers, eight wigmakers, seven booksellers, and just one china dealer.[43]

A mercer nominally specialised in silk and velvet, while a draper sold wool. But the advent of new materials in the early seventeenth century, together with the generally loose definitions of what any shopkeeper sold, means that the terms were blurred. Cloth retailers often just called themselves mercer-drapers. It was further complicated by the fact that many also sold ready-to-wear items, including stockings, gloves and caps, which were technically the province of a haberdasher. Others sold hats, officially made by a milliner.

Millinery was the most female-centric of the related trades, and it was as milliners that you'd find many women employed. There was still a lot of tension around women in shopwork, publicly visible – and accessible – as it made them. The *London Tradesman* thundered that parents should think twice about apprenticing their daughters into trade: 'nine out of ten creatures that are obliged to serve in these shops, are ruined and undone: take a survey of all the common women of the town, who take their walks between Charing Cross and Fleet-Ditch, and, I am persuaded, more than one half of them have been bred milliners, have been debauched in their houses, and are obliged to throw themselves upon the town for want of bread, after they have left them.'[44] But the appeal of millinery for women looking for a means to support themselves was precisely the same as the reason it terrified the men who fulminated against it: it was dominated by women, patronised by women, and gave women a reasonable chance of making money in a retail environment that was very much a man's world. Mantua-making was also largely a women's trade (a mantua was the open-fronted gown, which was the ubiquitous item of upper-class clothing at the time), and mantua-makers were a standard target of male writers wishing to criticise women for spending too much or being grasping and greedy. Rather predictably they were also accused of selling sex: 'The mantua-maker need must honest be, instead of one trade, she can practice three. And if at worst, two of the three should fail, she has still a good employment with her tail.'[45]

Female shopkeepers faced another hurdle, in the form of the law of couverture, which held that, once married, a woman had no independent legal existence, her identity subsumed by that of her husband. That not only meant that their businesses belonged to their husbands (and that they were liable for any debts he ran up), but that they were often recorded under their husbands' names (making it also very hard to find women traders in the historical record). That said, it was complicated, and many married women advertised under their own names, and occasionally went to court in defence of their independence as business people. The British Museum's trade card collection contains two identical designs from a London haberdasher, one carrying the name Benjamin Cole, and the other, Martha Cole and Martha Houghton. Benjamin was in fact an engraver, responsible for many of the other cards in the collection, and Martha his wife. The picture is more accurate than the wording, clearly aimed at female customers, with an interior scene showing well-dressed ladies being served by only slightly less well-dressed female shop assistants. The overall effect is cosy and elegant, with more than a nod to the intimate atmosphere of the female-focused galleries of the exchanges.[46]

You'd probably go into the mercer's shop unless you were in a hurry and just wanted a simple pair of gloves or other

Fig. 2.5. Trade cards for Martha Cole's haberdashery business, 1720s.
Note the inviting door at the back, hinting at a more private
space beyond.

ready-made item. At the bottom end of the market, or for
quick purchases, window-selling was still the norm. However,
if you had slightly deeper pockets and wanted to spend proper
time looking at what was on offer, the interior was both more
salubrious and sheltered. Windows were nevertheless vital ways
to attract attention. Richard Butler, a draper in Basingstoke,
had 'rolls of cloth at [the] window' in 1671.[47] Much depended
on the level of society the mercer was aiming at. In Wellington,
Shropshire, Benjamin Wright's shop in 1700 didn't even have
a counter, while his competitor Joshua Johnson had a 'large
glass [mirror]', plus a counter with drawers below and even
some wainscotting.[48] Twenty years later, William Monsford's
shop in London had furnishings including a pier glass, three
glass sconces, four leather stools, two chairs and cushions, silk

curtains, and ten 'Indian pictures'.[49] Definitely a place to enter, sit down and look around. Some shopkeepers even invested in glazed windows, which allowed for more elaborate displays of cloth and other goods, as well as enabling potential customers to judge from outside whether he or she felt this was a shop they'd feel comfortable in.

Inside the shop, bolts of cloth were set on deep shelves or displayed draped on rails. Smaller items such as lace were kept in drawers. You'd have to ask to inspect what you wanted and wait while an assistant laid it out on the counter. With several people being served at once, goods could quickly pile up, especially faced with an indecisive customer. Cluttered counters and crowded shops were a new and exciting opportunity for petty thieves, a less welcome aspect of the high street. In 1699 shoplifting was recognised as a crime. Defoe used it as part of the plot in *Moll Flanders* (1722), showing Moll being trained in the best way to steal from shops, though after seeing a colleague caught and carted off to Newgate she becomes 'very shy of shoplifting, especially among the mercers and drapers who are a set of fellows, that have eyes very much about them'. She favoured lace sellers and milliners who had just set up and hadn't yet learnt to be careful, keeping their counters clear and their customers under control.

One of the reasons shoplifters found so many opportunities to filch from laden counters is that shopping was increasingly associated with browsing without necessarily buying. This practice even gained a specific term, 'tumbling'. It was seen as a pleasurable way to spend time, as this gentleman found in 1709: 'this afternoon some ladies, having an opinion of my fancy in cloths, desired me to accompany them to Ludgate-Hill, which I take to be as agreeable an amusement as a lady can pass away three or four hours.'[50]

Bargaining over prices gave satisfaction as well, and could become something of an addiction. Pepys wrote happily of having 'cheapened a pair of gloves' in the 1660s, while a few decades later Horace Walpole shopped daily and pondered 'and is there greater happiness?'[51] There were complaints, though, from shopkeepers, as well as journalists who felt that all this shopping was achieving nothing. In *The Plain Dealer* of 1724, a fictional draper complained that 'they tumble over my goods, and deafen me with a round of questions, till, having found nothing in my shop, to their fancy as they call, they toss themselves again into their coaches, and drive on the persecution, to the terror and disturbance of most of the honest shopkeepers, from one end of the town, to the other.'[52] Women came under particular fire, but men were criticised for the same behaviour, as well as whiling away the day flirting with shopgirls.

Unlike those who merely lamented the way in which shops encouraged time-wasting and spending on frivolities, Defoe recognised that leisure shoppers might be persuaded to part with their money by a careful operator and that tumbling could be turned to profit. He quoted (at length) the tale of a wealthy lady who went to a shop merely to turn over goods and drive the shopkeeper to distraction, testing him, for she'd heard bad things about the shop. Not only does she examine cloth in the main shop, but also in the 'back shop', a further space reserved for select customers. Back shops were relatively common, and if you were well-dressed and obviously wealthy, or a known and prestigious customer, you might well be invited to sit in more comfort and look at cloth in a more private setting. It was also better for security. In Defoe's telling, the shopkeeper remains cool and calm, apologising for not having the right goods, and offering to order extra – with a promise to have it delivered within a few hours. In the end she is won over, and decides to make him her main supplier henceforth.

Defoe had a great deal to say about the temperament required to keep shop, especially in the fabric trades, and especially those aiming at the monied, who liked to browse. The shopkeeper must have 'no passions, no fire in his temper, he must be all soft and smooth; nay if his real temper be naturally fiery and hot, he must show none of it in his shop; he must be a perfect complete hypocrite, if he will be a complete trades-man.' It gets worse, since he quotes the example of one man he knew who got so wound up by his customers that he would go upstairs, and 'beat his wife, kick his children about like dogs, and be as furious for two or three minutes, as a man chained down in Bedlam, and when the heat was over, would sit down and cry faster than the children he had abused'. His point was that shopkeeping was not for the faint-hearted. Female readers might perhaps have seen it rather as a warning not to marry a mercer.[53]

Although there were mercers and drapers in every town, smaller shops inevitably had less choice. Plenty of people preferred to wait until they were in a larger town, perhaps making excursions specifically to shop. London continued to be a major draw. If you couldn't get there yourself, you could always send someone else. In Catherine Verney's case, it was her husband, to whom she wrote: 'My dearest – I hope you got safe to your journey's end and found all well. I have sent a pattern of the cloth with an account of all you needed to buy . . . Mr Gurney says that the cloth breeches will last a year very well. I think we had better . . . buy but nine yards of this coloured cloth, but pray let it be as bright, and I think we used to have a finer cloth for the same price.'[54] Alternatively, if you had established a relationship with a particular tradesperson, perhaps while you were in London for the season, you might just deal direct. Henry Purefoy wrote from Buckinghamshire to his London tailor asking for advice on the latest fashions, and requesting a new suit made up accordingly. He was laid-back about the specifics: 'as to my size I am partly the same bigness as I was when in town last', and, unsurprisingly, then complained that his clothes didn't always entirely fit.[55]

If you were titled, or a leading local dignitary, and not fussed by the fun to be had browsing, you could rely entirely on distance shopping. Retailers were more than happy to attend the more upmarket customers in person, bearing samples of cloth or examples of caps, and carrying out fittings at your home. In Manchester, wigmaker Edmund Harrold recorded the various clients he visited personally, as well as those who came to him. His day was a constant round of fittings, meetings and hagglings, as well as the actual process of making the wigs. Harrold's diary is also remarkable for his frankness towards sex. Anyone peering in through his window on 18 July 1712 might have glimpsed him as he 'did my wife standing at the back of the shop titely [quickly].'[56]

You've selected your lace, arranged to pay at a later date, and are ready to depart. If you came in your carriage, it may be parked some way off. The mercer will send his apprentice to fetch it, standing at a respectable distance before handing you into the carriage and either arranging with the coachman where to put your purchases, or agreeing to deliver them to your house. Time, if you are a man, for another quick break.

The coffee house

The first British coffee house opened in Oxford in 1651, swiftly followed by London. By the 1720s you'd find them in every urban centre. In York they were along the main shopping areas of Coney Street and Stonegate, off which you could find Coffee Yard. Coffee Yard was also adjacent to Gropecuntlane (later sanitised to Grape Lane), for coffee was heavily masculinised, and no respectable woman would be found in a coffee house.

As with the chophouses, you might well have found a woman manager, and depictions often include a woman standing in a sort of kiosk at the entryway to take payment and guard

Fig. 2.6. The coffee house politicians, n.d., (late seventeenth century). Complete with coffee, snacks, broadsheets and a stack of punch bowls behind the neatly dressed woman presiding over proceedings.

against the wrong type of customer. Some women became notorious. In Covent Garden, Moll King ran a coffee house with her husband Tom, which was well-known as a place to meet prostitutes. Not every woman was a bawd, though, despite the enthusiastic efforts of pamphleteers to describe them as such. In Bath you could visit Elizabeth Taylor's coffee house, which was also a jewellers and toyshop, and, unusually, open to women (who could always claim that they were mainly there to shop).[57] Tea was also served in coffee houses, but much less talked about. It was supposed to be the woman's hot beverage of choice, and, very much a case of cause and effect, was associated with drinking in domestic settings.

Coffee houses were controversial, though they were becoming less so by the early eighteenth century. In their early days they were thought to be dangerously liberal venues, where classes could mingle freely, a man merely paying the entry fee of a penny and then gaining access to newspapers, broadsheets, gossip and a whole host of like-minded people. The Earl of Clarendon branded them 'the places where the boldest calumnies and scandals were raised, and discoursed amongst a people who knew not each other, and came together only for that communication and from thence were propagated all over the Kingdom'.[58] They provided an alternative forum to the Court for plotting and politicking, as well as for business and pleasure. Charles II even tried, unsuccessfully, to ban them.

In time, some developed specialisms, especially in London where you could choose from over 500 outlets. Lloyds was known for shipowners and merchants (Lloyds List emerged from here), while the Chapter was best to hear the latest news. Will's was a literary salon, Nando's was favoured by lawyers, and Forrest's was the best place to encounter a Scot. Some were overtly political, others renowned for their libraries. They acted as a poste restante for their regulars, and you might also have bought your coffee there for home consumption. Thomas Twining, who ran Tom's Coffee House just off the Strand, could get you everything from coffee cups to coffee grinders (invented in 1687), though he'd also supply such things as gaming dice and jewellery, if asked.

Entering, you'd be hit by the noise, the smell of tobacco, and the sound of people taking snuff. The coffee was pretty dire, as it was usually roasted in house, sometimes with a mechanism made for the purpose and attached to a spit, before being milled and made into a drink in a simple lidded pot.[59] It wasn't exactly an even roast, although it was greatly improved from the early days when it was roasted in a pan over the fire. Plus, advice on making it from this period suggests it was disturbingly weak. The spout on coffee pots was at the bottom so that you could pour the drink without disturbing the grounds, which rose to the top. Milk and sugar helped. You might opt instead for tea, chocolate or even alcohol.

There were worries, too, over the health impact of coffee. In the 1660s, hack journalists slogged it out in the pages of lurid pamphlets containing ever bolder claims. Along with the (not untrue) accusation that coffee caused bad breath, you could have read that it was 'Pluto's diet drink, that witches tipple out of dead man's skulls'. Even better quality ranting was available in 'The Women's Petition Against Coffee' (nothing suggests it was actually written by women), which featured both chauvinism: 'Certainly our Countrymen's palates are become as Fantastical as their Brains; how else is it possible they should Apostatize from the good old primitive way of Ale-drinking, to run a-whoring after such variety of destructive Foreign Liquors, to trifle away their time, scald their Chops, and spend their Money, all for a little base, black, thick, nasty, bitter, stinking, nauseous Puddle-water', and that reliable way of getting attention, sex. Apparently coffee 'has so eunucht our husbands . . . that they are become as impotent as age, and as unfruitful as those deserts where that unhappy berry is said to be brought'. There was a response, 'The Men's Answer to the Women's Petition', which explained that actually coffee stopped premature ejaculation and aided sexual performance, as it 'Collects and settles the Spirits, makes the erection more Vigorous, the Ejaculation more full, adds a spiritualescency to the Sperm, and renders it more firm and suitable to the Gusto of the womb, and proportionate to the ardours and expectation too, of the female Paramour'.[60] If that failed you could always ask the manager to procure you some candied eryngo root, supposedly an aphrodisiac, on the sly.

We'll leave the coffee house, reeking of tobacco but with a clear head and a bouncy step. It's late afternoon now, and if the daylight is fading, you'll see some shopkeepers lighting oil lamps in their windows. Shoe buckles are the last items on our list, and perhaps the one you are looking forward to the most. They are, after all, a great way to add some glitter as you strut your stuff. Both men and women wear heels. Skirts are high enough to show shoes, and a well-turned male calf is always noticed. Your choice of buckle matters. You might try your luck at a shoemaker, but it's better to head to a specialist, and that means a toyman.

The toyman

The term toyman first came into use in the 1680s and denoted a trader who sold a mixture of fashionable things made mainly from precious metals. One guidebook described the toyshop as somewhere where 'curiosities are sold'.[61] Many toyshops were pure retailers, selling goods made in Sheffield and Birmingham, but others also operated as engravers or metalworkers. They sold everything from jewellery to cutlery, as well as technical instruments such as telescopes, plus antiques, taxidermy, and anything else that would sell.[62] Most of it was at least nominally useful, but it was more about demonstrating your wealth, intellect and – a concept which was becoming so important that it was invariably capitalised – Taste. London and a few other places had toyshops by the 1690s and by the 1740s all the larger towns had at least one outlet. They were often found at the sign of the Parrot or the Seven Stars – but their signs were as varied as the wares they sold, and there are records of toymen at the Three Rabbits, Three Herrings or even the delightfully whimsical Elephant and the Rising Sun.[63]

By the second quarter of the eighteenth century some towns were pulling ahead as social centres. Town authorities in places such as Bath, Harrogate, Newmarket, York and Scarborough consciously sought to attract visitors with a range of activities, which included horse-racing, promenades and shopping. Some, such as Tunbridge Wells, took advantage of natural resources

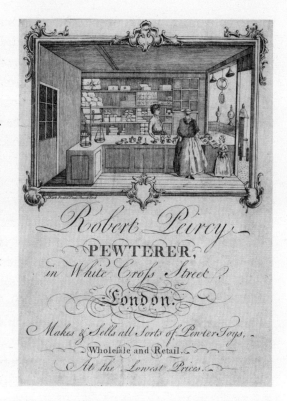

Fig. 2.7. Trade card of Robert Peircy, a seller and maker of pewter toys in London, *c.*1758. The shop still has an open window, with a stallboard projecting on to the street, but inside are shelves holding various goods while more are set out for inspection on the counter. Among them are cups, teapots and candlesticks.

Robert Peircy
PEWTERER,
in White Cross Street
London.
Makes & Sells all Sorts of Pewter Toys,
Wholesale and Retail.
At the Lowest Prices.

and marketed themselves heavily as spa towns. Celia Fiennes visited Tunbridge Wells in the 1690s, recording as she walked through the town 'a row of buildings on the right side which are shops full of all sorts of toys, silver, china, milliners and all sorts of curious wooden ware'.[64] In 1714 apparently 'the chief diversion of the wells is to stare one at another, and he or she who is best-dressed, is the greatest subject of the morning's tittle-tattle'.[65] Wandering the high street, peering into the shop windows, was an ideal opportunity to see and be seen. In the late 1730s an enclosed gallery was added to the Pantiles (the main shopping area) from which musicians played.[66] Shops started to be mentioned more and more in town guides, which had hitherto concentrated on the elegance (or otherwise) of the roads, along with notable churches, monuments and houses. Thus, in

Cambridge in 1725, 'the streets though narrow have many handsome and well-appointed shops which are well accustomed by the great resort of nobility and gentry to this place'.[67]

By the 1720s you would almost certainly be able to stop and enjoy window displays. Many shop windows remained unglazed, especially in less fashionable towns or streets. But in major centres, shopkeepers, at least those aiming at the elite, had realised that a window was good for security, stopped draughts and acted as a showcase for goods. A good window display allowed a level of painless browsing, and, done well, could entice a customer to come in for more.

César de Saussure visited London in 1725, commenting that 'the choicest merchandise from the four quarters of the globe is exposed to the sight of passers-by. A stranger might spend whole days, without ever feeling bored, examining these wonderful goods.'[68] Glass-making technology didn't yet extend to large expanses of plate glass and so windows consisted of multiple small panes behind which was a board with a display.[69] Some went further, with a clever construction of shelves against the window frames, which enabled each pane to show something different. Booksellers or printers might use a board with pages pinned to it, while drapers and mercers used the whole expanse of the window to drape attractive cloth in luxurious folds. Some windows extended above the interior of the shop, with the top of the window decked out with swags of fabric or moulding to disguise the bare brick or wood.[70]

Typically, Defoe had views on all of this. He did not think that glazed windows were necessary. The idea that traders should spend their money on fittings made him even more apoplectic than the idea of shopping for pleasure. He bewailed 'painting and gilding, fine shelves, shutters, boxes, glass-doors, sashes and the like', partly due to the expense when starting out, and partly because in his view it was all just indicative of the decline in morality of the general public. The debate over luxury shopping was still rumbling on, and he was not the only one convinced that people were too easily swayed by sales techniques and that it should be enough for a shop to be 'decent and handsome, spacious as the place will allow, and let something like the face of a master be always seen in it; and, if possible be always busy, and doing something in it, that may look like being employed'. Because it was the eighteenth century, he blamed the rot on the French.[71]

The French were, indeed, present on the high street. In Bath you could find the toyshop of Mary and Paul Bertrand. Paul, who was born in London to French refugees, listed his profession as a goldsmith, as did Mary's family, whose main shop was in London. However, like many fashionable London retailers, they operated seasonal pop-up shops in the main social centres so that their hard-won aristocratic customers could continue to spend their fortunes, and didn't suddenly find a new supplier. The Bertrands' shop was not on the marketplace, but was instead on the highly fashionable Terrace Walk, an open street which led to the bowling green and the river. One of their apprentices later opened a shop on nearby Orange Grove (at the sign of the Hand and Solitaire).

By the 1730s, you could expect the shopping area in richer towns to be paved, with both the road surface and the sidewalk – now, of course, called a pavement – rendered less dusty or muddy, and more hard-wearing. You might even find streetlights. Some towns levied taxes – a 'lamp rate' – or insisted that individuals hung a light outside their houses. It didn't really work, and slowly the town authorities took over. Liverpool had forty-five town-administered streetlights in 1718, while in Coventry the town took responsibility in 1725. There was a real, if highly sporadic, effort to improve the streetscape, and occasionally you would also find street cleaners paid by the authorities. Chester had a 'scavenger' appointed in the 1670s.[72] However, that was rare, and even the most upmarket streets were still mucky – and the alleyways off them remained decidedly dubious.

Toyshops did not, as a rule, sell from the window. Instead, you'd find a well-appointed shop fitted out with shelving, mirrors and glazed cabinets. Most provided upholstered chairs for customers to sit upon while discussing their purchases. Not all toyshops aimed at the very wealthy, though. In places like Bath, York and Edinburgh there was a roaring tourist trade, and toyshops very quickly cornered the market in souvenirs. Painted fans with scenes of town life were particularly desirable. This was an era where inventions tumbled from workshops at quite a rate of knots, and if they could be made into something small and largely unnecessary, the toyshop was their natural home.

In the 1740s, transfer-printed enamel was all the rage, and your toyshop would have been full of enamel snuff boxes and patch boxes (patches are another term for beauty spots, painted or stuck to a person's face, ostensibly to enhance their natural beauty). Japanned wares were another popular item, japanning being the technique of lacquering with a black gloss, often applied to furniture or trays. Small items lent themselves to being slipped into pockets or suitcases, or used to fill gaps in a cargo hold, and ornamental wares from around the world found their way into the display cabinets of Britain's toymen. This included shells, which were polished and displayed in velvet cases and were phenomenally popular. Lady Lovetoy, a character in a play of the early 1700s, described the way her purchases enabled her to 'walk around the globe without going out of [the] house', and some toyshops seem to have been more akin to a museum or a cabinet of curiosities than a simple shop.[73]

As with any other shop, the shop assistant was a gatekeeper. There was no self-service, and prices were still predominantly open to negotiation. However, by the 1740s for small items such as buckles, the price tended to be set. Bertrand's was the subject of a puff piece in 1731 which stated that 'the nobility and gentry, who frequent this place, seem to be greatly pleased with the new and elegant toyshop lately open'd by Mr Bertrand; and what is more agreeable to them is the manner in which all the toys, curiosities and plate are sold; and that is by the price being mark'd upon the goods, and sold at a word.'[74] The quality of the clientele wasn't an idle boast. Frederick, Prince of Wales spent a whopping £714.4s there in October 1738.[75] Most of the cost lay in the materials – so a silver sauce boat at Bertrand's would cost you nearly £8 in silver, but a mere £3.15s for the labour.

The sums involved in selling such fine wares meant that security was always an issue. In addition to the petty shoplifting which dogged so many traders, the more serious crime of shopbreaking was now popular. One of the Bertrands' competitors was broken into in 1744 by burglars who wrenched off the staple and stout padlock on her folding doors. She advertised for the return of the lost stock, which included rings, seals, tweezer cases (a catch-all term for a case containing personal implements including pins and toothpicks) and watches. In other towns the breakers also pillaged the domestic quarters of the shopkeepers, taking food and tableware along with the contents of the shop itself. The glazed windows had stout bars fitted at night, and thick wooden shutters were still ubiquitous, chained shut at the end of every day.

Make your choice, and stow your buckles away in your purse. As evening falls and you emerge into the gloom of the street, you can congratulate yourself on a day well spent. You are heading home now, for supper awaits. The high street is still buzzing, though, for the shops remain open until 9 or 10pm most days of the week. Around you, lights shine down on doorways and catch the gilt of tens of signs promising tactile pleasures and the thrill of the hunt.

The taverns are still open, of course, for where people come, tradespeople will always gather. Perhaps you wonder about the economics – where does it all come from? Are there too many shops? – or worry over whether you are paying too much or putting local makers out of business because you prefer the more fashionable imported goods of their competitors, but it's unlikely. Dwell, instead, on your remarkable show of taste (or Taste) in your purchases today. You can look forward to finding even more choice ever closer to home as the high street expands amid the industrial boom of the late eighteenth century.

Milsom Street, Bath, 1792

Ah, Bath, a social centre, a shopping centre, and according to writer Tobias Smollett, a 'sink of profligacy and extortion'.[76] And yet, here you are. Have you come for your health? Plenty claim they are here to merely take the (sulphurous) waters, and that the town's reputation for pleasure is entirely coincidental. It was put on the map for the fashionable set largely through the efforts of one man, Beau Nash, who became master of ceremonies here in 1704 and dragged the town from being a slightly seedy backwater into one of the most elegant resorts in Europe. Its population went from 2,000 in 1700 to 30,000 in 1800.

Now, as the eighteenth century nears its end, Bath is renowned for a heady mix of sociability and healthy living, all performed against a backdrop of classically inspired architecture. The new town sits at the top of a steep hill and includes the Circus and Royal Crescent, a sweeping statement piece which looks out on to meadows and cows, but which is linked to the old town in the valley below by a series of carefully planned streets.[77] The old town is messier, and behind its stage-managed facades lie the usual slums, along with light industry. Avon Street is particularly disreputable: one in eight buildings houses a drinking den, and it's known for its brothels and high levels of crime.[78]

Bath can be undeniably grim. It's got a reputation for attracting fat, greedy men and women looking to snare a half decent husband. But it is still the place to be, at least for now. Jane Austen writes that it is a good place for 'learning what was mostly worn, and buying clothes of the latest fashion'.[79] It is highly seasonal. Writer and traveller Johanna Schopenhauer

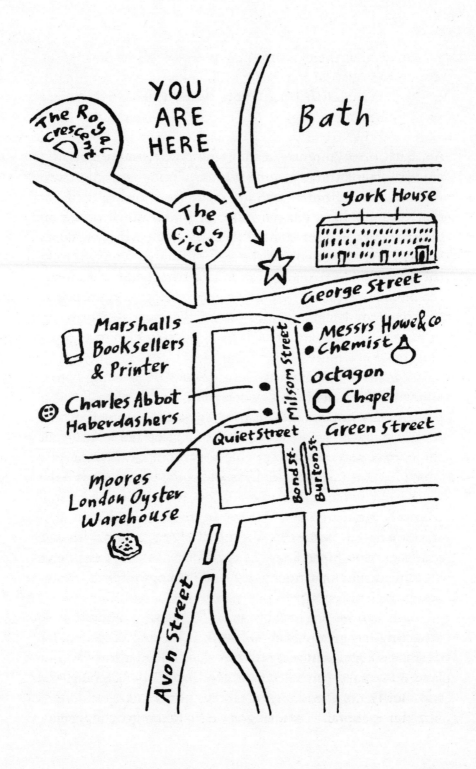

says, 'in winter there is life and pleasure while during the summer the old and lonely die sadly away', and from June to August it is mainly a place where those who have overspent can live cheaply yet elegantly until they've retrenched enough to have another try at going bankrupt. It's too hilly to keep a carriage, for one thing, which does cut down on expenses.

Let's assume you're a winter visitor. If you live in Bath, you probably can't afford the shops on Milsom Street, scene of today's perambulate. For centuries, Bath residents shopped on the streets around the market and Abbey Churchyard. When the town first started to develop in the 1740s, the Orange Grove and Terrace Walk developed with it, and they are still important shopping areas. However, the construction of Bath's upper town necessitated new streets, an opportunity to reorientate its geography. Milsom Street is rapidly becoming the place to be, built not quite as one from 1762. Unusually for British shopping streets, its architecture is relatively uniform, all flat-fronted buildings with classical proportions.

Start at the top of hill. You may have lodgings at York House on George Street, which runs perpendicular to Milsom Street. According to a 1778 guide it is 'the only house of reception which is situated in an open, airy part of the city'.[80] Most of the inns are in the older part of town. If you are planning to stay for some time, as most people do, look, instead, for more permanent lodgings. Milsom Street has thirty-two lodging houses, located on the upper floors of the buildings. You could also take a furnished apartment or house. You can rent anything in Bath, or if you prefer to buy, can pick up furnishings for an entire house from one of the auction houses on the street. John Plura, who has an upholsterer's shop at number 10, is one of the pre-eminent auctioneers of the town. He and his business partner Mr Bally run sales from the Great Room behind the shop. But Henry Cross at number 18 is also an auctioneer (and upholsterer, appraiser, undertaker and lodging house keeper).

Fig. 2.8. Milsom Street, Bath, 1794. This is the start of our walk, with Marshall's bookseller on the left, and a perfumery on the right, behind the trellised wall. You can just see the curve of the Bath and Somerset bank further down the street on the left.

At the top of the street on the left is number 24, Marshall's, a bookseller and printer, which also has a very popular circulating library. Their subscribers include royalty, nobility and celebrities including Emma Hamilton, Nelson's mistress. The shop changes names regularly and for a long time was Tennent and Marshall, printers of the most up-to-date map of the town. On the opposite corner, at number 23, is Elizabeth MacKinnon's perfumery, though she also sells tooth powders, hairpieces and soap. Her shop is one of the few to have a protruding window – not quite a full bay, but notable nonetheless. Although there are oil lamps hanging from the buildings, little else interferes with the line of the houses. Her window, like several others at this end of the street, is surrounded with iron railings to stop you plummeting into the basement area below. Next door, William Ward's shop is about to change hands. He's specialised in Wedgwood since the 1770s, but has never done well.

Now William Ellen is taking over, diversifying into porcelain and glass.

Quite a few of the houses here are entirely devoted to private lodgings, and it's a very sought-after address. The pavement is properly paved and curbed, no bollards necessary, and the road has stone cobbles, or setts. Keep walking, and look for Messrs Howe and Co at number 34, a chemist and druggist warehouse with a window full of brightly coloured jars and adverts for patent medicines (and boot blacking). They're about to move out too, to be replaced with John Coles, a tea dealer who advertises that customers can return the tea if it is not to their liking. He was at the Golden Cannister on Northgate, but the tea market in Bath is ferocious and this is a better address. Almost opposite are three much larger stores, including Percival and Cunditt, who claim to have the largest drapery stocks in the country and have an excellent end-of-season sale. Not tempted? There're plenty of others on the street – including one with an in-house tailor and Lillington's children's frock shop.

Cross back over to the right-hand side of the road and admire the long street frontage of the Bath and Somerset Bank. The site was occupied by the poorhouse until 1781, so the bank building is significantly different to the rest of the street. It's formed of five terraces, with the bank in the central section. There's an impressively curved entrance and the building groans under the weight of pilasters and balustrades, pediments and rustication. For all that, there are rumours that the bank is in trouble and indeed, by January 1793 it will have gone bust, part of a general financial crisis which will also put paid to the grandiose building works currently going on over Pulteney Bridge.

Carrying on, you might pause to look into Elizabeth Mandell's millinery shop, resplendent with ribbons and bonnets. It's sufficiently well-known to be the subject of some of the terrible poetry Bath sometimes inspires. It's said that:

You may stroll for an hour up and down Milsom-Street,
Where misses so smart, at ev'ry fine shop
(like rabbits in burrows) just in and out pop
Where; booted and spurr'd, the gay macaronies,
Bestride Mandell's counter, instead of their ponies.

Try not to wince. As for the ponies, look across the road, where a sedan chair is just pulling up. John Partridge, a dealer in horses, is at number 5. Two doors further on is Charles Abbott, a laceman and haberdasher. You may know the shop better as the sign of the three pigeons. Perhaps nip up the narrow passageway to the side, to take a moment of peace in the Octagon Chapel (admire the gardens stretching out to either side behind the shops as you do). The chapel is very popular, described as 'the only safe place of worship in Bath as there are no steps to climb and no bodies buried below'.[81]

You're nearly at the end of Milsom Street now. As you pass number 2, the scent of cake and almonds reaches you, for this is where Nicholas and Dorothy Molland bill themselves as 'cook and confectioner'.

You may have been surprised, walking down the street, at the lack of more practical shops. Everything here is about smelling and looking nice, and buying the right accoutrements to look like a person of taste. Now, though, you have a choice. You could continue down Bond Street or Burton Street, two narrow parallel roads divided by a row of tiny terraces with nine small shops underneath them, built specifically to alleviate pressure on this most desirable of streets. Maybe admire the statuary on the end nearest you, including an incongruous naked cherub rescued from the rebuilding of the Cross Bath a few years ago. The shops are broadly similar to those you've just walked past, all drapers and china dealers and such like – although you will also find William Ashley's umbrella shop here (much use is made of old silk petticoats), a music dealer (more of a toyshop really), Benjamin Smith's scientific instrument dealer and optician (he also offers electric shock therapy for a shilling per shock), and Robert Ricard's print shop, from where you can both buy and rent prints and artists' materials. Ask nicely, and he might show you some of what the Bath magistrates call 'the most indecent, scandalous, and disloyal prints'.[82] Promises, promises. The turnover of shops is just as high here as on Milsom Street itself, and in 1805 a wide new road, New Bond Street, will replace Frog Lane, halfway down Burton Street on the left.

You may decide you've had enough. To your right and left are Quiet Street and Green Street, which do offer more useful outlets. Milsom Street might be all fabric and frivolities, but it's only one part of the shopping area. Jane Austen, newly arrived in Bath a few years later, will send her brother out for provisions, writing, 'I trust the bustle of sending for tea, coffee, and sugar &c., and going out to taste a cheese himself, will do him good.' Green Street, you may be reassured to know, has a pub, a baker, a butcher, a poulterer, a brewer and a grocer and tea dealer, while Quiet Street has a hairdresser, a couple of grocers, an apothecary, and a tailor. Both also have eating houses and caterers. Why not allow yourself to be tempted by the pickled salmon advertised outside Moore's London Oyster Warehouse – after all, you do need something for supper.[83]

Chapter Three

1750–1815

The ladies . . . prefer a shopping party to all other promenades.[1]

– Johanna Schopenhauer (1803–5), diary notes, published as
a travelogue and translated fully into English in 1988

Shopping list: *Teapots for a friend, tea, a novel, Daffy's Elixir, wine biscuits and some sugar*

In this chapter, you're not quite as wealthy as you were, but you're still firmly at the upper end of the middle class. You're the type of person who spends a few weeks in Bath at the tail end of the season, but lives quite happily in a more provincial – but still important – county town. The head of your household may be a doctor or a banker, though he's probably hoping to procure a very small estate and retire to the country. This is a shopping list suggestive of an occasional trip to town, rather than a quotidian one: browsing on behalf of a friend, stocking up on luxuries and medicine, and visiting a confectioner for items which will keep.

The second half of the eighteenth century is famous for many things: big wigs, tight breeches, a mad king and a profligate Regent. It's also full of big, globally significant events including the growth of Empire and concomitant horrors of the slave trade, the American War of Independence, the French beheading their royal family and drowning lots of lawyers before unleashing Napoleon and taking over much of Europe. On domestic soil in Britain, it's known for the first industrial revolution. The term can be misleading – the changes which occurred were more of a speeding up of existing trends, and large parts of the population were relatively unaffected for several decades. But there's no doubt that Britain by 1800 was very different to Britain 100 years before, and that many of the developments had happened in the previous half century.

Two key shifts for the development of the high street were huge population growth and urbanisation. Figures are notoriously unreliable, but between 1700 and 1800 the English population rose from around 6 million to at least 9 million, while the number of people living in towns of more than 5,000 rose to around 23 per cent. Some towns grew particularly quickly, off the back of factories and mills: between 1700 and 1841 Birmingham grew from 8,000 to 183,000, Leeds from 7,000 to 152,000 and Manchester from 8,000 to 311,000 people.[2]

The experience of living in a town was hugely divergent, and for every rapidly expanding industrial town, there were tens of traditional county towns, along with spa towns in the early part of the era and, by the end, several nascent seaside resorts. Scarborough was very popular, but by the turn of the century the south coast had started to develop, especially once George III started sea-bathing there. His son converted a modest villa into a flamboyant new palace in the small fishing port of Brighthelmston (or Brighton, as it then became known). The majority of the population was working-class, not given to promenading down fashionable high streets and spending their money at goldsmiths and toyshops, but the middle class was also expanding, in number if not proportion. As industrialisation brought ever cheaper goods to the market, it wasn't just the rich who could express their identities through their choice of tableware or wallpaper, pictures or printed fabric.

Walking down your high street in the 1750s and 1760s, you'd have seen more shops, and a wider variety of them. In 1689 most of the taxable residents of King's Lynn's High Street were makers or manual workers, including cordwainers, glaziers, plumbers and carpenters. The street housed five draper/mercers, two milliners, and a scattering of butchers and grocers. By 1764 the manual trades were in decline, and far more buildings contained shops. Now there were booksellers (one a printer), a cheesemonger, fishmonger, spirit merchant, china seller and a coffee house. The latter two were kept by women, as were all but one of the milliners, along with an ironmonger and two of the drapers.

It wasn't just newness and novelty on display, for as the range of goods expanded, the age-old second-hand market flourished as well, especially in clothing and furniture. Second-hand dealers, along with pawnbrokers, were often – though by no means always – in poorer areas or side streets. The market was huge, driven not just by the price of new goods, but by a long-standing tradition of reuse and a moral abhorrence of waste.[3] In all but the most prestigious of towns the cycle of use was very much in evidence because the streets frequented by the lower classes were right next to those occupied by shops aiming at the rich. Shopping areas remained incredibly mixed, with shoppers mingling with residents, workers, entertainers, traders and tourists. There were also many people who used the street primarily as a thoroughfare, generally to the market.

Despite the increasing range of shops, markets remained vital, especially for fresh foodstuffs, and were the mainstay of the working class for most of their needs. This included wares which the wealthier bought from fixed shops. In 1818 shoe-makers in Sheffield who were threatened with removal from their market pitches petitioned to stay on the grounds that they weren't a threat to those selling 'fancy articles' in the shops.[4]

The changing town

Markets were changing too, though, driven in part by tension between pure market traders and fixed shopkeepers. This was less about competition, and more about noise and nuisance. Where a few decades ago proximity to the market was seen as an advantage, now it was increasingly viewed as problematic. In Birmingham, you might have encountered groups of bored youths hanging round the market cross, still used as a site of punishment, 'hooting and yelling and pelting the unfortunate offender in the pillory with mud, bad eggs and offensive garden stuff'.[5] Mixed-use marketplaces were now seen as old-fashioned and annoying for traffic. But official reaction to complaints was piecemeal. Some towns merely shifted a few stalls, while others moved or enclosed their marketplaces. Bristol built a new market on the back of the Exchange in the 1740s, Halifax added one in 1790 and Plymouth in 1804, all with smart new entrances and ordered arcades.[6]

Butchers were a particular target. In Newark in 1773 the new town hall included a purpose-built shambles, kicking off a heated row with the butchers who refused to move until the turn of the century. Sheffield's 1787 regulations outlawed butchers sharpening their knives on the walls, along with the playing of rowdy games, gambling, encouraging dogs, and urinating on walls and in passageways. In Halifax a toilet was provided to tackle the latter problem, but the butchers complained that it was too close to their stalls, meaning customers thought the meat was putrid.[7]

Civic authorities were very conscious of their responsibilities in shaping the town. They weren't the only interested parties – some local aristocrats still had a huge role, as they both owned the land and had the money to reshape the townscape. Public subscription funded other elements. As a local, you may well have given money to help pay for Burslem's town hall (1761), Stafford's infirmary (1766), Birmingham's New Street Theatre (1773), Chester's assembly rooms (1777), Halifax's marketplace (1788) or Hanley's library (1794).[8] (Yes, this was essentially crowdfunding, with subscribers getting extra benefits as well as their name recorded somewhere official.) One of the most important concepts in the late eighteenth century was Improvement. As with Taste, the term was invariably capitalised, to give it the seriousness it deserved. In the urban environment,

Improvement included better street lighting, rubbish collection, civic facilities and the demolition of buildings regarded as eye-sores in an otherwise reasonable town. Street-widening schemes were popular: in York, Coney Street was widened in 1769, while Liverpool's Dale Street underwent a similar process in the 1820s. Liverpool is a good example of the shift away from the market, with the main shopping street leading from the docks to the amenities frequented by 'polite' society: the assembly rooms, the theatres, and, beyond them, the more upmarket residential areas.

There were limits to what could be achieved from above, though. For example, the quality of the paving, if present, was often dictated by individual effort, for each property owner was supposed to pave his or her bit of street. Then, as now, some people took enormous pride in a job well done. When Francis Place, a tailor in 1790s London, was renovating new premises he extended the shop front and sealed off the wooden hatches which gave access to the shop vault directly from the street (a little like the delivery hatches still used by some pubs today). If that wasn't enough, he then 'paved the places where there were wooden flaps in the footpath in front of the shop'.[9] He was a rare case, and across the country the authorities issued and then exasperatedly reissued the town regulations, exhorting shopkeepers not to slaughter animals in the street, obstruct the footpaths, leave rubbish or dunghills in the road or, as in Blackburn in 1793, 'not to throw pea and bean shells, or other offals of greens upon the foot pavements'.[10] Offal, at the time, meant any waste product.

Light was still an issue. The looming metal and wooden signs which hung, creaking, above so many shops had been quietly proliferating over the last few decades. They were now even more puzzling to the uninitiated – Bath had an excellent sign with a golden knife and fork and stocking legs – William Evill's fine cutlery and hosiery shop.[11] They jostled with more

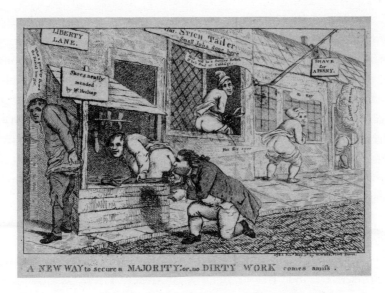

Fig. 3.1. Anon., *A new way to secure a majority*, 1784. This satire
on the Westminster election campaign of 1784 shows that nothing
is new in politics. It's also a really good illustration of a bulk
(you can see why people complained about them obstructing
the pavement), along with the painted street signs now
replacing pictoral signs.

makeshift signs, basically a wooden stick with whatever was
being sold slung from it. You might see tattered trousers blowing in the breeze, pairs of shoes tied up and looped over a beam,
or collections of battered cooking vessels. There were constant
rumours that a sign had fallen and crushed someone, and the
overall impression could be quite disorientating. Down the side
streets they had the additional unfortunate effect of diverting
whatever was thrown from above. Apparently 'the renters of
single rooms, in first, second and third floors, in mean streets,
feel themselves above restraint. Those people empty dirty water
mixed with their offal into the gutters, the stench of which
is appalling.'[12] In 1762 London banned all overhanging signs.
Street names and numbers started to take off, changing the

way people navigated the town, and changing, too, the way it was mapped.

Another pet peeve was bow windows, though few places went as far as Chester, where they were banned. Shopkeepers rarely bothered with permission, and their eye-catching bow fronts not only illegally obstructed the pavements, but in doing so risked causing bad air to linger. This was an era obsessed with miasmas, and in which bad smells and foul air were still suspected of causing illness. Ventilation was a bit of an obsession, and things protruding into the street were therefore seen as very bad indeed. As ever, implementation of the rules was patchy, but by 1805 Johanna Schopenhauer wrote that 'to see the many signs, emblazoned on houses in beautifully drawn golden lettering, that alone is entertaining'. She was especially taken with the number of royal crests in London, indicating that a purveyor supplied one of the (very many) members of the royal family, and was understandably amused by 'Bug-destroyer to Her Majesty the Queen'.[13]

Still, the streets were far from minimalist and even early in the day, the level of noise, dirt and crowds could be intense for the out-of-towner. In Bath, Jane Austen wrote of 'the heavy rumble of carts and drays, the bawling of newsmen, muffin-men and milkmen, and the ceaseless clink of pattens'.[14] (Pattens were metal overshoes worn to protect soft leather boots from dirt and wet.) One, somewhat satirical, commenter in 1761 gave a strangled list of things he wanted banned in London. This included: delivery boys going too fast, derelict houses dropping bits on the street, knackered hackney carriages (cabs), cheesemongers putting their firkins (casks) in the pathway 'by which many a good coat and silk gown may be spoiled', workmen carrying ladders, sedan chairs on the paths and not on the road, prostitutes, longswords, and people who deliberately splash mud on 'a gentleman with white silk stockings'.[15]

Even the more upmarket streets were a cacophony of sounds, smells and sights. When Francis Place opened his shop at 16 Charing Cross, complete with illegal bow window glittering with expensive glass, it was a prestigious address on a street leading to the Strand. This didn't stop it housing several brothels, a tavern, milk cellars (for storing often fairly rank milk), barbers and gin houses along with more finely appointed shops. There were bulks and stalls, as well as residential premises, and narrow passageways leading to downmarket lodging houses and yet more brothels. Down in Brighton it was similar. Johanna Schopenhauer complained that while there were 'elegant little shops where London merchants sell their prettiest and most exclusive fashions', the local fishermen insisted on stretching out their nets 'just where one wants to stroll, so spoiling the air'. She was also less than enamoured with how new, fine houses mingled with much older ones 'giving the place a motley and not very agreeable appearance'. Perspicacious as she was, she was also well aware that the influx of London merchants wasn't fair on local tradesmen, who missed out on potentially lucrative commissions.[16]

Shops were differentiated by class as well as by specialism. You could spot a shop aiming at an upper-class clientele a mile off (well, a few hundred metres anyway: the shopping streets weren't that long yet). Some places had streets from which all signs of such plebeian things as buying bread or underwear seemed to have been banished. London's West End was so well known for being the haunt of the painfully fashionable *bon ton* that it attracted crowds of lesser-born tourists who came to gawp. But even the West End was far from homogeneous, and there were still fishmongers and butchers, bakers and grocers down the lesser streets. It was also far from typical, not least because it was so seasonal. Trade was dictated by when parliament was sitting, and the social scene that surrounded it as MPs (all male) descended upon London and their wives and children partied. When 'the season' ended, the *bon ton* departed. Some shops even used end-of-season sales to get rid of the 'fripperies', which would be unfashionable by the autumn. Then they either shut shop, or reduced their expectations. Some moved for the summer to the resort towns (including Brighton and Bath), hoping to retain the custom of their best customers, or to find new ones.[17]

Let's assume you've started early, attempting to dodge the traffic (fail). You can expect a paved road, the pedestrian area marked with metal or wooden bollards, and a drain in the middle of the road ostensibly clearing the worst of the liquid muck, though by midday it'll still be clogged with straw and horse manure. At this hour, the coffee houses are full of bachelors tired of their housekeepers' cooking, and fops who haven't yet gone to bed but are instead drinking coffee to sober up. There will be businessmen on their way to their offices, and bakers' boys and milkmaids returning from their morning rounds. Step carefully on the uneven stones, breathe shallowly to avoid the unhealthy miasmas, and make your way to your first shop, the china merchant.

The china warehouse

China was an upmarket item. Everyday pottery was generally earthenware, while for centuries the rich had opted for pewter, silver or even gold, both for tableware and display. But then came the quiet revolution that was the introduction of tea (and coffee and chocolate) in the mid-seventeenth century. Chinese hard-paste porcelain was used partly as ballast by the ships of the East India Company, but rapidly found a market among fashionable tea drinkers. English makers quickly started copying the tiny little red teapots of the Chinese, along with tea bowls, saucers, plates, bottles and anything else they could successfully sell.

Initially, English china, along with that of the rest of Europe, was made of lightweight stoneware, glazed and often painted to look like the Chinese imports. In the Netherlands, tin-glazed blue and white china became such an important product that it became known as Delft, after the city at the centre of the new industry. Delftware was, in turn, exported to Britain. By the 1740s the British pottery industry was booming, with dinner services, vases, figurines, chamber pots, knick knack pots and pretty much anything else you could imagine. One of the biggest sellers was a fine earthenware in a warm cream colour, called, unimaginatively, creamware. It was harder wearing than the soft stuff that had come before, and oh, so elegant.

Your china shop would certainly have a properly glazed window. Not only that, but you'd probably find a suitably upmarket door with Georgian architectural detailing, some of which can still be seen in the twenty-first century. Today, you're here on behalf of a friend, and your primary task is to examine what's on offer and report back. You could get a good idea of what was inside from the pieces in the window. The most expensive items would be made of porcelain, the holy grail of china. The Chinese had perfected the process in the medieval period, but it proved hard to replicate. However, by the 1760s soft-paste porcelain was being produced quite widely in Britain, and a harder porcelain would be introduced around 1815. The secret was the inclusion of bone, and for this reason it became known as 'bone china' in England.

Teapots were some of the best items for window display. They were easy to recognise from a distance and were produced in a huge variety of designs, meaning lots of choice for an eye-catching presentation. However, as we've seen with so many luxury goods, there was an undercurrent of unease. Tea, and by extension china, was often negatively feminised, and the tedious trope of women gossiping at the tea table was blamed for an ascending list of ills from individual bankruptcy to the emasculation of the nation. Jonas Hanway was a particularly apoplectic anti-tea advocate, claiming that 'some of the most effeminate people on the face of the whole earth, whose example we, as a wise, active, and warlike nation, would least desire to imitate, are the greatest sippers'.[18]

In reality, men were equally keen china buyers, but they tended to favour one-off, frivolous purchases of enormous vases or dinner services which happened to feature their country house on one of the plates (well done, Mr Wedgewood). Women bought more quotidian items, including those which, like teapots, enabled them to experiment with identity and dare to show their personalities in a highly patriarchal world.[19] You might use your embossed white one for talking business, your floral one

Fig. 3.2. Advert for Charles Hancock's silversmith, 'opposite the Hen & Chickens Hotel' on Birmingham's New Street, *c.* 1810. This was a very smart row of shops: Sarah Bedford's glassware emporium was particularly impressive, with an upstairs showroom, and a staircase whose balusters were made from cut glass.

when you wanted to emphasise your domestic side, your black basalt one when you wanted to show off the whiteness of your hands (nightly applications of hand pomade helped), and you might even have a rather dashing pineapple one when you were feeling, well, fruity.

High street china sellers were rarely makers, ordering instead from potteries in Staffordshire, London, Worcester, Bristol, Leeds and Lowestoft. Popular designs were swiftly copied, so competition was stiff and pricing competitive. There were twenty-seven factories in Britain in the 1780s, rising to 106 by 1820.[20] By the 1790s around two-thirds of English towns had at least one china dealer.[21]

Shopping in person for other people was a common practice, especially among women, whose networks were maintained by constant letter-writing, exchanging gifts and carrying out commissions such as that which you are undertaking. It could be a frustrating experience. Mary Noel went shopping for her aunt, based in County Durham, in 1783, writing that 'I fear you will not like your China much, but Mr Cooper has no choice . . . I saw only one set of twelves & that was that old pattern, foreign, with a great deal of blue, & gilt edges, but he did not shew me any new or pretty patterns.'[22] Then there was the issue of men getting involved. Here's Bessy Ramsden explaining away the lurid silks she sent to her cousin 'Dear Cuzz, the plot against your peepers was not of *my* laying. The patterns were of my husband's chusing, to shew (as he says) his *Taste*. I tell him he had sufficiently shewn that before in his choice of a – wife.'[23] Overall, though, better to trust someone you know than to risk buying blind. Lancashire-based Michael Hughes found out the hard way, ordering a new carriage from a London carriageworks in 1809, only to discover it was 'the most mean paltry thing that ever was sent out of London'. To add insult to injury, the springs went after only thirty miles and had to be replaced.[24] Manufacturers' guarantees were a thing of the future.

It's a good thing your friend trusts you. Going inside the shop, you'd expect a well-furnished interior. It was normal now for upmarket shops to have mirrors, glazed cabinets, wall sconces, and a range of storage and display cabinets. For breakable goods like china, there were real and obvious dangers with open shelves. China shops frequently appear in satires in the late Georgian period, often illustrated as a scene of disaster, with upset goods and shrieking ladies as a bull runs riot within them. China broke easily, and had long been used as a metaphor for female virtue – add in a rampaging male animal, all rippling flesh and animalistic violence, and you had an irresistible mix for a guaranteed smirk. The phrase 'bull in a china shop' as a metaphor for being dangerously clumsy in a delicate situation wasn't recorded until the 1840s, but behind the metaphor lay a genuine risk. Bull-baiting was still popular, despite being actively discouraged. Birmingham's militia was called out to disperse a crowd – and capture the bull – in 1798.[25]

There was a more illicit and altogether more awful version called bullock hunting, which involved youths staging a fight with drovers bringing cattle to market. Others would then descend, with the aim of separating one animal from the others, which they would then chase, poking it with sticks until 'the noise and the blows soon forced him to his utmost speed which was kept up either till he was blown when he would stop and very often turn round on his pursuers: this was fine fun, the beast partially exhausted was easily avoided, and he was teased and tormented until he became perfectly furious, the sport was then at its height, as there was more danger.'[26]

Back to the business in hand. The craft of selling was recognised as an important one. Some writers still ranted about luxuries and morality, or complained that nowadays shopkeepers just sold and didn't make, but it was an old-fashioned attitude. The middleman was still hated, but for different reasons.

George Cruikshank.   A BULL IN A CHINA SHOP.   *September 5, 1808.*

Fig. 3.3. Not just a bull in a china shop (from 1808), but also a good example of the way in which each pane of a glazed window could be used to display a different item, all individually framed.

When the government proposed a shop tax in the 1780s the justification was based on the supposed wealth of the shop-keepers themselves. The inevitable accompanying pamphlet, 'A Vindication of the Shop Tax', claimed that 'do not . . . a considerable portion of them live in a style of opulence and even of splendour? . . . Have they not their country lodgings, and their country villas? . . . Their private entertainments, and their public dinners, where luxury if not riot predominate? . . . Do they not, in general, enjoy a much greater share of the conveniences and superfluities of life, than landholders of far superior property?'[27]

Let's be honest, this screams sour grapes, probably penned

by a jealous small landowner in dire financial straits. Most shopkeepers were small scale, prone to bankruptcy, and far from enjoying a regular weekend riot. Of course, there were undeniably some wealthy men (and occasional women). Lists of civic officials – mayors, sheriffs, councilmen and the like – are stuffed full of shopkeepers. Between 1750 and 1815 around a third of the mayors in York were shopkeepers, mainly druggists, apothecaries and drapers, and a further quarter were listed as merchants, who may have operated a shop as well. Why not, given their livelihood relied on the way in which the town was run?

Francis Place was quite explicit about his role as the owner of a tailor's shop intended for the better-off gentleman about town, employing men to do the cutting and making while he concentrated on its appearance. He admitted that 'the most profitable part for me to follow was dancing attendance on silly people, to make myself acceptable to coxcombs, to please their whims, to have no opinion of my own, but to take especial care that my customers should be pleased with theirs. It was all a matter of taste, that is of folly and caprice. I knew well that to enable me to make money I must consent to much indignity, and insolence, to tyranny and injustice.'[28]

For your china seller, inspiration may have come from the way in which the furniture makers and upholsterers displayed their goods, arranging their wares in mocked-up rooms, so that would-be purchasers could walk through and get an idea of what a sofa would look like in their house. Abner Scholes was doing this in Chester by 1736. Showrooms were exciting places, but even better were those shops which called themselves warehouses or warerooms. Only the larger shops had the capacity for this, as it tended to mean a series of rooms, often extensions to the back of existing premises, top lit with skylights and full of things to buy. They had connotations of immensity and choice and became quite the trend. In 1765 one commentator complained, 'Have we now any shops? Are they not all turned into warehouses? Have we not the English warehouse, the Scotch warehouse, the Irish warehouse, the shirt warehouse, the stocking warehouse, the hat warehouse, nay, even the buckle and button warehouse.'[29] (Scotch and Irish were both cloth – wool and linen, respectively.)

The most pre-eminent china dealer was, of course, Josiah Wedgwood. Wedgwood had showrooms in London, Bath, Liverpool, Dublin as well as in Staffordshire where he was based, renaming his factory Etruria to make it sound classical and therefore achingly fashionable. In London he was based at Portland House on Greek Street from 1774, where he laid out the rooms as showrooms, complete with set tables, display dressers and comfortable seating. He explicitly mixed the domestic setting with the business of selling (and if you are thinking in a modern context about the less painful part of Ikea, you aren't far off). He changed the displays frequently, explaining that 'I need not tell you that it will be poor interest to amuse and divert and please and astonish, nay, even to ravish, the Ladies.'[30]

Wedgwood was a very canny operator, schmoozing the *bon ton* by offering them exclusive viewings and sending them free samples. He called himself the 'potter to her majesty' and marketed his creamware as 'Queen's Ware' after making a couple of services for Queen Charlotte. He took every opportunity to fulfil difficult commissions at a loss, knowing that he could first exhibit the final pieces and then produce versions of the services at various price points having whipped up demand. In 1775 he wrote that that he would 'astonish the world all at once, for I hate piddling as you know'. That year he completed a set of nearly 1,000 pieces of china, each showing a different English house or landscape, each named, and featuring a frog crest in the border. It was destined for Empress Catherine of Russia (Catherine the Great), and when he exhibited it in London the coaches full of eager, wealthy, viewers blocked the street.

The company successfully gained a reputation for quality

and novelty and established its wares as deeply desirable. But Josiah was clear-eyed about what was really going on, and that in business 'fashion is infinitely superior to merit in many respects'.[31] His success lay in convincing the upper classes that he was there just for them, before promptly selling lots of pottery to anyone who could afford it, which very much included the middle classes. Wedgwood's friend and occasional collaborator, the metalworker Matthew Boulton, summed up his own attitude, which resulted in very similar sales techniques to Wedgwood, when he was ticking off an agent who'd suggested restricting trade only to the upper class: 'We think it of far more consequence to supply the people than the nobility only; and though you speak contemptuously of hawkers, pedlars and those who supply petty shops, yet we must own that we think they will do more towards supporting a great manufactory, than all the lords in the nation.'[32]

At Portland House, Wedgwood made good on this promise by setting aside a section of the showroom for seconds or inferior quality goods, allowing people to 'come at them and serve themselves'.[33] This is the earliest known example of self-service (i.e. helping yourself to goods from the shelf, with no intercession from shop assistants). It was definitely not the norm elsewhere. Instead, an assistant would set out items on a counter for their seated customer to examine, watching as they picked each one up and hefted it, inspecting the patterns for mistakes, and considering how it would feel in use. Shopping was very much a tactile experience, highly interactive in terms of both the goods and the people. Shopkeepers were expected to have a great knowledge of their stock, advise on what was in or out, and what else might be coming up soon. Price-wise, there was some wiggle room, but increasingly many of the items on sale now had fixed prices. The habit was spreading, not just from other established businesses, but from the rash of pop-up shops that had started appearing.

Such pop-ups were arranged by London or other big city merchants, who took a large room in a provincial inn, or even rented a market hall, and operated on the pile 'em high, sell 'em cheap principle. Think cash sales, fixed prices, big splash advertising. They took out adverts in the local press and made much use of people with signs standing in the street (sandwich-man was an 1860s term, but the principle was established a century before). Usually, they claimed to offer goods intended for the 'nobility, ladies and gentlemen', but given the size of their venues, the reality was rather more plebeian.[34] Local traders complained that such sales affected their business. Thomas Turner, a draper in Sussex, fulminated that 'this day came to Jones's a man with a cartload of millinery, mercery, linen-drapery, silver etc to keep a sale for two days, which must undoubtedly be some hurt to trade; for the novelty of the thing (and novelty is surely the predominant passion of the English nation, and of Sussex in particular) will catch the ignorant multitude, and perhaps not them only, but people of sense, who are not judges of goods and trade, as indeed very few are.'[35] In fact, pop-ups like this brought people to the town, and probably helped boost trade, as well as slowly change trading practices.

Fully specialised shops remained rare, and opportunistic traders were quick to offer lines that went with their main stock-in-trade. Given the link between china and tea, it was a natural fit for an extra sales opportunity, and while it could sometimes be found at the grocers' shops, until the very end of the century you'd more often buy your tea from a china dealer, a mercer or a toyshop – all upmarket outlets that catered to the same clientele as tea itself. The government issued licences to sell tea, and by 1784 there were 32,754 licence holders across the country (roughly one for every 234 people). They bought from the big London dealers, companies like Twinings and Antrobus, both on London's Strand. By the 1780s fixed-price selling was standard, and local tea retailers, such as William Tuke, a grocer in York, sent circulars to their regular customers stating their latest retail prices after each big tea auction.[36] Tea dealers carried several different types of leaf tea, and often blended them to order. Price lists include different grades of both black and green tea, with enticing names such as twankey (the pantomime dame was later be named after it), bohea, hyson and congou. Black tea was now more popular than green, but both were commonly drunk. If you couldn't decide, help was on hand. John Gibson took out an advert in the *Newcastle Courant* in 1752, declaring that he had taken over a shop at 'the door above the Black Swan in the Fleshmarket, Newcastle', had rechristened it a warehouse, and that he stocked a variety of teas procured from Edinburgh and Leith. He listed his prices and went on: 'the above teas are all very fresh and good, and upon trial will recommend themselves. The tea kettle will be always boiling. Gentlemen and ladies may try the teas.'[37]

Of course, not everyone paid market price from a reputable dealer. Those who did were making a bit of a statement, of wealth or perhaps political belief. It's not known exactly how many people bought tea from smugglers or smugglers' agents, but when the government reduced the duty on tea from 119 per cent to 12.5 per cent in 1784, the number of official tea dealers rose by 60 per cent within nine years as all the illegal ones reluctantly started to pay their licensing fees.[38] The official import figures, which were previously meaningless as a real guide to consumption, rocketed, as the smuggling trade went into a sharp decline (in tea, anyway; brandy and lace from France remained staples, especially during the Napoleonic wars). Estimates that around two-thirds of the tea drunk in Britain was illegal seem pretty accurate, making something of a mockery of the number of officially licensed shops. At least by buying your tea from an official dealer you could be guaranteed that it was, in fact, tea. Richard Twining, who was instrumental in persuading the government to drop the duty on tea, argued that when the price was too high, unscrupulous chancers would profit. Food adulteration would be one of the burning issues of the Victorian period, but it started gaining attention in the 1780s through the publicity given to tea. Twining gave 'recipes' for adulterated teas, some of which weren't merely adulterated but completely fake. Ash leaves were usually the base, coloured with iron sulphate and flavoured with a heady mixture of sheep poo and whatever was to hand in the 'factories' (don't forget this is the industrial age) which made them. To those in the know the result was called smouch. To the poor who thought they were getting the genuine article, it was probably known, at best, as a reason to go back to drinking water or beer.

Your tea chosen, the assistant will wrap it expertly in paper, tie it up and pass it to you to stow in your bag or basket, along with your notes on teapots for your friend. Now you know what you like, you can order it to your home, and ensure you never go short. Best to leave now, though, for there's a commotion outside in the street, and you want to see what's going on. You'll need to skip round the coach parked outside as you exit, mind. Elite customers remain attached to being served at their convenience. As you pass, you can hear the shopkeeper being as obsequious as he can to a barely glimpsed figure inside. If you tiptoe, you may glimpse a towering wig or catch a puff of perfume from within. Mind the man drawing chalk pictures on the pavement (give him a coin if it's half-decent) and head to where the street is wider in search of a quick pick-me-up.

The salop-seller

You could buy a huge range of food on the street. Whether they sold breakfasts to early risers, or more substantial fare to workers who lacked time or facilities to cook at home, the streets teemed with men and women pushing barrows, carrying trays, or set up in a convenient corner. The various 'Cries of London' broadsheets and ballads of the time listed biscuits, gingerbread, buns, dumplings, oysters, plum pudding, muffins and baked fruit (of which biffins and wardens – types of apple and pear, the former dried out until delightfully wrinkled and sweet, the latter more likely to be roasted until tender – were the most common).[39] Pies provided a more substantial option, often with a local twist. On Whitehall in London you could find 'bow wow' pies, 'made of meat very highly seasoned. It had a thick crust around the inside and over the top of the very large deep brown pans which held it. A small plate of this pie was usually eaten on the spot.'[40] Sounds delicious? Contemporaries worried over the relationship between price and quality, and rumours were rampant about bad meat, horse or cat meat inside pies. Then again, everything was risky according to some people. Tobias Smollett described one apple seller as a 'dirty barrow bunter in the street, cleansing her dusty fruit with her own spittle'.[41]

There were less dubious options, and more permanent sellers, who relied upon reputation and were less likely to poison their punters. Hot food vendors were more likely to have fixed pitches, sometimes even extending to shelters or stalls. This included the remarkably popular salop, usually sold by elderly women who could sit down while stirring their cauldron of liquid. Salop (or salep) was made from the dried powdered root of certain orchids. It came from Turkey. In both countries it was known as an aphrodisiac because the orchid roots looked like testicles, but it also had a reputation as being nutritious and good for invalids and children. It was commonly drunk mixed with water and rosewater or, more fashionably by the 1760s, orange flower water, and sweetened with sugar. Other people preferred to add spices or citrus peel, and some drank it like coffee or tea, with milk. Sherry was always popular as an additive as well. Undoubtedly some of the flavourings disguised the fact that sometimes there was very little actual salop powder added, as other starches such as sago and tapioca were cheaper. This was a real issue and contributed – along with its association with the poor, and the increasing affordability of tea – to its eventual decline.

Salop was cheap, and although it was most popular with early-rising or late-to-bed workers such as the nightwatchmen many towns now employed, it was also enjoyed by the (slightly) wealthier, especially if they were out carousing and needed to sober up a bit, or hungover and wanted to feel less mangy.[42] Catherine Baker, a salop seller in London, plied her trade between 3.30am and 7.30am.[43] It was easily made into a light

SALOOP.

Fig. 3.4.
Thomas Rowlandson,
Saloop Seller, 1820

meal with a hot spiced bun or roasted chestnuts, depending on the time of day. Mealtimes were in a state of confusion, with people dining at a bewildering set of different hours depending on their social status and where they lived. By the late eighteenth century, a wealthy early adopter would be looking forward to luncheon (or nuncheon, or noonings) around midday, with dinner to follow any time from 6pm onwards. If you were less fashionable, you'd be more likely to have breakfast, followed by dinner mid-afternoon, which wasn't quite late enough for luncheon to have crept in, and substantial snacking was very much a part of the daily routine.

Drink up, return the dish, and don't think about how many other people have drunk from it before you – it'll be over a century before germ theory takes off. Leave the salop stall, a spring in your step, and head back to the main high street in search, now, of something to feed your mind.

The bookseller and circulating library

Booksellers, like china shops, were characteristic of the changing shopping scene in late Georgian Britain and present in over 80 per cent of towns. Some combined bookselling with publishing or printing, others branched out into lending services. The circulating library was one of the key elements of the civilised town, courting both permanent residents and seasonal visitors as potential members.

The 1818 edition of *The Book of English Trades*, in a somewhat belated recognition of booksellers, noted that 'the Bookseller of the present day is a person of considerable importance in the republic of letters, more especially if he combines those particular branches of the trade denominated Proprietor and Publisher: for it is to such men our men of genius take their productions to sale: and the success of works of genius very frequently depends upon their spirit, probity and patronage.' The author waxed lyrical: 'it is by the diffusion of knowledge by books that all species of tyranny and oppression can be most effectually resisted; it is by the diffusion of books, that mankind become acquainted with their moral and religious duties; and it is also by books that men generally become distinguished for their intelligence, probity, and worth; for where the diffusion of knowledge by books has not taken place, there we most commonly find the relative and social duties at a very low ebb.'[44] He was biased, of course; after all, this was written in a book, and booksellers themselves did a lot to encourage a view of their shops as repositories of knowledge, havens of learning, as well as of their own persons as people to be relied upon.

The eighteenth century produced a huge volume of printed material, both fiction and non-fiction. Booksellers produced regular catalogues listing the titles they had in stock by subject and by size. Categories included sermons, philosophical tracts, self-help guides and acts of parliament. Would-be readers were spoilt for choice. In York, John Todd's 1775 sales catalogue listed over 10,000 books, rising to 50,000 by 1792. Todd sold both new books and those acquired from private collections – not exactly second-hand in the modern sense, as they would have been carefully bound, stored and cared for, with a price to match. The 1792 catalogue was swelled by the private libraries of the gloriously named Marmaduke Tunstall of Wycliffe and Lady Fagg of Wood End.[45] Todd operated at the sign of the bible (the wooden sign still exists, on York's Stonegate). One of his rivals, Thomas Wilson, was at the sign of the Dryden's Head, about a five-minute walk away, and listed 20,000 volumes in his 1783 adverts. He was good at targeted advertising, with one ad making much of the thousand legal books he had in stock, and others highlighting specific volumes, including *Every Man His Own Gardener*, written by the gardener to his Grace the Duke of Leeds.

Many booksellers explicitly puffed their London connections. Here's a bookseller in Worcester, promising 'all sorts of books, pamphlets, acts of parliament, the several magazines, and all other periodical publications, are continued to be sold by H Berrow, Goose Lane, Worcester; who procures them from London as soon as possible after they are bespoke, which is the usual method with country booksellers, whose orders are supplied weekly from thence.'[46]

London wasn't the centre of the known universe, but its inhabitants were prone to considering it as such. It was massive – 650,000 people in 1751 – and inevitably both imported and exported a lot of goods. It's undeniable that its shopping districts were very developed, its facilities advanced and aspects such as lighting were introduced there before anywhere else – but it is too easy to allow it to obscure developments on high streets elsewhere. London snobbery was particularly evident versus the industrial north. Here's a Londoner on Sheffield in 1798: 'shops all shut, place extremely dull and not a person to be seen of a tolerable, decent appearance'. Apparently the town was 'completely dirty, and strewed with Nutshells from one end to the other, as if all the inhabitants had been eating them the whole day'.[47] Meanwhile Oldham's high street was so narrow as to be 'disgraceful to the town itself', and Manchester was 'offensive, dark, damp and incommodious'.[48] Visitors from overseas, who tended to spend most of their time in London, echoed these rather jaundiced views. Johanna Schopenhauer dismissed Manchester as being 'dark with smoke from the coal fires', noisy with 'the rattling of the looms of cotton mills', and complained that the otherwise pleasant botanical gardens were bordered with hospitals and lunatic asylums 'with the result that one constantly hears the screaming and babbling of the poor mad folk'.[49] Residents fought back, and another category of book was the town guide, always full of civic pride and reasons to love your town over any other.

Booksellers were influential by their mere presence. This was the great age of satire, and while Rowlandson and Gilray are the names best known to us today, in the 1790s they were just two artists among many poking fun at society or viciously lampooning its rulers. Prints were popular, looking was free, and crowds around the bookseller or printshop's window helped to draw attention to the shop. It was not without its hazards, mind you. One game played by the unoccupied youth was to creep among the crowds jostling for position and pin people's clothing together, leading – apparently – to great mirth. As ever, you needed your wits about you when navigating the street.

Inside, the emphasis on windows as a showpiece rather than a means of letting in light meant shops tended towards the gloomy. Oil lamps helped, but real browsing was still best done in the limited daylight which filtered in above the window display boards. A good shop would offer a series of counters with bookstands on them displaying interesting volumes, along with further stacks of carefully selected books at intervals along the surface, inviting you to spend time flicking through them. Shelving reached right up to the ceiling on all sides, crammed with books, mainly bound in brown, but with frequent flashes of green, red, blue and black. It was deliberately a little overwhelming and relied on staff to recommend and locate suitable volumes. Browsing a catalogue was easy: browsing the bookshop was discouraged.

Most booksellers were men, often working alongside their wives. Women were involved in all areas of the business, from writing to printing and selling.[50] In Regency London, for example, you could buy from Ann Lemoine, a prolific writer and publisher of cheap pamphlets, aimed mainly at middle- and lower-class women, and which included tales of female adventurers and plucky prostitutes. One of her contemporaries, Martha Gurney, printed and published abolitionist literature.[51]

In York, meanwhile, Ann Ward took over the printing of the *York Courant* after her husband's death in 1759, and also printed fiction including the first two volumes of Laurence Sterne's *The Life and Opinions of Tristram Shandy, Gentleman*.[52]

It could be perilous. James Lackington, who ran a wildly successful bookshop in London, the Temple of the Muses, recounted in his memoir The Story of a bookseller in Taunton, 'a beautiful young lady of irreproachable character; and one whose fine understanding and polished taste did honour to the profession'. Enter, one day, a well-dressed customer claiming to her shop assistant that he had 'private business' with her mistress. The proprietor, a Miss 'A-d-n' (Lackington, like so many eighteenth-century writers, keen to preserve anonymity where possible), took the gentleman into a back room reserved for elite customers, whereupon he 'clasped her in his arms, called her a divine creature etc.'. Unsurprisingly, she screamed and struggled. The assistant and maid rushed in, to find 'Sir Harry Wildair taking improper liberties'. Neighbours arrived, and seeing a sexual assault in progress, 'desired him to desist'. The mayor now turned up, and finally the would-be customer put the shaken bookseller down. It turned out he'd asked at his inn for a place where they 'took in the news', a euphemism for a brothel, but not one which the innkeeper had recognised, directing Sir Harry instead to the bookshop which sold actual newspapers. Sir Harry being an aristocrat, no real consequences ensued – he merely left the town rather quickly.[53]

Gender tension extended into other areas. Shops themselves were not explicitly gendered (apart from clothing), but there were social norms and therefore assumptions. Saddlers and leather shops were very masculine – indeed men seemed to spend as much time ogling fine leatherwork as women were reputed to spend pawing over millinery. All those (horse) whips and (greyhound) collars displayed in a dark panelled room really seemed to get men going.[54]

Fig. 3.5. Todd's Warehouse, Stonegate, York, in around the 1820s. This is probably the circulating library, built when Todd expanded his bookshop into the premises next door.

Booksellers welcomed both sexes, but there was sometimes a slight preference for the male consumer. This was partly due to literacy rates, which hovered around 60 per cent for men and 40 per cent for women, skewed, of course, towards the wealthy.[55] It meant that as a man, you might have used your bookseller for purchases you wanted to keep a little on the sly. Pornography was a flourishing part of the bookseller's trade and was aimed largely at men. But they also had a sideline in certain types of healthcare, an area which usually fell under the control of women. A man who didn't care to explain his latest STD to his wife, or ask his mother to procure a hangover cure, might choose instead to procure suitable products through a male-oriented outlet. Booksellers therefore commonly sold patent medicines.[56] Our shopping list includes a bottle of Daffy's Elixir, one of the best-known patent medicines, and which claimed to be 'a certain cure (under god) in most distempers, viz the gout and rheumatism, with all those torturing pains attending them'.[57] Puffs for it included glowing letters from people saved from imminent death, and warned about fakes in dark tones.

Another service offered by many bookshops was that of a circulating (subscription) library, generally run from a back room and offering several thousand more books. The catalogue for Todd's in York promised that 'Besides what are already specified, four or five of every New Book, or Sett of Books, (especially of the instructive or entertaining type) shall be purchased as soon as published, for the sole Use of the Subscribers; so that they may be morally certain of never being disappointed of Things that are NEW'.[58]

As ever, novelty sold – or in this case could be borrowed. There were good reasons for using a library. Books were expensive, and

Fig. 3.6. Thomas Rowlandson, *The Library*, from *Poetical Sketches of Scarborough*, 1813. An elegant room for elegant people – and their book-carrying servants. The sign at the back proclaims 'just published', for customers always looking for the latest thing.

you didn't always know if you would like them. Jane Austen borrowed *Alphonsine*, a moralising novel about illegitimacy and education, from a library in Southampton. A few days later she wrote, "'Alphonsine' did not do. We were disgusted in twenty pages, as, independent of a bad translation, it has indelicacies which disgrace a pen hitherto so pure; and we changed it for the "Female Quixotte".'[59] She was equally sniffy about one of Egerton Brydges novels, which she disapproved of her father buying (rather than borrowing), on the grounds that it was semi-autobiographical, and Brydges' family were ashamed of it.

The library was a more exclusive space than the shop at the front. They were large rooms, often lit from above (natural light – what a relief), with counters and staff on hand to help. As with the bookshop itself, catalogues allowed a certain level of browsing, but in real life the shelving system was usually incomprehensible, making it quicker just to ask. The decor was upmarket – libraries weren't for the working class, and you'd expect a decent fireplace, paintings (sometimes hung in front of the books, to judge from contemporary depictions), as well as a scattering of tables in the latest fashion. Some shops provided breakout rooms nominally for reading, but really for socialising (some even had water closets). Libraries were recognised as social spaces. Johanna Schopenhauer again, this time bored in Bath: 'what bliss then to refuge in those lending libraries. There one always meets company, exchanges a few politenesses with acquaintances, staring at strangers who stare back at one. And then there are the many novels, newspapers, journals and pamphlets, most elegantly presented, which can be browsed through or taken home.'[60] She enjoyed the stationery section as well, and the artist supplies which the seller kept to one side just in case. Using shops as a meeting point wasn't at all unique to libraries – McGuffog's drapers in Stamford was 'a kind of general rendezvous of the higher class of nobility'.[61]

To balance out the masculine focus of some bookshops, others, including those with libraries, were keen to capitalise on the female market. This was also the age of the novel or, as they were often known, the Romance (most did tend in that direction, fantasy and sci-fi not yet having made an appearance). They were yet another cause of friction. Reading, apparently, was supposed to be serious, and it was disgusting to some that 'books are no longer regarded as the repositories of Taste and Knowledge, but are rather laid hold of, as gentle relaxation from the tedious round of pleasure'. One critic called booksellers 'those pimps of literature', complaining particularly about women who read. As usual, he fell back on unsubtly sexual language: 'female readers in particular have voracious appetites, and are not over delicate in their choice of food, everything that is new will go down'.[62] Scottish poet James Beattie went even further, thundering that 'romances are a dangerous recreation'. He found the fact that they were (sometimes) well-written particularly insidious, for they would therefore 'corrupt the heart, and stimulate the passions. A habit of reading them breeds dislike to history, and all the substantial parts of knowledge; withdraws the attention from nature, and truth; and fills the mind with extravagant thought, and too often with criminal propensities.'[63] If you are a woman, therefore, beware, for you risk becoming a frivolous, impulsive, easily swayed nymphomaniac by simply thinking about reading a cosy gothic romance. The fact that most readers – including of novels – were men was quite conveniently forgotten.

Amazingly, the steady growth in fiction titles at the time didn't lead to the degeneracy of the reading classes of either sex. But grab yourself a copy of The Castle of Otranto *in the hope of interesting times to come, and don't forget to stash your Daffy's Elixir in your pocket and pick up the publicly admissible volumes you've bought on account on the way out.*

The tavern

Our mid-afternoon pause is probably for dinner if you're of the middling sort, especially outside London. You might also fancy a drink. There was plenty of choice in drinking terms, but for decent food as well, you'd have been best heading for a tavern or an inn. Alehouses were fairly primitive: just lots of men standing up drinking, while a serving man or woman went round with a jug. Both taverns and inns catered for a better type of customer (though the line was quite blurred between them all) and had room to sit and eat. Inns were unmissable, for their primary purpose was accommodating travellers. Coaches left from inns, with published timetables and scheduled departures, and stops at other inns to change horses. Many were substantial complexes with stabling and lots of rooms. Residents would be offered a choice of provisions, often displayed in a cupboard for them to inspect. Food would then be cooked to order and served in bedrooms or in a side room. Inns were also venues for public entertainments, including music recitals, dances and auctions. Inquests, bankruptcy proceedings and business meetings were also frequently held in them. Eventually, as the railway network took over and stagecoach travel declined, some would develop into hotels. As the distinction between alehouse and tavern disappeared, the smaller inns became largely indistinguishable from their companion establishments, and all would end up under the broad heading of the public house.[64]

In the eighteenth century, though, taverns remained slightly apart. In theory they specialised in wine, and catered for a clientele which was nominally slightly less intent upon getting drunk than the one in the alehouses. They also served food. As with the coffee houses, they were masculine spaces, though you might find a woman waiting tables or touting more personal services. Some taverns saw this as a chance for extra profit, providing rooms 'to receive prostitutes and their gallants'.[65] Your tavern would, of course, operate under a sign – common names included the King's Head, the White Hart, the Crown and Anchor, the Globe and variously coloured bears (if you were lucky, there'd be a stuffed one displayed outside). Otherwise, the architecture varied from the splendid to the homely, though most favoured a domestic style, with neatly glazed windows and a couple of steps up to the door. Inside, clients sat at communal tables in the same room. More upmarket venues had booths. Kitchens could be off to one side, but many had a basic open fire and spit providing heat, light and food from the same, communal space.

Taverns didn't provide much choice to the casual dropper-in. Like chophouses, there was a fixed menu, and you'd simply agree on what you wanted to eat. However, it was also possible to arrange for private dining, with a menu designed to order. Some taverns were renowned for their food. The White Hart Inn in Lewes boasted a chef called William Verrall. Verrall trained under the French chef to the Duke of Newcastle, a man lampooned for his extravagance, and in 1759 published *A Complete System of Cookery*, defending French cuisine and showcasing the most *à la mode* ways of cooking. The introduction is a masterclass in bitchiness and self-aggrandisement. Other tavern cooks also published. Richard Briggs (*The English Art of Cookery*) advertised himself in the 1790s as 'many years cook at the Globe tavern Fleet Street, the White Hart tavern Holborn, and now at the Temple coffee house'.[66] John Farley of the London Tavern meanwhile called his book *The London Art of Cookery*. Both books were largely plagiarised, a fairly normal state of affairs in the publishing trade, and not an impediment to healthy sales.

London was particularly well furnished with taverns: you could even buy a guide to them (and other eating venues) in the shape of *The Epicure's Almanack* of 1815. A quick flick through its pages reveals such delights as the King's Head on Newgate Street, 'a celebrated steak and chop-house, with soups always ready', the Dolphin on Ludgate Street, 'in the winter evenings roasted potatoes are to be had here, served up with butter and pepper, at three-pence each', Morins on Duke Street, 'the dinners are cooked by French artists, who are at stated times carefully physicked and dieted, in order to preserve their palate in all its original delicacy of tact', or, in Wimbledon, the White Lion, where 'you may have a good dinner drest here to order, in which order you ought not to forget to include stewed eels, or fried flounders'.[67]

The primary draw of the tavern was its wine list, with wines decanted for each customer from the barrel and kept well. Overseas travellers couldn't get enough of English inns and taverns. Over in Paris 'restaurants' were becoming popular – serving restorative bouillons and soups, hence the name. In 1782 a restaurateur called Antoine de Beauvilliers opened an upgraded version, modelled on the English taverns he so admired. He called it La Grande Taverne de Londres. It was one of the first true restaurants, a concept which dribbled back into Britain as French cooks fled across the Channel following the demise of their employers during The Terror. It would take another century to fully catch on, by which time restaurants had developed an identity of their own, and were able to take off as a glamourous French innovation.

For now, enjoy your mutton and claret, and engage, if you like, in a spirited discussion with your fellow diners. Unless you are dining privately, you won't be served a dessert, though you may indulge in a sweet pudding (or two) if the place offers more than one course. Your next stop will provide the opportunity to rectify this, though, if you so choose. Step into the street and gingerly sniff the air: it's time to salve your abused olfactory senses, and if you're lucky, the scent of boiled fruit and sugar-syrup may reach you as you draw near.

The confectioner and pastry-cook

According to *The Book of English Trades*, 'a confectioner is one who makes sweetmeats, preserves of various kinds, jellies, jams, gingerbread, &c, and is generally combined with the pastry-cook, who makes tarts, cheese cakes, pies, &c'.[68] It was a new entry for the 1818 edition, for a trade which exploded in the first decades of the nineteenth century. There were four confectioners in Norwich in 1784, but twenty-nine by the 1820s. In York, the respective figures were four and twenty-two. Meanwhile Bath had four in 1790, rising to twenty-six by the 1840s.[69]

Fig. 3.7. Billing and Cooing at the Jelly Shop, 1798.
Everything about this suggests quiet luxury, from the stand full of jelly glasses, to the carving around the mirror in which the dandy is admiring the cut of his coat.

The Book of English Trades only told half the story. Confectioners' shops – normally called simply 'confectioners' were a riot for the senses, and confectionery was associated with glamour, wealth and exoticism. The exteriors were often gorgeous, all rococo fripperies and gilt detailing. Even in the 1720s, when confectioners were just getting going (and were still known as pastry-cooks), they were among the most lavish of premises. Defoe had (unsurprisingly) moaned about the expense of them, listing as typical fittings including sash windows, tiled walls in both front and back shop – the latter additionally 'finely painted in forest work and figures', large multi-branched candlesticks, several 'great glass lanthorns', sconces, silver candlesticks, endless silver salvers to display sweetmeats, plus 'twelve large high stands of rings, whereof three silver, to place small dishes or tarts, jellies etc at a feast'.[70] Now, eighty years on, the lighting was even more splendid, the gilding brighter, the silver shinier, the plasterwork fancier – while the goods they offered would make your mouth water just reading their names. The wine biscuits you've come in for (literally intended for dipping into wine at the end of a meal) are small fry. This is a shop of magic.

What was confectionery? In the modern sense, it's mass market chocolate bars and disappointingly dusty boiled sweets. In the Georgian era it referred broadly to anything sweet and light. It came out of the dessert course, itself a descendant of the early modern banquet, which generally referred to the sweet course at the end of a meal which was entirely geared towards showing off and titillating the palate. Dessert did not refer to sweet puddings or fruit pies, the kind of thing which we erroneously lump under the category of pudding (meaning the sweet course) today – they were served as part of the main meal. Instead, you'd serve fresh fruit and nuts, along with goods bought specifically from the confectioner. Think jellies and meringues, set creams and blancmanges, syllabubs, ices (ice creams), wafers and waffles, many of which you would need to

The Confectioner.

Fig. 3.8. *The Confectioner*, from *The Book of English Trades*, 1818.
Confectioners were luxury shops: all that slave-produced sugar
didn't come cheap. The stand to the left probably holds whipped
syllabub rather than jelly, while behind the shopkeeper you can see
jars which might hold sweets, meringues or biscuits.

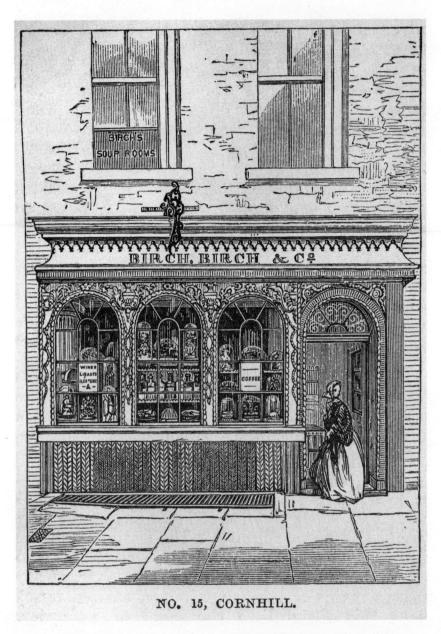

NO. 15, CORNHILL.

Fig. 3.9. Birch's confectioner, 15 Cornhill, London. The shopfront
was installed around 1800 and remained in use until 1926.
It is now at the V&A.

order in advance. Behind the counter, glistening in the light, you'd see fruits in liqueur and syrup, candied flowers and glass jars full of delicate, hand-made sugar sweets and intricately moulded sugar sculpture (available for rent, but maybe don't tell your dinner guests). You might also feast your eyes upon cakes, especially iced or very fancy ones, and there was a grey area around some other baked goods such as biscuits. Many confectioners retained elements of the pastry-cook's art and sold tarts and pastries which shaded into the more certain definition of confectionery.

Some confectioners in the early nineteenth century also operated as sit-down snack joints, offering a range of wares to be consumed at the counter or at little tables to one side. What you ate depended on the time of day. Johanna Schopenhauer was a fan: 'The cake shops, where it is the fashion to call in the morning and for breakfast eat several small cakes hot from the oven, also present their wares in the most pleasant manner. Everything the baker and the pastry-cook have invented is to be found there, arranged enticingly on tables covered with snow white linen clothes. Everywhere there are flowers, jellies, ices, liqueurs and dragees [sugar-coated nuts] of all shapes and colours in fine crystal jars.'[71] In Bath, Lady Luxborough liked a daytime visit: 'from the bookseller's shop we take a tour through the milliners and toymen; and commonly shop at Mr Gill's, the pastry-cook, to take a jelly, a tart, or a small basin of vermicelli'.[72]

Gill's of Bath was famous – at least among a certain set. For the first time, some shops had achieved a degree of status – brand awareness, if you will – which meant that you could talk about them in letters and know that your correspondent would know what you were on about. Jane Austen mentioned another Bath stalwart, Molland's, in *Persuasion* (we passed it on our way down Milsom Street earlier), while in London, Gunter's on Berkeley Square was known for its ices. Also in London was

Birch's, which from an enviable location opposite the Royal Exchange served not just confectionery but one of the most iconic of show-off dishes. You can almost feel the quiver of excitement from Ralph Rylance as he writes, 'on the tables are placed lemons, cayenne and other condiments, with toasted French bread for the free use of the visitants. Throughout all the turtle season, is served up in positive perfection that maximum of high diet, real turtle soup.'[73] Not every shop was quite so elevated, and the more standard offering was of simple jellies, creams and ice creams in individual glasses along with tea, wine and riffs on the theme of sponge cake.

Birch's turtles were imported live from the British West Indies and then slaughtered on site. It was impossible to miss Britain's imperial connections as you shopped, but they were especially in evidence at the confectioners. The trade was founded on sugar and spice, all of which was imported, much of it from British colonies. Many trades were exploitative, but sugar took exploitation to new lows. The wealthy clientele of the confectioners' shops enjoyed products reliant on slave labour. Did they consider the human misery behind their cakes? The reality of production was all too easily ignored in the face of fashion and desire. Those who opposed slavery drew on the tropes used in previous centuries as part of the debates over shopping itself. Some blamed shopkeepers, for dangling temptation in the face of powerless consumers. Others pointed out that consumers were complicit too, so blinded by their own desires that they ignored morality or ethics. A small group of abolitionists set out to prove that public opinion could be swayed, and that money really could talk. Even before mass media it turned out to be possible to effect change through concerted, organised action, proving that shoppers did (and do) have agency, even if they rarely chose to exercise it.

In 1791 William Fox wrote *An Address to the People of Great Britain on the Utility of Refraining from the Use of West India Sugar and Rum*. It was published by Martha Gurney, the abolitionist printer we met on page 124. It was one of many attempts to influence the government to abolish, first the trade in enslaved people, and then the institution of slavery itself, and it was hugely influential.[74] The key was to persuade women, the buyers of everyday household goods, and the keepers of the sugar-laden tea-table, to boycott slave-produced sugar, using their purchasing power to the good. Around half a million people joined the campaign, which gained enormous traction.[75] Some confectioners switched to East India-produced sugar in response to consumer pressure, and all reported that sales were down. Wedgwood, finger as ever on the pulse, produced commemorative items with a kneeling slave and the motto 'Am I not a Man and a Brother?' You might have noticed them in the china shop, printed on snuff boxes, medallions and tea wares. The campaign had a real – if slow – effect, and contributed to the abolition of the trade in 1807. However, while Britain made much of its humanitarian bent, the practice itself continued until 1833 – and the debts incurred in paying off slave owners weren't fully paid until 2015.

Like catering generally, confectionery was a trade where women were slightly more common, although local trade directories still listed shops under the male head of household, regardless of who ran the business. That was the case, for example, of Elizabeth Raffald, the Manchester-based ex-housekeeper turned confectioner, caterer, cookery teacher, innkeeper, newspaperwoman, recruitment agent and author. Raffald's husband, an ex-gardener, kept a florist, while her own shop promised 'cold Entertainments, Hot French Dishes, Confectionaries, &c'.[76] It was very successful, boosted by the publication of one of the best cookery books of the eighteenth century, *The Experienced English Housekeeper* (1769), which in turn supplied many of the recipes published by the plagiarising tavern cooks we've already come across. Also in Manchester, a little later, was Jane Clowes, described as 'industrious, persevering and successful'. She clearly had an eye for a business opportunity, for 'in the summer of 1812, when several regiments of militia were encamped on Kersal Moor . . . so great was the demand for sweets to vend to the numerous visitors to the Moor, that all her hands worked almost night and day for some time, to meet this extraordinary demand'. (Britain was at war with France from 1793 to 1815, and redcoats swarmed the streets of Britain – wealthy bored officers were good customers for confectioners offering sit-down delicacies.)

Sugarwork was not for the faint-hearted. Pastillage and moulded work might well involve carving your own moulds, building highly intricate architectural pieces out of delicate sugarpaste, applying filigree sugar lace to vertical surfaces and transporting the end result to whichever client had ordered them, but at least it rarely involved actual physical danger. For that, order some boiled sugarcraft. Apparently Clowes 'would often herself take an active part in the labour, for severe labour it was, of pulling the boiled sugar into long ropes; and when her step-son, who worked in this part of the business, one day fell exhausted and fainting on the floor, overcome by the severe toil in a necessarily heated atmosphere, while his comrades got him water, she only looked at him and said, "Thou'rt a poor soft thing."'[77]

As a result, confectionery was rarely made in domestic settings, except in very large establishments. By the 1860s Queen Victoria was one of only a handful of people to employ a confectioner directly, and the royal kitchen took to poaching chefs from Gunter's, among others. Many confectioners operated as full-scale caterers, preparing and setting out elaborate desserts for those who could afford it, and, by the nineteenth century, branching out into supplying full dinners and catering large events such as weddings and garden parties. The larger companies could also look after marquees and furnishings, while even smaller shops might find it prudent to offer specialist dessert services and cutlery. Then, as now, you could rent a lot of goods for one-off occasions. Over in York, the mayors habitually rented their tableware and glasses for parties at Mansion House from a shop further down Coney Steet run by Mr Surr. The dinners involved copious quantities of wine, and the list of breakages was significant: perhaps a good reason to stick to simple desserts and use your own plates.

Resist the lure of splashing out on anything too ornate. You're only in town for a while, and your family would look aghast if you came home brandishing a bill for a grotto made of nougat with sugar moss, or a classical pavilion wrought in carefully coloured pastillage. Take your biscuits, arrange delivery for your sugar, and tear yourself away.

By early evening you want to be safely at home, unless you're preparing for an Assembly or a rout. By nightfall the scavengers will be out in force picking up refuse, and the cry of the dustmen collecting dust for fields and brickyards will echo across the streets: 'Dust ho.' On the high street the shops shut around 10pm, the last few shoppers haggling for bargains at the grocer, while around them the apprentices clear goods from the street and the shopfront. Some shops still have full shutters, others now prefer half shutters, allowing the windows to reflect light and advertise the wealth of the shop within. Others just have bars for security, leaving their oil lamps burning. Christian Goode, in London in 1804, marvels at 'the shops displaying their elegant lamps . . . in such profusion as to produce a very brilliant effect'.[78] While most shops still aim for a reasonably wealthy clientele, even the poorest person can enjoy a shop window. And it's only a short step from looking, to wanting, and that means opportunities to come.

Gentleman's Walk, Norwich, 1869

It's the mid-point of Queen Victoria's reign, and you're in Norwich. City chronicler A. D. Bayne says it was 'formerly a great manufacturing city; but it has declined much of late'. Reliant on the cloth trade for centuries, and still well known for its fine printed shawls, it has lost out to Manchester and France. However, Bayne does it a disservice, for in the last decade the boot and shoe-making industry has taken off, employing thousands of people turning out stock for the ready-to-wear market. Engineering is another key industry, and down by the river (and in Norwich over-the-water) there are myriad warehouses, workshops and factories. The biggest employer is Colman's, who make starch, paper and laundry blue, though all of that pales beside their award-winning mustard. Like many of Norwich's leading families, the Colmans are non-conformist – in this case Baptists – and support the Liberal party. They play a large part in the governance of the city, and Ethel Colman, currently aged six, will go on to be Britain's first female mayor. Norwich is known for its religious non-conformity and independent bent, and punches above its weight as a regional centre, particularly in the area of banking. Another leading family is the Gurneys, who are Quaker. Their bank will merge with Barclays at the end of the century to form a banking behemoth. Other names you'll see on every city dignatary list include the Chamberlins and the Jarrolds, both of whose money comes partly from shoppers like you.

You're standing, a little indecisively, at the north-west corner of the market square. Unlike the planned streets of Bath, Norwich retains an essentially medieval layout with impractical narrow streets and a great deal of light industry within even the

most upmarket commercial areas. But its civic authorities are strong and much given to modernising. Bayne likes that 'the old street architecture . . . is rapidly vanishing before the hand of improvement'. Behind you lie the rather unimaginatively named Post Office Street and Exchange Street, one of very few post-medieval routes into the city centre (the Corn Exchange itself was rebuilt just eight years ago). Perhaps you've come from there, buying seeds at Ewing and Child (their nurseries are a mile or so out of town), or picking up 'the noted square meat biscuit' for dogs at Chamberlin's feed merchant. The smell of cooking bran drifts down the street, for they manufacture on site. Not the best odour while enjoying the 'experienced French assistant' at the hairdresser nearby. There's also Thorns the ironmonger, which will survive until the twenty-first century, lending its name to the only pub in Britain called the Ironmonger's Arms.

The corner of Exchange Street where London Street leads off to your left is home to one of Norwich's foremost booksellers and printers. The Jarrold family are well represented on the town council, and known for their philanthropy, as well as for the extensive series of religious tracts they produce, promoting abstinence and temperance. In 1877 they will publish *Black Beauty* by Anna Sewell and go on to be a leading publisher as well as taking over the entire block as they add other selling departments to their premises. For now, though, they are content merely to outshine the three other booksellers on the street.

You may be momentarily tempted by London Street. Norwich can be challenging for shoppers. It has two main shopping streets, and it's not easy to decide which is the pre-eminent. But the many large drapers and other shopkeepers on London Street are constantly complaining, for it is cramped and in a permanent state of disarray. Widening works have been ongoing to improve access from the station to the centre of the city since 1848. The *Norfolk Chronicle* says, 'the whole street is a bungle . . . The lower part of the street remains as bad as ever, and in the upper part years have been required to make a fourteen feet passage.' No wonder the city walls are being razed for rubble to build a new road.

Unlike the other shopping streets in this book, Gentleman's Walk directly borders the market. Indeed, it is more properly called Market Street, though nobody ever calls it that. As you start walking, the market square is on your right, shops to your left only. If it's Saturday, the market will be in full swing. Even on a normal weekday you can find quite a few stalls dotted about the place. Three sides of the square have shops – looking a short way up to your right you can see the flags and uniform frontage of Chamberlin, Sons & Co, drapers – they occupy one of the largest buildings on the marketplace, and sell not only cloth, but furniture, carpet and soft furnishings. They even

have a refreshment room, 'for the convenience of country customers, many of whom have come long distances'. The building
is somewhat obscured by the black and white flint of the medieval guildhall, but you suppose it's good to retain something
of the past.

As you start along 'The Walk' proper, you will notice that
the buildings here are mainly late-eighteenth-century (at the
front, at least). More modern, plainer fronts contrast strongly
with the rusticated stonework and almost too much glass of
converted townhouses, and down the side streets lurks many
a medieval gable. Right next to you now is Lammas Bros., a
tea dealer that has been there for several decades. However, the
building is a bit shabby, and they face stiff competition now
from Ladyman's a few doors down. In just a few years' time
Howlett and Sons, a pianoforte and harmonium seller currently
at number 2, will move sideways, rebuilding the prestigious
corner site in a vaguely neo-gothic style. For a kitchen range,
or some good wrought iron, the city showroom for Barnard,
Bishop and Barnards is at number 3. They advertise noiseless
lawnmowers which even a child can work. Next is Thomas
Brighton, a bootmaker, who retains his sign – the Golden Boot
– for those who, be warned, can't quite grasp the many names
and odd numbering system applied to this street.

The street is well paved, with proper kerbstones, which is
very necessary given the habit of boys selling firewood from
carts to park up against it – 'a glaring disregard of the public
convenience', as one correspondent to the *Norwich Mercury*
thunders. Step round them – ooh, a private house (have a quick
peek in the window and be disappointed, as it is just full of
drapery assistants like so many of the rooms above the shops)
– and admire the goods on show in the Mary Rump's fancy
repository on the corner of one of the alleyways leading to the
street behind. All fashionable life is here: another bookseller,
Snowdon's linen-drapers and milliners, and the hard-to-miss

premises of Etheridge & Ellis, one of several jewellers on the street. Their main competitor is Theodore Rossi, back near the Guildhall, who is also a silversmith as well as an optician. Etheridge & Ellis have much bigger signs though, affixed to the upper walls as well as above the windows – plus a huge eagle with its wings outstretched above the door. They promise 'the largest selection of plate, jewellery etc in the Eastern Counties' and are also very good for electroplate, which is very popular now.

On your right is a statue of the Duke of Wellington. Give him a nod and look beyond, to the upper marketplace, gradually closing in on you. It's all taverns – the Waterloo, the Two-Necked Swan, the Sir Garnet Wolseley, plus a set of dubious-looking bulks which house the butchers' shambles tacked along one side. Thankfully, the fishmongers were rehoused in a splendid neo-classical building just nine years ago. Back on the shop side of the street, it's all about the grocers. Copeman's is the largest – John Copeman is another Norwich dignitary, having founded the Norfolk News Co (along with Jeremiah Colman and Thomas Jarrold). Naturally he also sits on the city council. At number 13 is Marston's confectioners, and then Henry Brown, covering all possible bases as a 'family grocer, provision merchant and Italian Warehouse'. Numbers 15 and 16 are the imposing Royal Hotel. This is one of the city's foremost inns, used for mayoral parties (including celebrating royal weddings, christenings, etc.). You may remember its less dignified previous incarnation as the Angel, from which the Norwich Whig supporters threw flour bombs at the Tories in the 1840s elections.

Also here is Cubitt's druggist and one of James Gore's two cutlery and fancy goods stores. His other shop is at 10½ Haymarket. The numbering is so erratic that it's no wonder grocer and fruiterer William Lake advertises himself as 'three doors away from the Royal Hotel'. Incidentally, Cubitt is also an insurance agent, while the glass dealer at number 22 will sell you fishing tackle. The notion of specialising in one thing is still far from established.

At this point, the open space of the market finally closes in. The street remains wide, though, enough that you can see the tall tower of St Peter Mancroft still looming above you as you walk. Confusingly, it also becomes (officially) Haymarket, for just seven shops (and some more taverns) further on is the former site of the actual hay market. Now it's partially filled with the White Horse Inn. You'll also find the Star and the Lamb just opposite – all coaching inns hanging on for dear life as the railway slowly puts coaches out of business. The shops here are a bit bigger, presumably as rents are just a little bit lower. Back & Co are a large wine and spirit dealer, while Israel Jacobs sells china, glass, earthenware and more general furnishings, and has another outlet in London. Not to be outdone with the London connection, Henry Stacy advertises that the book club he runs from his print shop is better than buying from London as there's no delay in postage.

As you might imagine, given the business travellers coming and going from the inns, this bit of the street also has services: banks, solicitors and the like. As Haymarket turns into Briggs Street, watch out for the Savings Bank on your left. The sharp corner on which it sits will be swept away and the frontage done up in the latest style at the end of the century to enable the newly installed tramway to make the turn.

Briggs Street itself is a little more downmarket. Here you'll find ready-to-wear shirtmakers, and four milliners. S. D. Page & Sons are here too, selling wires and brushes. They are also 'manufacturers of paper bags by patent steam machinery'. However, don't despair – for if you do keep going (and it really isn't a long section of the street), you'll come to Rampant Horse Street at the T-junction at the end. If you're still thinking about London Street's drapery emporiums, fear not, for here are two more draper's stores with multiple departments. Curls and Buntings are rapidly becoming Norwich institutions, having set up as a partnership in 1860, to split up and open rival stores just a year later. Competition being good for the consumer, you can now choose between Bunting's brazen claim of 'Latest, Cheapest, Best', or Curls and their determined attempt to take over the whole of the block directly opposite as they expand. Already they sell china and furniture alongside the drapery, millinery and haberdashery, and they've recently installed a new outfits department in the former billiard room of the hotel they've bought out. Unconvinced? They make much of their own stuff, with 500 people employed in workshops in the higgledy-piggledy streets back at the other end of the marketplace. Shop local or shop for exotica from London and beyond: your money, your choice.[79]

Chapter Four

1815–70

If, some years ago, our neighbours in sneer, called us a nation of shopkeepers, we think that they must now give us the credit of being shopkeepers of taste.[1]

– *The Book of English Trades* (1818)

Shopping list: *Mutton chops, a plaything for a child, and a bolt of decent light wool (followed by a dress or suit fitting)*

We're moving steadily down the social scale: as shops have become more established, their clientele has expanded. Today's shopping list suggests you are a lower middling sort of a person, the kind targeted by aspirational mid-century self-help literature such as Beeton's Book of Household Management. *If you're a man, think George in Jerome K. Jerome's (slightly later)* Three Men in a Boat, *a clerk who 'goes to sleep at a bank from ten to four each day, except Saturdays, when they wake him up and put him outside at two'.[2] If you prefer the female viewpoint, it's the classic bored suburban model: a nursemaid, a daily help and the determined desire to create the impression of slightly better-off circumstances than your actual income might allow.*

And so, we sweep into the nineteenth century. In 1815, the Napoleonic Wars had just ended, and the country, victorious and revelling, was emerging into a new era. The Regency, with its restrained classical fashions and heavy tax burden, gave way to a much more confident time. In 1821 the florid, flamboyant Prince of Wales finally became George IV, one of the least liked monarchs ever (the competition is stiff). He's best known for his dramatic coronation complete with bouncers refusing entry to his estranged wife, for eating too much, and his exuberant personal taste. Sixteen years later Queen Victoria's accession signified the end of the Georgian era. Against this background the population more than doubled between 1811 and 1871, while by 1851 Britain had become the first urban nation in the world. For the first time, more people lived in towns than in the countryside. Meanwhile, waistlines (for women) dropped and tightened, crinolines came and went, trousers (for men) came and stayed, and fashion in furnishing and architecture slid towards the gloomy spikiness of the neo-gothic.

This was an age of hyperbole, when writers could happily purr without a blush that 'under [Victoria's] benign sway the old semi-barbarous state of society has passed away like a dream, and we live in new social era, the result of the progress of education, of the march of improvement, and of the spread of true religion'.[3] An orgy of street-widening schemes, building work and the reordering of town centres was funded by both civic authorities and private enterprise, with the removal of older fabric praised as necessary and useful by the writers of town guides, as well as town planners. Shopping for pleasure was now expected, encouraged, and increasingly open to the working classes as well as the wealthy.

The high street increased in range and physical size. Even allowing for the vagaries of categorisation and patchy coverage in trade directories, overall retail provision increased faster than the general population. In some northern towns, the number of shops relative to the size of each town tripled in the first half of the century.[4] Elsewhere, the number of shops stayed constant, but they grew bigger and reached more people. Working-class towns saw the biggest change, as demand for goods increased among the lower classes: a reflection both of higher living standards (for some) and of a drop in prices due to continued industrialisation and mass-production.

Change wasn't limited to the bigger towns either. Although we're mainly looking at regional hubs, even tiny places were affected by the desire for a fixed set of shops. Wirksworth (Derbyshire) didn't even manage the requisite 5,000 inhabitants

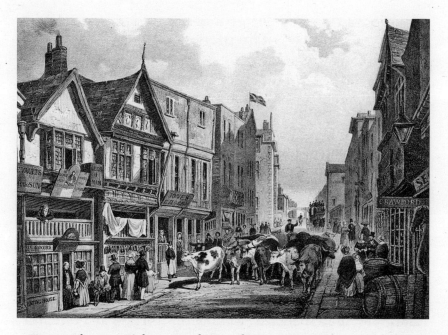

Fig. 4.1. Thomas Picken, *Northgate, Chester, c.*1840. The atmosphere
is typical of the early Victorian era with both animals and people
crowding the street. The buildings are less typical, for this is part
of the Chester Rows. The lower shops slope (or step) down from
the street and occupy undercrofts, while on top of them runs
a continuous, covered walkway with more shops (originally in
very small units). They still survive today, but have been heavily
Victorianised, with faux black and white timber framing and
alarming turrets.

usually taken as the definition of a town. Yet by 1828 its main
shopping streets boasted three booksellers, two druggists (one
also sold glass), a jeweller-perfumer, a second perfumer, and
two watchmakers, all of which would have counted as markers
of an upmarket high street just fifty years before. Outside this
cluster of shops – inevitably around the marketplace – were the
usual mainstays of drapers, hatters and milliners, along with
butchers, grocers and such like.[5]

The market

In all but the largest of towns, market day was still the busiest day of the week. As well as providing cheap cloth and furniture to those who weren't tempted by the shops, the market remained the main place to buy fresh food and flowers. For around two-thirds of the population, shopping meant the market.[6] As ever, the earliest arrivals of the day were other traders, and the growing suburbs were serviced predominantly by pedlars who bought market goods early in the morning and sold them on to customers at their doors or windows.

The presence of an officially sanctioned market was a mark of civic pride as well as genuinely necessitous. In the fast-growing industrial towns of the north, their lack was deeply felt. Traders set up in the street, causing obstruction and nuisance. In Blackburn in 1824, 'the want of a good spacious market place is much felt', and 'the confusion and danger which prevail in the town on the market days from the deficiency of room to carry on the necessary traffic incident to a place of this magnitude are very striking to strangers'.[7] Over in Birkenhead, a planned town which expanded fast after the opening of a steam ferry service from Liverpool, residents lobbied hard for a market in the 1820s. It took a while, but in 1835 they got not just an open square with temporary stalls, but a dedicated market hall, with a mixture of shops, stalls, tables or stands and vaults providing accommodation for everything from tripe to tulips. Ten years later it expanded, and the breadth of goods on offer by the 1850s included furniture, shoes, ceramics and live poultry.[8]

Street markets were increasingly seen as problematic. It was one thing to have a purpose-built square, where stalls could be (mainly) contained within a given area, but quite another to have to fit markets into an existing streetscape. In Scarborough there were mutterings that 'wherever a street market existed

Fig. 4.2. The London poor at their Christmas marketing, 1872. Brightly lit shop awnings in the background, a busy food market in the foreground, and a cheap drapers sticking to the pile 'em high principle of displaying goods to the right.

it tended to keep down the standard of public taste'. Experiments in decentralisation in Manchester worked to clear the main market, but then led to suburban street stalls, which were deemed to 'generally lower the tone of the immediate neighbourhood'.[9] The solution, especially in the midlands and the north, where suitable sites could be snapped up by the authorities as the town expanded, and grandiose building works were used as a symbol of industrial and civic pride, was a new type of public edifice: the market hall.

Market halls were the big shopping story of the mid- to late nineteenth century. They weren't exactly on the high street but are nevertheless important in its history. The format was related to the selds and exchanges of previous centuries. Once again, here was an orderly space full of individual retailers, sheltered from the elements as well as from bothersome street hawkers and anti-social behaviour. But to the early nineteenth-century consumer – and retailer – it was all quite new and exciting.

The sense of market halls as something 'a bit different' was often reflected in their architecture. Some were truly gigantic. An example is Liverpool's St John's Market, opened in 1822, which had sixty-two lock-up shops and a vast, well-lit internal space divided with columns. It had its own water supply, a central clock and space for 404 stalls. In 1835 Newcastle's Grainger Market was even bigger – probably the biggest market hall in Europe. Birmingham's market hall was smaller, but 'one of the finest buildings in the kingdom'. For once, London was left behind. Yes, Billingsgate was grand, but it paled into nothingness set against Leeds Kirkgate, or the halls of Stockport or Bolton, all of which were inspired by the Crystal Palace and soared above the townscape in a glorious mixture of cast iron, wood and glass.[10] Not all market halls were huge or magnificent, though. Bath's Guildhall Market opened in 1863, and was really just a (very nice) glass roof on an existing site along with some reorganisation to impose order by moving the slaughterhouses and improving access.[11]

Market halls helped turn certain places into real destinations. They were an especially important draw for the working classes, for they provided a wide choice of cheap goods. This was also the age of the railway, and as the network spread across Britain, some operators put on special third-class carriages on market days.

Like the high street, the new halls weren't just for shopping, but for socialising and catching up on the latest trends. They were also a draw for the upper classes, who went just to look. Actor Fanny Kemble visited Bristol market one morning in 1831, admiring the 'quaint-looking rustic people' and writing that 'it is most beautifully clean; the fruit and the vegetables look so pretty, and smell so sweet, and give such an idea of plentiful abundance, that it is delightful to walk about'.[12] Some market halls opened every day, and the mixture of interior and exterior stalls, lock-ups, small shops and fixed premises on the surrounding streets become a good way to start a business. Infamously, Marks & Spencer, later known for its department stores, started out with stalls in Leeds Kirkgate and Birkenhead markets.

Markets weren't the only area of change. Your experience of shopping could differ wildly depending on where you lived. Many towns still lacked any paving, let alone raised pavements for pedestrians, and in most places roads were still divided from sidewalks with nothing more than the ubiquitous bollard. In the East End of London, captured cannons from the Napoleonic wars were repurposed as bollards – later on replica cannons became a popular design across the country. From the 1820s onwards, though, the range of street furniture increased. One week you'd see protective iron bumpers being installed on the kerbs to stop carriages cutting off the corner; the next time you might find cast-iron road signs, a drinking fountain or a trough for your horse. By the mid-century you'd be able to watch the local lamplighter do his rounds as gas lighting became the norm. The first post boxes were erected in 1852 in St Helier, Jersey, and by the 1860s there were several standardised designs, all painted a fashionable leaf green. In 1874 they were repainted red to increase visibility.

Improving the high street

What of the atmosphere on the high street? Mainly it remained filthy, noisy and crowded with people, horses and occasional escaped cattle. Mostly the roads were cobbled, but some did have paving slabs, while still others had wooden setts, which were quieter, but slippery when wet. Macadamised surfaces, with ground-in gravel and stones, were easy to lay, but dusty. Bad weather was a nightmare. On rainy days in Chatham 'the streets resounded with the clicking noise made by the iron rings of the women's "pattens", who, mounted upon a pair of these, carried a strong gingham umbrella of large size'. The ubiquitous pattens preserved your shoes, but could also make things worse, for they often had sharp metal bottoms which cut up any surfaces not well paved. They had their uses, though, if your shopping trip went bad: 'with the viragoes of the age the "patten" was not unfrequently a weapon of offence, and has been flung through shop-windows before now, as well as at people's heads'.[13]

Mud was sometimes the least of people's problems, for although urinals had been installed in some towns, provision for women was woeful. The first dual-sex public conveniences didn't open until 1855 (opposite the Royal Exchange in London), and then there weren't any more for thirty years.[14] Much though the civic authorities might moan, women were left looking for a convenient drain down a side street, unless they had a carriage handy, at which point they could retreat for a moment of communion with a chamber pot.

Talking of carriages, they were yet another issue. Richer people still insisted on being served from them, which blocked the road. Sedan chairs were also still in use, their bearers frequently drunk, and in towns which still retained their narrow, medieval layouts, frankly it was all a bit much.

All of this meant that many towns invested enthusiastically, if not always wisely, in road widening, particularly when linking new railway stations to the centre of the town. Outdated buildings were ripped down with gay abandon, to make way for more aesthetically pleasing and practical solutions. In York, a splendid new curved terrace, St Leonard's Place, was built on council-owned property, replacing an area of low-value houses and yards to form a wide new road allowing carriage access to the theatre, assembly rooms and shopping areas. Meanwhile Coney Street was widened for the second time in 1841. Over in Bath, New Bond Street had been constructed off the bottom of Milsom Street in 1805–6, while in Norwich, endless attempts to improve London Street ended in the construction of the brand-new Prince of Wales Road, which punched a hole through the city to provide wide, easy access to such delights as the new Agricultural Hall, as well as the city centre. Typically, the council ran out of money before they finished the railway station end.

Small towns weren't immune to grandiose plans for improvement, either. In Haverfordwest (Pembrokeshire, population 4,328 in 1831), the council happily swept away the picturesque but disordered frontages of the steep high street, adding a new square, inevitably named for the monarch. In, too, went a grammar school, Literary and Scientific Institution, a library, billiard rooms, police station and asylum.[15]

Piecemeal improvement of this type did not mean that every British high street was suddenly transformed into a modern-looking shopping mecca. Even if parts of a town were rebuilt, elsewhere old and new still jostled together, and in reality, 'new' was frequently merely a fascia on top of the old. Behind some of Norwich's surviving Victorian facades you can still find medieval undercrofts or stairways, and the National Trust own one building on York's Coney Street precisely because of its early-seventeenth-century ceiling.

It's time to get started on your shopping list. Brush the dust from all those building works off your skirts or trousers, and work out where you are if the street layout has changed. We're starting with the butcher because refrigeration doesn't come in until the late nineteenth century and, while cold stores and free-flowing air work quite well, it's still advisable to purchase meat earlier in the day. You can arrange for delivery to your home while you attend to the more pleasurable items on your list.

The butcher

If we define the high street as a place of leisure, pleasure and shopping, the butcher is not exactly an integral part of it. Even today in towns of any size, butchers' shops are generally on the edges of the high street, and this was equally true in the past. As ubiquitous as they were – numerically often the most important type of vendor – they tended to be grouped together, a reflection of the centuries' old tradition of butchers' rows and shambles.

Lots of places still had a street explicitly dedicated to butchery. In Leeds, a major redevelopment of the Briggate area saw the shambles installed in Cheapside and Fleet Street, both streets leading to Briggate itself (the main shopping street). These units were intended purely for retail premises, and part of the new development included a dedicated underground wholesale carcass market, 'where 150 beasts, besides sheep, calves &c may be killed and dressed'. Not only did it stay cool in summer and frost-free in winter but 'it is plentifully supplied with water, and kept perfectly clean and free from offensive smells'.[16] Smells, noise, gore and unpleasant refuse were all age-old reasons to keep butchers at a certain distance from the high street. Equally, the butchers themselves didn't need to be there. They hardly relied on passing trade, and didn't need to compete with luxury shops paying much higher rents for their more prestigious premises.

Don't worry, though: you absolutely can't miss the butchers' shop. They were generally festooned with carcasses to the point where you'd be hard-pressed to locate the entrance: advertisement and storage conveniently rolled into one. Some premises were barely changed from a century ago, still featuring open windows and protruding wooden bulks, sometimes with cutting tables on the road outside. Increasingly, though, the blood and guts were restricted to a back room, and bulks were rare after the 1830s. Instead of spreading horizontally – out on to the street – butchers' displays now went vertically – up and up and, in some cases, right over the roof. You might find your eye drawn first to the rails and hooks holding medium-weight stuff – perhaps a few half pigs, some heads and such like – but look further up, as particularly for poultry dealers there was almost no limit. At Christmas, in particular, the displays of whole, feathered geese, turkey and chickens was mind-boggling. No wonder so many authors of the time referred to the 'hecatombs' of meat consumed during the festive season (a hecatomb comes from ancient Greek, and means a massive public sacrifice, originally of 100 bulls).

The vast majority of butchers bought 'on the hoof', with slaughter either at a local small abattoir or on the premises. Conditions were basic, and even in the early twentieth century: 'there was no gas up the slaughterhouse, only candlelight, and if they were working late the slaughtermen, like the coalmen, used to have a bracket round their head with a candle stuck in the front'.[17] In larger towns there might be a public abattoir, and a minority of butchers bought 'dead meat' from wholesale markets. As a shopper, you wouldn't have witnessed the killing, skinning, debristling and basic butchery, but you'd still have known exactly what you were eating. The smell of a butcher was quite distinct: an iron tang of fresh blood, a woody backnote from the sawdust on the floor, and the slightly musty scent known to anyone who has ever hung game (or buried their face in the fur of a slightly manky family pet). Every butcher had a huge cutting bench in the shop itself, and while meat hung all around you, perhaps on wheeled rails for easy manoeuvring, there were no refrigerated cabinets or neatly packaged up cuts devoid of blood. Instead, you'd enter into a discussion with your butcher, who would cut up and weigh out in front of you.

Many shops had a separate paying desk so that the butcher didn't have to handle money with gore-splattered hands – or, indeed, handle meat with fingers made filthy from grubby coins. However, if you knew your butcher, and shopped there regularly you might still have an account, rather than paying in cash. The sign 'family butcher' indicated that a trusted local family might keep a tab.[18] Given that cash remained problematic – the plethora of local banks were prone to go bust, rendering their banknotes about as much use as your shopping list – settling up at monthly or three-monthly intervals was not a bad idea.

Butchers weren't all men, despite the stereotype of John Bull the butcher and his sirloin of beef, which still held sway in the popular imagination. In King's Lynn (Norfolk) in the 1820s, of the forty-seven butchers, four were women. Later in the century, twenty-five miles down the road, the small town of Ely managed three women out of a total of ten.

The trade was widely distrusted. Meat was expensive, and a large proportion of the population rarely ate it due to cost. Bad meat was not only a waste of hard-earned resources but could be dangerous (and no, people did not use spices to disguise tainted meat in the past. Spices were even more expensive than the meat). Butchers were known to leave blood, bone or fat in joints to increase its weight, or to pass off bad meat as good. Advice manuals emphasised that you should always watch the sausages being made, and who knew what was in those curiously cheap meat patties?

Hygiene was a primary concern. You could witness the spread of ideas about hygiene, as well as the desire of butchers to be seen as hygienic, in the replacement of wooden display boards with marble or glazed tiles. By the last half of the century many butchers had tiled the whole shop, often buying

Fig. 4.3. Francis Donkin Bedford, *The Poulterer*, 1899. Clearly a Christmas scene, but also an accurate depiction of just quite how much death was on display at the average butcher or poulterer. No wonder the dog looks happy.

purpose-made tiles with sepia depictions of peacefully grazing cows or emblazoned with adverts for pickled tongues or home-made sausages.[19] The displays of hanging meat stayed, though, and in summer must have been a magnet for flies. Cold rooms were usually used to store cut joints, but by the end of the century, imported ice helped to bring basic refrigeration into use. In Ashford, Kent, one shop had a pulley system rigged up so that the window display, in all its fleshy, pink glory, could be winched up and down into an ice box in the cellar. Brine tanks were used 'for pork, beef, bullock's tongues, ox tongues and so on'. Meanwhile the offal was made into blood puddings and haslet, and bladders were used as storage containers for lard.[20]

Bladders were surprisingly versatile. Stretched out over a stone jar and left to dry, they made a convincing, if initially somewhat fragrant, tight lid. (They are quite difficult to remove, though.)

By 1870, the chances are that your butcher would look quite different to that of fifty years before. Instead of relying mainly on British or western European-bred animals, livestock was increasingly being imported from Australasia and South America, to be killed in large abattoirs at ports, and shipped out as carcasses. Just a few years later, frozen meat would start to come in, to be defrosted and sold on, leading to a range of shops specialising in cheap imported meats for the working class. Names such as Eastman's or the American Fresh Meat Company became common in working-class areas. Not that imported meat was new. Australian meat was widely sold as tinned meat, and its availability had already slowly started to improve the diet of the poor. One cookery lecturer lamented that 'in this country a diet of animal and vegetable food is most acceptable, but the high price of meat, except fat pork and bacon, excludes fresh meat, except in small scraps from the homes of a large number of families'. He lauded the use of preserved meat, though added the exasperated note '[an] objection is, that kangaroos and elephants and horses are cut up. I do not know how they obtain the elephants and horses; and kangaroos are far more costly in Australia than oxen and sheep'.[21]

Assuming you've ordered your mutton, this is the point to have a break. We're venturing, now, to the gin shop. They aren't the most salubrious of places, but you can always make the excuse that you need a bottle for household purposes. Gin was much used for cleaning, as it was very cheap. Got a stained silk waistcoat? Try 'four ounces of soft soap, four ounces of honey, the white of an egg, and a wine glassful of gin'. Work it in, give it a good scrub, rinse well, and iron while still damp. According to the author of Enquire Within Upon Everything, *this recipe has never been made public before but can be used 'with perfect success'.*[22] *(My own experiments on this front suggest otherwise, but maybe I'm doing it wrong.)*

The gin palace

Gin was the most consumed spirit in Britain, driven mainly by working-class consumers. It had been introduced into Britain by soldiers returning from European wars in the late sixteenth and early seventeenth centuries, who'd picked the habit up from the Dutch. It was supposed to cure the plague, and, due to various bad moves by the government, became the dangerous drug of its time. The gin craze of the late seventeenth and early eighteenth century was an urban phenomenon, and mainly a London one. Gin was everywhere, distilled in cellars and back rooms, and sold, despite inevitably futile attempts at prohibition, cheaply and widely. The upper classes went wild with worry, fearing civil disorder and unproductive workers. Lurid stories circulated of murder in the name of gin, and government-appointed inspectors were dragged through the streets even as mock funerals were held for 'madame genever' (the Dutch name for gin) as successive crackdowns failed.

By the 1750s, though, the craze was dying out. Now, in the middle of the nineteenth century, it is respectable enough for Isabella Beeton to include it in a recipe for noyau (almond liqueur). It had always been consumed by the middle and upper classes, largely as a medicine, but now it was marketed as both medicinal and tasty. After 1830 and the invention of the continuous still it was generally also free of dead rats and could be made in large, quality-controlled batches. Distillers such as Greenalls, Gordons, Booths and Tanqueray were all producing high-grade gins by 1830. In 1863 Beefeater was founded. London

Dry Gin was developed, and by the 1860s cocktails, as well as gin and tonic, were making a very occasional appearance. The first aerated tonic water was patented in 1858, though it was slow to take off until the British living in the Far East adopted it as a dual-purpose digestive and fever remedy – adding gin in the late 1860s. Schweppes, who'd commercialised carbonated water back in the 1780s, launched their Indian Quinine Tonic from their base in Bristol in 1870 and rapidly cornered the British market.

The idea of going to a gin palace might well have you raising a lower middle-class eyebrow. Given the history of gin in Britain, it's hardly surprising that they've got a dubious reputation, but by the 1840s this was slowly changing. In previous centuries nipping down the gin shop would have been strictly for the impoverished wastrel (at least according to the upper classes, who could order it from the spirit merchant and not have to resort to back-street dives). But while they remained largely the province of the working class, some were at least marginally respectable, despite the opprobrium of pretty much every middle-class writer. Here's George Dodd, writing about the transformation of London's gin houses in 1856. They'd gone 'from painted deal to polished mahogany, from small crooked panes of glass to magnificent crystal sheets, from plain useful fittings to costly luxurious adornments', with service from a 'smart damsel', or possibly an older woman (not, it has to admitted, a lady), done up with the latest in hats.[23] In 1834 one Westminster grocer described the conversion of a dingy pub opposite his shop into a gin palace which was now a 'splendid edifice, the front ornamental with pilasters, supporting a handsome cornice . . . the whole elevation remarkably striking and handsome'.[24]

This does all sound convincing, but let's be fair, quite a lot of them were still situated down back alleys and were frequented by the same class of people who once gave gin a truly bad name.

These were not places for cocktail drinking: neat or nothing (well, maybe some hot water). The *Illustrated London News* described the average clientele as being working-class married women (who should be getting dinner on for their husbands), itinerant street-sellers, costermongers, and 'the poor, the old, and the miserable', who relied on gin to get through the day. You might also encounter children, for 'even these young miserable creatures are fond of drink, and may sometimes be seen slily drawing the cork outside the door, and lifting the poisonous potion to their white withered lips. They have already found that gin numbs and destroys for a time the gnawing pangs of hunger, and they can drink the fiery mixture in its raw state.'[25] At least there was now an acknowledgement that sheer bloody misery was a factor in drinking gin, while the gin sellers themselves made stringent efforts to raise the reputation of their venues, as well as of the product itself.

The decor in gin palaces was very much faux-rich, dripping with crystal, stained glass, wood panelling and hissing gas chandeliers. Gin was decanted from large barrels, which in the various depictions of them crowd the walls, looming above the heads of the happy drinkers. According to Charles Dickens, the names were evocative: as well as the standard Old Tom (slightly sweeter than today's gins, genuinely very nice), you could choose from such delights as Cream of the Valley, The Out and Out and The No Mistake.[26] Some venues had ladies' bars, away from the rowdiness and potential sexual assault by drunk men. And yes, it's clear drunkenness remained the main aim, and that you'd almost certainly find yourself stepping over a body on the floor and avoiding groups of men and women shouting merrily at the tops of their voices, or fighting, or snogging. Being sozzled by lunchtime has a very long history, but really, genuinely, you're only here because you need gin to mix with tonic for back home.

Whether you stumble or sail out of the gin palace, I hope you're ready for more shopping. You're after a plaything for a child, perhaps a wooden horse or lead soldier, hoop or doll. Something cheap and cheerful. When we visited the toyshop in the 1720s, a toy was a fanciful thing intended for mainly adult amusement, but in the intervening decades it's come to mean an item for children to play with.

You can buy toys in all sorts of places, including specialist shops. In London, Hamley's Toy Warehouse is known as 'Noah's Ark' by the 1830s, after its most popular toy (educational, fun and suitable for playing with on a Sunday). A wooden ark hangs over the door. But you can also find toys in more general shops. In Norwich, the pattern manufacturer, fancy repository and Berlin wool shop Ganley's advertises itself as 'the only toy shop in London Street!' and sells 'games, puzzles, balls, swings, whips, tops, noah's arks, bows and arrows, and drums', the last few guaranteed to strike fear into any parent's heart and start them looking up boarding schools.[27] *You're after something cheaper (and quieter), so let's pop to a phenomenon which peaked in the mid-century: the bazaar.*

The bazaar

Not every town had a bazaar, but for those that did, what a genuine delight. The concept was yet another riff on the exchange theme. They were very close cousins to market halls, though smaller than some of the vast examples of the north. Unlike exchanges or markets, they looked like normal buildings from the outside. However, inside you'd find one or more large halls, nicely decorated, and fitted up with mini shops which were rented by the day. Some also had galleries, exhibition spaces, auction rooms and upper floors with a further shopping space. They were privately owned and managed, and came, inevitably, with a set of regulations, including that all goods were to be clearly marked with a price and sold with no haggling.

The first bazaar was in London, in the form of Trotter's on Soho Square. John Trotter had been an army supplier, but the end of the Napoleonic wars left him with a big warehouse and no job. By 1818 his Soho Bazaar was quite the craze. It was carefully furnished to appeal to the middle classes, with an interior liberally furnished with red drapes and mirrors, 'fitted up with handsome mahogany counters, extending not only round the sides, but in the lower and upper apartment, forming a parallelogram in the middle'. Each counter had lockable drawers and an access flap, then a novelty, later commonplace.[28] They were 'let upon moderate terms to females who can bring forward sufficient testimonies of their moral respectability'.[29] Trotter went large on the feminine side of things, promoting the bazaar as a charitable enterprise designed to stop war widows falling into poverty. According to one contemporary, it opened 'an immense field of usefulness' and also stopped women wasting their time over novels, which was only marginally less awful than the risk they'd turn to prostitution.[30]

The format spread rapidly – to elsewhere in London, Leeds, Margate, Blackpool and Exeter, to name just a few. In Brighton there was a bazaar on the Grand Parade, which 'affords an hour's amusement to the numerous fashionable visitors, who honour it with their presence'.[31] In Bath, James and Thomas Jolly started a seasonal bazaar on Milsom Street, before opening permanently from 1825. Initially, many bazaars proclaimed their patriotism by selling only British goods, though this lapsed as memories of the war receded. Respectability remained key, though, with bouncers to bar 'persons meanly or dirtily dressed, or otherwise calculated to lessen the respectability of the place', and early closing to allow female customers and vendors to get home before the evening riffraff descended, in an attempt to stop the bazaars becoming associated with sex. It wasn't entirely successful. Here's 'Humphrey Hedgehog's' 'The London Bazaar':

What bargains there are sold and bought,
But, 'faith, I mean of female sort;
For, you must know, th' industrious fair
There get a living by their ware.

'Speak softly, sir,' returned the maid:
'We shall be heard, I'm much afraid:
'Though I've of you but little seen,
'I understand the thing you mean.'

'This is the thing! Could I procure it'
'In fact I will! – if you'll insure it!
'By Heaven! Tis fine,' quoth he, 'I swear,'
Laying his hand upon her ware.[32]

It's not subtle. However, the largely female stallholders were also part of the appeal for more upstanding types. One 1818 children's book, *A Visit to the Bazaar*, explained in great detail the joys to be found within, explaining 'a more pleasing and novel effect can hardly be imagined, than is here produced by the sight of these elegant little shops, filled with every species of light goods, works of art, and female ingenuity in general'.[33] The book takes the form of a family trip to Trotter's, where at each stall the horribly precocious children show off their knowledge of geography, botany, diamond mining, etc., in return for being allowed to buy something tacky. As a healthy, moralising text, the children are also suitably horrified by another child being gluttonous at the pastry-cook's, and we, as readers, are encouraged to laugh – but not too obviously – at a 'short thick made vulgar looking woman' with a regional accent trying to force a small hat upon her large child's head. Elsewhere we meet an elderly lady trying on hats at the milliner, where the youngest child points out that 'unless she can hide the wrinkles in her face and neck, and the loss of her teeth, and the leanness of her body, she will only the more expose her age, by dressing so ridiculously'.

George Sala visited London's Pantheon Bazaar in the 1850s in a rather more cynical mood, commenting that 'I fear the price of the merchandise which the pretty and well-conducted female assistants at the stalls have to sell. I have been given to understand that incredible prices are charged for India-rubber balls, and that the quotations for drums, hares-and-tabors, and Noah's arks, are ruinously high.' He went on: 'I have yet another reason for not patronising the Pantheon as a toy mart. It frequently happens that I feel slightly misanthropic and vicious in my toy-dealing excursions, and that my juvenile friends have sudden fits of naughtiness, and turn out to be anything but agreeable companions.'

Sala's solution for childhood naughtiness was to 'warm them' by taking them into the bazaar's toyshops and buying them ugly toys. He gives a list, which for a modern reader is a useful reminder that shops sold just as much junk 150 years ago as they do now. How about an 'old gentleman impaled on the area railing while in the act of knocking at his own street door, and who emitted a dismal groan when the pedestal on which he stood was compressed', a wizened monkey on a stick, or a magnificent selection of animals made from cheap rubber, all of which seem to have too many legs?[34]

It's easy to imagine getting bewitched by the level of merchandise on offer (don't forget you're here for a simple wooden horse), but bazaars really did provide endless entertainment. The world was on offer through the lens of the optician, the plumes of the feather merchant, and the buffed woods and barrels of the gunsmith. There were bird sellers (to cage, not eat), musical instrument makers, silk flower makers, furriers, brush makers, house plant specialists and – well, the list goes on. It didn't last, though, and by the late 1830s bazaars had peaked. In Manchester the Deansgate bazaar now emphasised 'various interesting and amusing exhibitions and works of genius'.[35] Shopping was almost a sideline. There were refreshment rooms and 'dressing rooms' (hoorah! A ladies' loo). Others had live entertainment, including a demonstration of laughing gas at the New Royal Bazaar in 1831.[36] Some started charging entrance fees. As with any venue trying to push the boundaries in search of custom, there was always a slight risk attached. In 1829 the Royal Bazaar on London's Oxford Street burnt down thanks to an unfortunate diorama of 'the city of York with the Minster on fire'.[37] Bazaars became associated with tawdry goods, sold, not by sweet-faced young ladies, but by established shops opening a second branch on the cheap.

It was hard to make a profit running a bazaar, especially given the lavish architectural flourishes that customers loved. The Norfolk and Norwich Bazaar had a gallery supported by iron pillars shaped like palm trees and a double stair leading up to it – and it struggled for all its short life. Less than two years after its grand opening in 1831, it flopped and was turned into a single, large, store full of books, stationery, fancy goods and toys. Over in Bath, Jolly's also rebranded, seizing on the next buzz term and advertising that 'the distinguishing feature of the EMPORIUM will be ECONOMY, FASHION and VARIETY'.[38] The Manchester bazaar became a draper, while in London the Baker Street bazaar was already best known as the home of Madame Tussauds' waxworks. The last bazaar to be built was London's Corinthian Bazaar in 1868: by 1871 it was a circus.[39] The term bazaar would survive, but change in meaning, becoming a catch-all term for a motley collection of items for sale. Returning, briefly, to Leeds Kirkgate market and the Marks & Spencer origin story – it was as a Penny Bazaar that the first stall operated.

Another refreshment pause, and let's make it a morally upstanding one. There's a pervasive idea that consumers – shoppers – in the past were just cattle, easily sold to and without agency, but that was as untrue in 1870 as it is now. People make choices all the time, including how to show

*their belief systems through the goods and services they purchase. One of
the big causes of the mid- to late nineteenth century was the Temperance
movement, which campaigned for teetotalism across the classes. Drink
was held to be the root of many evils, especially for the working classes,
and the easy access to pubs (and, yes, all right, gin palaces) was thought
to be a root cause of alcoholism. Off we go, therefore, to an alternative
venue, where you can both assuage your conscience and demonstrate
your credentials as a fine, upstanding and sober member of society.*

The temperance rooms

Temperance had its roots in middle-class condemnation of
working-class drunkenness in the late eighteenth and early
nineteenth centuries. It was a mixture of somewhat hypocritical
outrage and genuine social concern. It was apparently fine for
someone like Charles Dickens to calm himself after a bad day of
travelling by quaffing a pint of brandy and a pint of champagne,
but lower down the social scale, wanton beer-drinking could
lead to public brawling, lack of personal control and the much-
feared reduced productivity. Anyone with money drank steadily
in private, but never appeared publicly inebriated (much). More
nuanced social reformers pointed out that drinking was not
always bad, that 'anyone who frequents public houses knows
that actual drunkenness is very much the exception', but
equally they worried that excessive drinking could lead to crim-
inality, loss of work, destitution and degradation.[40]

By the 1830s there was a small, yet very vocal, movement
urging temperance, which quickly started promoting complete
abstinence. In 1829 the Glasgow and West of Scotland Temperance society became the first of a rush of such organisations, all
emphasising moral purity and self-improvement. Despite their
good intentions, they became renowned for heavy-handedness
in recruitment, as well as a tedious love of processions and

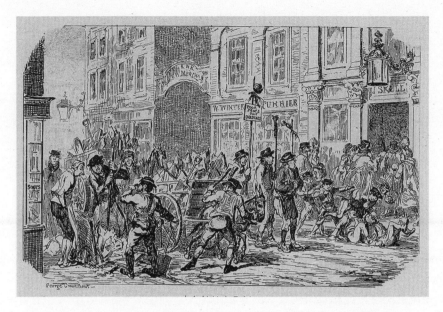

Fig. 4.4. George Cruickshank's 1848 *The Drunkard's Children* was a series of plates, with an accompanying poem, which started with innocent children neglected in a gin palace and led remarkably quickly to the boy being convicted for robbery and dying of dissipation while the girl throws herself off a bridge in despair. The gin palace might be alluring, but temperance is a decidedly better option.

demonstrations. One contemporary referred to the 'rabid sons of abstinence', complaining that 'to insinuate that those who by reasoning you have failed to convert to your opinion will end their career on the gallows or in the madhouse, and that the transition stages to those undesirable consummations will consist of wife-beating, bankruptcy, moral degradation, premature physical decay, and unutterable sottishness, is to show a decided want of that medium which ought to characterize discussions of all matters of opinion'.[41]

Despite the self-defeating moralising of a few zealots, the movement grew and broadened in scope. As it became more genuinely working-class, it became associated with workers' rights, while the membership of many women also led to strong connections with the suffrage movement. As early as 1837 Norwich's Temperance Festival was so over-subscribed that 'upwards of one thousand persons were present, and five hundred applications for tea tickets were refused. The Lord Bishop of Norwich delivered an address. Supper followed, and everything was conducted in good order.'[42] Building on this, the mainstream movement now moved into temperance rooms and hotels. By the 1860s they were everywhere. In Loughborough, the Temperance Hotel on Swan Street offered 'plates of meat from 12 to 2 o clock', 'well-aired beds' (you'd hope), and 'coffee ready from half past five am to ten pm'.[43] Over in Belfast, the proprietress of the Temperance Refreshment Rooms on the corner of Donegall and John Street promised 'proper management and strict attention to the comfort of her visitors', while up in Wick (Scotland) a Mrs Taylor renamed the former coffee rooms the Temperance Coffee Rooms and advertised both lodgings and refreshments.[44]

Taking refreshments in a temperance café at this point was, however, often more of a moral stance than an entirely pleasurable experience. In 1903 Charles Booth noted that 'at first cocoa rooms, or coffee palaces as they were then called, were the result of philanthropic or religious effort. They were to pay their way; but they did not do it. They were to provide good refreshments; but tea, coffee, cocoa and cakes were alike bad. It was not till the work was taken up as a business that any good was done with it.'[45] By then, a new breed of more commercially minded owners had taken over the early, well-meaning, but not great, cafés. They particularly favoured the popular working-class beverage of cocoa, which boomed in the wake of the reduction in sugar tax in the 1870s. The most well-known of these was Lockhart's, the first of which opened in Liverpool in 1875 (complete with teetotal pledge book for customers to sign). It allowed consumers, who were frequently destitute and desperate, to bring their own food, or to bring bread and butter and buy a sausage. Mahatma Gandhi lauded them as being the cheapest way to live in London. Lockhart's Cocoa Rooms subsequently opened across the country, becoming one of the earliest chain cafés, all driven by a genuine sense of social injustice and a desire to do good (though they also made a tidy profit). In the Edwardian era they would open in more salubrious areas as well, calling these smarter outlets 'refreshment rooms' rather than cocoa rooms. Their blue and white branded crockery and trade tokens still occasionally crop up in antique shops today.[46]

Hopefully you feel restored, with renewed verve and purpose in your step. This is good, because our next shop is another key one on the high street. A lot of shopping history is concerned with drapers, partly because they were one of the major innovators of the era, and partly because some of them got very large, expanded beyond drapery, and eventually morphed into department stores, the later collapse of which would leave large holes on the high street. But that's not happened yet. You're after a bolt of decent light wool, and, although many drapers have expanded well beyond mere cloth, it is the very heart of the trade. Every town has a draper, most towns have several, and some are very rich and very well respected. The drapers are high on the list of people from whom the civic authorities elect their leaders, and some will go on to found veritable dynasties through which to safeguard their future good names.

The draper

The 1818 *Book of English Trades* waxed lyrical on the subject of the draper. Apparently 'there is no trade in England, in which more efforts are made to captivate the public, and more especially the ladies, by a display of goods'. In London especially, 'this display is carried to a most costly and sumptuous extent. In most of the principal streets of the metropolis, shawls, muslins, pieces for ladies' dresses, and a variety of other goods, are shown with the assistance of mirrors, and at night by chandeliers, aided by the brilliancy which the gas lights afford, in a way almost as dazzling to a stranger, as many of those poetical fictions of which we read in the Arabian nights' entertainment.'[47]

Drapers were a draw. They were vital retailers, clothing being a necessity as well as a fundamental way to show status and, assuming you got it right, take pleasure in one's appearance. In small towns, in the early nineteenth century, the draper might well still be part of a mixed shop, part grocer, part ironmonger, part everything anyone wanted. Even then, there might be a rival, selling some of the same items. In Elizabeth Gaskell's *Cranford*, we hear of the Barker sisters who set up a millinery shop in their front room and 'piqued themselves upon their "aristocratic connection". They would not sell their caps and ribbons to anyone without a pedigree. Many a farmer's wife or daughter turned away huffed from Miss Barkers' select millinery, and went rather to the universal shop, where the profits of brown soap and moist sugar enabled the proprietor to go straight to (Paris, he said, until he found his customers too patriotic and John Bullish to wear what the Mounseers wore) London.'[48] Certainly, by the 1820s, the majority of drapers sold far more than just cloth, and crossed easily into the realms of haberdashery, mercery, millinery and fancy goods.

There were drapers and there were drapers. In Macclesfield, Swanwick's was 'a very aristocratic and first-class tailoring establishment and was called the "top shop" in contradistinction to the "ready-made clothes shop" which was a little lower down'. At the upper end, they often operated as undertakers as well, for mourning was big business in nineteenth-century Britain. At Swanwick's 'in those days, when silk-sashes and hat bands and gloves were sent out to the mourners and friends, they drove a very lucrative and first-class business'.[49] At the lower end there was more of a move towards ready-to-wear, still in its infancy, and very much associated with badly fitting clothes bought mainly by the poor. In Droitwich, described as 'a small straggling dirty looking town on the banks of the Salwarpe', all the main drapers sold ready-to-wear. Even the most upmarket draper carried farmers' smocks and clothing intended for clothing workhouse inmates.

Charity clothing and uniforms really kick-started the ready-to-wear market.[50] The association with poverty wasn't entirely fair, for with hot competition, drapers, particularly in provincial towns, were very good at catering to their local market. Bainbridge's of Newcastle was definitely not low-class. It had a French Room for Parisian imports, and by 1850 had expanded to list twenty-three different departments. Yet it stocked pit clothes for coal miners until the 1890s and happily promoted ready-made clothing.[51]

Regional preferences even extended to design. William Ablett, who wrote the pompous, but endearing, *Reminiscences of an Old Draper* about his time in the trade, recounted his experience of replacing some prints he found to be ugly when working in a Manchester store, only to find his rarefied London tastes didn't sell at all.[52] Ablett painted a vivid picture of life in a low to mid-range drapers' store. Looking back from the 1870s, he 'cannot help contrasting the abundance of clothing that even servant girls now possess to the scanty equipment that the poorer people of decent station had to put up with then'.[53] Technological change, global connections and the enthusiastic exploitation of workers known as 'sweated' labour all helped to bring prices down, making the working class an increasingly important group of consumers.

The shop Ablett started out in in the 1810s had only just adopted fixed prices, largely because it was a 'pushing and ticketing shop' where the assistants, who got commission, bullied their customers to the point of tears and embraced decidedly sharp selling techniques. Some shops still offered credit to trusted customers, but in this case ready money was preferred as it didn't bounce. The shop was full of long alleys and towering shelves, stacked with fabric in wrappers – the less popular items at the top, and the fast-selling stuff behind the counters. For ease, some fabric was pre-cut. Later on still it would be sold cut into shapes ready for sewing. Skeins of silks were individually laid out on paper, rolled up and placed in a further roll of coarse cloth, with the heads of the different colours arrayed 'in a brilliantly variegated mass, from which the customer drew out the shades that were needed'.[54]

The owners knew their market. They did a lot of business on a Sunday before church, selling ready-made shirts to men still drunk from the night before, and used flash sales to get rid of unwanted stock. Classics such as the closing-down sale and the damaged stock sale pulled in massive crowds, unaware that much of what they were buying had been carefully burnt on the edges by an increasingly inebriated huddle of shop assistants, downing pints and giggling to themselves behind carefully blacked-out shutters in the days before. The punters went wild for a few genuine bargains and an awful lot of rubbish, making the shop look like a jumble sale, but 'this mattered but little, people bought the goods, right and left, using but little judgment, and appearing to care only for being served with something or other'.[55]

The apprenticeship system was still in place for drapers, but slowly the gender bias towards men was shifting, and the percentage of women rose from 15 per cent of sales staff in 1851, to 26 per cent in 1871. By 1911, when around 150,000 people were employed in selling drapery and mercery, over half the workforce would be female.[56] Women were cheaper and assumed to be more pliable. Plus, women liked being served by other women. In 1859 the Society for Promoting the Employment of Women (admittedly biased) exhorted women shoppers to ask for women shop assistants, crying, 'why should bearded men be employed to sell ribbon, lace, gloves, neckerchiefs and the dozen other trifles to be found in a silkmercer's or haberdasher's shop?'[57] One shop assistant in London recounted her day in 1861. She 'lived in', one of four women and four men, all sharing a common sitting room and kept in good order by the cook. Shop opening hours were 8am until 9pm, with very limited breaks: 'We have to get our meals as we can,' she said: 'sometimes when you've gone down to get dinner, the shopbell rings, and up you've to come without tasting a thing.' She sometimes went for a walk after closing, and had Sunday evenings to herself.[58]

Church attendance was obligatory. One East Anglian draper's list of employee rules included giving a guinea a year to the church and attending Sunday school. The men got an evening off a week for courting and an extra one if they attended prayers. Women did not. Potential employees were carefully vetted for that all-important quality of respectability – but they also sometimes had to send a photograph to check they weren't ugly – and some West End stores also imposed a minimum height.[59]

Shopping in a draper's was as varied as the shops themselves. In a smaller, family-run affair, you might enter, be seated, and have a lengthy discussion as to your needs, with everything brought out for your inspection. Drapers acted as intermediaries between customers who wanted to be in fashion and trend-setters in London or Paris. Popping back to the fictional town of Cranford, the local draper (also a tea seller) held a show of the new fashions, to be exhibited on market day, and held in an upstairs room up a spiral staircase. Buying wasn't the point. 'We inspected the fashions with as minute and curious an interest as if the gown to be made after them had been bought. I could not see that the little event in the shop below had in the least damped Miss Matty's curiosity as to the make of sleeves or the sit of skirts. She once or twice exchanged congratulations with me on our private and leisurely view of the bonnets and shawls.'[60] Meanwhile another of the characters 'was in the habit of spending the morning in rambling from shop to shop, not to purchase anything (except an occasional reel of cotton or a piece of tape), but to see the new articles and report upon them, and to collect all the stray pieces of intelligence in the town'.[61] Shopping was just a pretext.

Drapers tended to be larger establishments than most of the shops we've so far encountered. Expanding stock meant expanding premises, and you could expect the drapery emporiums to occupy double units or even more. Enterprising owners bought up neighbouring shops, knocking down walls to form what could be a bewildering labyrinth of interlinked rooms. You might find the facades had been 'forced into a semblance of eternal unity by means of a coat of stucco'.[62] By the 1870s you might equally have found the various buildings being demolished entirely, to be replaced with a new, purpose-built shop which stood out among its lower, older, neighbours.

Not every large shop was a draper, of course: furniture sellers were also keen buyers-up of property and vied with drapers over rebuilding their stores. These new constructions were able to take advantage of the latest technology, including plate glass, which was now being produced very efficiently, meaning windowpanes could get larger. Duty on glass had been dropped in 1845, so that it wasn't quite so prohibitively expensive to enlarge your windows and maximise your displays. Dickens nevertheless took on the mantle of Defoe, and had a good pop at them in the 1830s:

> Quiet, dusty old shops in different parts of town, were pulled down; spacious premises with stuccoed fronts and gold letters, were erected instead; floors were covered with Turkey carpets; roofs supported by massive pillars; doors knocked into windows; a dozen squares of glass into

one; one shopman into a dozen; and there is no knowing what would have been done, if it had not been fortunately discovered, just in time, that the Commissioners of Bankruptcy were as competent to decide such cases as the Commissioners of Lunacy, and that a little confinement and gentle examination did wonders.'[63]

His other complaints included the use of large royal crests, too much gilding, gas lighting and illuminated clocks on every street corner.

Shop fittings hadn't yet caught up. You could buy or make wooden frames for display, but it was a bit primitive. Canny window dressers improvised with rolls and bales of fabric, trying to create an idea of how cloth would swirl and drape in use. Displays might be changed daily, or in reaction to the weather – you could expect to find umbrellas on display on rainy days, swapped with straw hats and parasols in more clement weather. Minimalism was definitely not the aim, and it was common to pile or hang as many things in the window as possible, labelled, in a lot of cases, with prices. Even with all of this, and a clear idea of what you wanted, it could still be a nerve-racking experience going through the door.

In larger drapers, occupying several units, you could expect to be met at the door by a shopwalker: part security guard, part greeter. He would usher you through the interlinked rooms to the relevant counter, all natural light vanishing as you walked. Later writers satirised such shops. One 1890s account describes how 'an afternoon's shopping was a solemn and dreary affair, when one was received at the door of the shop by a solemn gentleman in black, who in due time delivered one over to another solely gentleman, and perhaps again to a third, who found one a chair, and in a sepulchral tone of voice uttered some magic words such as "silk, Mr Smith", or "velvet, Mr A" and then departed to seek another victim. One bought what

1. Thomas Rowlandson, *An Eating House*, c.1815.

2. Pellatt & Green's china shop near St Paul's in London, 1809. The goods on open display, though not quite self-service, are a far cry from shops just fifty years before.

3. *left*. James Gillray, *Sandwich-carrots*, 1796. Faulder's bookshop was a real shop, though it's quite obvious books aren't the main thing being bought or sold in this depiction of the 5th Earl of Sandwich and a carrot-seller.

4. *below, left*. John Dempsey, *Black Charley of Norwich*, 1823. More properly, the Norwich shoeseller Charles Willis Yearly, *c*.1785–1829. His fortunes waxed and waned, but here he is resplendent, a good reminder that black faces were not unknown in the shops of the past.

5. *below*. John Burgess's Italian Warehouse at 107 Strand *c*.1830–70. Burgess's was particularly renowned for its anchovy essence, for which it won prizes. They were mainly sauce manufacturers, but were not alone in deciding that Italian Warehouse sounded more interesting in the mid-nineteenth century.

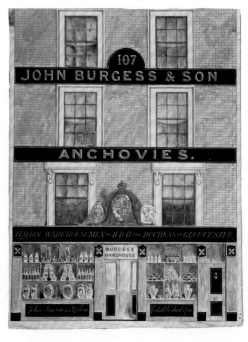

6. The Royal Bazaar, *c*.1828 (that's a lot of bonnets on the lower floor).

7. The first of the magnificant market halls of the north, St John's Market opened in 1822. With gas lighting, pumped hot and cold water, decent ventilation and a central clock, it set the standard for many of the market halls which followed. It was demolished in 1964 to make room for a shopping centre.

8. Tinned foods were a stock-in-trade for provision merchants such as this one in Colwyn Bay in Wales, and McCall's were leading importers of tinned meats from across the globe (Paysandu is in Uruguay, but they also advertised Australian rabbit, among other things). The bill here shows the range of goods available at a decent grocer – everything from gravy browning to strawberry jam.

9. Dale Street had long been Liverpool's main commercial thoroughfare. Numbers 65–67 were rebuilt as the Pioneer Building in 1906, mainly to house the Pioneer Assurance company, but with lots of other businesses as well. The Snackeries pub was on the ground floor, but there was also this café-restaurant, The Gainsborough, advertised in 1911 as having 'popular prices'.

10. Plans for Hepworths tailors in Kings Lynn, *c.*1923, show the fashionable new frontage with its recessed door and standardised design details.

11. This ideal interior from an Edwardian trade manual has it all: neatly stacked produce, hygienic glass display cabinetry, well-placed advertising signs and chairs for customers to sit on while they discuss their orders. There's even what looks suspiciously like that early-twentieth-century cliché, the aspidistra.

12. A tray of Bettys fancy goods, *c.*1930. these include 'cauliflowers' (third across, second down) made from sponge cake, green marzipan, maraschino and buttercream.

13. Eric Ravilious, *Baker and Confectioner*, 1938. Baking in the early hours, with a delivery cart outside.

14. The escalator hall at D.H. Evans on London's Oxford Street was an eye-catching element of a completely new store, opened in 1937 with a brochure to publicise it (and tie into that year's coronation). It featured pale pink marble walls, cork floors for aesthetic and sound reasons, and shimmering bronze and silver metal finishes.

15. Manchester's Arndale Centre, built between 1972 and 1979 and universally loathed by architectural critics. Work began to improve it within a few years of opening, and despite the anguish from anyone with a sense of aesthetics, it thrived as a shopping centre.

16. The interior of Manchester's Arndale Centre after the improvement plan of the 1980s, with (limited) natural light introduced, along with plant pots ideal for stubbing out cigarettes. Its atmosphere is far from the unruly, ever-changing high street outside.

one wanted and nothing more, and having secured one's goods left the shop as seriously as one arrived.'[64] This view, which has coloured a lot of later accounts of mid-nineteenth century shopping, reflected only one reality: quite clearly the writer hadn't encountered William Ablett and his 'pushing'.

An equally critical account, this time a contemporary one, complained in contrast that the new style of emporiums were full of 'assistants, male and female, who bustled about, and asked if you wanted "anything more", before they served you with what you came to purchase, and teased you with "wonderful bargains" of gloves and flowers, when you were inquiring the price of flannel'.[65] Some people grumbled that shopping wasn't what it used to be, when personal service mattered, and assistants were ready to spend time with you, and shops sold quality British hand-made goods instead of these mass-manufactured industrial things and – well, you get the picture.[66] But others enjoyed the game of shopping, and embraced the new world of selling and being sold to. Gradually a gulf opened between those who were up for less personal service and could cope with aggressive sales techniques and those who still craved the personal touch and the illusion of friendship. Even while the numbers of paid shop assistants burgeoned, one writer advised would-be shopkeepers that 'a kind and obliging manner carries with it an indescribable charm. It must not be a manner which indicates a mean, grovelling, time-serving spirit, but a plain, open, and agreeable demeanour, which seems to desire to oblige for the pleasure of doing so, and not for the sake of squeezing an extra penny out of a customer's pocket.'[67]

Times were changing. By 1870 drapers and other large independent retailers with multiple departments were firmly at the forefront of retail change. Elias Moses, a draper in the East End, offered not only a returns policy, but now had several outlets. He wasn't alone. The draper you're in may well have more branches, possibly in the same town or county, but was

Fig. 4.5. Chamberlin, Sons & Co (later Chamberlins), a large drapers on the corner of Dove Hill and Guildhall Hill in Norwich, 1869. By now it sold furnishings, carpets, and houshold linens and had a refreshment rooms – well on the way to becoming a Big Shop.

equally likely to be spread across the country. Clark & Debenham started in Cheltenham in 1826, and opened in Harrogate in 1844. Marshall & Snelgrove had stores in Scarborough and Harrogate and would expand ever further in the next fifty years. By the second half of the century, nearly every draper offered an in-house making service, employing tailors and dressmakers to make up the cloth you bought into the garments it was destined for. Of course, you could still go elsewhere. On Bath's Milsom Street, you could now buy your cloth at Parton & Co (numbers 2 and 3), Foard & King (8); Jollys (11 and 12), or Horatio James (39 and 40) and then choose from seven different dressmakers and a tailor all on the same, short, street. The dressmakers, some of whom were also milliners or corsetmakers, didn't all have ground-floor shops, but instead occupied showrooms and workrooms on the upper floors. Madame Laroche, who advertised herself as an 'artiste for corset-making', was at 15A, above a chemist and druggist, while Miss Russell shared number 14 with a bootmaker and a dentist.[68]

In the hotly competitive world of the drapers, racing to add services, ladieswear was a natural addition. In Dunfermline in 1863 John Johnston 'begs to intimate that, at the request of numerous Ladies, he has added a DRESSMAKING DEPARTMENT to his Business, under the Management of an Experienced Forewoman, long in one of the First Establishments in GEORGE STREET, EDINBURGH'.[69] By 1870 London's Debenham & Freebody had twenty-seven different departments, including the standard silks, shawls, gloves, lace and haberdashery, but also now venturing into household linens, millinery, ball dresses, costumes, coats and the ever-so-of-its-time 'India outfits' to equip those heading off to impose their rule upon the native populations of the British Empire. By now consumers were benefiting from easily reproduced clothing patterns, artificial dyes (bright and colourfast as well as cheap), sewing machines and a plethora of new and improved fabrics and manufacturing processes. Business was booming.

In all of this, it's easy to forget the human side of the changing high street. Ethical debates now concerned quality and price, along with access and the reality of what cheapness meant in practice. As early as the 1830s one critic wrote that 'nothing can be more erroneous than the idea, that everyone has a right to get any article as cheap as he possibly can'.[70] Pressure to produce cheap goods inevitably led to pressure on workers. In 1863 a young dressmaker died, and, because she was employed by a court dressmaker, her case hit the headlines. According to reports, 'The unhappy young woman appears to have been of a delicate constitution, little suited for long hours of hard work in a crowded and unwholesome room.' She was taken ill, saw a doctor but just two days later 'she was so much better that she was beyond the reach of Fashion and Fashion's milliners – she was dead! Her bedfellow, herself so tired and listless to observe how deep and placid was her companion's sleep, had probably lain by the side of a corpse all night.'[71] For now, the case sparked only momentary outrage – after all, so many of the working class laboured in terrible conditions that destroyed their health. The issues remained, however, and would only worsen as the high street continued to grow.

You're done with shopping now. Dusk is fast approaching and nobody genteel is out after dark. (On the other hand, you may not be that genteel, in which case keep going, by all means – but dinner is at 8 and unless your daily help is also a cook, you will need to attend to it yourself.) Once the factories kick out, the streets will fill with life again as workers flock to the bazaars and market halls. The poor crowd into the butchers to buy fly-blown meat or offcuts. Some of the lights in rooms above the shops blaze out as the pieceworkers carry on stitching and cutting. The shops themselves will start to close around 9pm, though some stay open until 11pm to catch the last of the trade. After that the shop-floor needs tidying, and items need to be processed and put out ready for the next day. The pubs are still open, and the gin shops, and if it's a Saturday the drinking will go on until the small hours. Let's end here, with Charles Dickens summing up the end of the mid-Victorian day: 'There were few passengers astir; the street was sad and dismal, and pretty well my own. A few stragglers from the theatres hurried by, and now and then I turned aside to avoid some noisy drunkard as he reeled homewards, but these interruptions were not frequent and soon ceased.'[72]

Briggate, Leeds, 1903

Leeds has come a long way in the last few decades. For most of the Victorian age it was derided as part of the grim and industrial north. Cornish quaker Robert Barclay Fox was typical in his critique, claiming it was 'amongst all others of its species . . . the vilest of the vile', going on to denounce the 'vast dingy canopy formed by the impure exhalation of a hundred furnaces. It sits on the town like an everlasting incubus, shutting out the light of heaven and the breath of summer.'[73] Rude as he was, it was not without some element of truth. Throughout Victoria's reign a fierce battle of words and ideas raged on the subject of industrial towns, with their pollution and overcrowded slums held up as emblematic of everything bad about the modern, capitalist age. The issue of rural poverty and exploitation was conveniently overlooked. But since the 1850s town leaders have fought back hard, beautifying the streets, building grandiose statements of wealth and intent, and making northern towns destinations for those seeking to spend time in a thoroughly modern city. It worked. Leeds was granted city status in 1893.

You're starting your walk at the junction of Briggate with Boar Lane and Duncan Street. You may have come via the lower part of Briggate, perhaps crossing the bridge over the river which originally gave the street its name. The lower end is very mixed and includes shops aiming at the less affluent residents of the city. There's a pawnbroker, several grocers, a mourning draper and some light industry including a margarine manufacturer and a whitesmith (a metalworker specialising in lighter metals such as tin or pewter). The buildings all look modern(ish), but this is a street which until very recently had a lot of elderly single-storey shops. Indeed, one of the ginnels

(a local term for alleyways) off it still leads to a jettied house that was built around 1600. Now they've been rebuilt or, more often, refaced. Thus Dyson's jewellers, at the top of the street near where you are standing, is all stucco outside and Parisian chandeliers inside. It also has a flamboyant clock with a ball which drops at 1pm every day; locals refer to it as the Time Ball Building.

Cross the road and pass the striped awning of Suttons mantle maker (mantles are coats) on one corner (number 33) and Emma Sillers' furriers (number 150) on the other. Mind out for the trams – you can't miss them, for they are festooned with advertisements. The city council has only this year banned advertising vehicles from Briggate, which has helped alleviate the traffic, but between the electric trams and the horse-drawn carts and the mass of people it is often very crowded. The pavements are laid with close-fitting slabs and have steep kerbs with drainage alongside. Small, ornate electric streetlights are set at intervals along them, with larger ones marching down the centre of the road (they also support the tram cables).

Over on your right is a passage leading to the *Leeds Mercury* offices, plus a fancy repository and a large wine merchant. Then there's the gleaming tiles of the Maypole Dairy, which has several hundred branches throughout England and Ireland and specialises in butter and margarine. It's not the only food seller on this part of the street, for number 129 is Mary Walker's butcher's shop and opposite that at number 51 is a grocer's. Number 45 is Klosterman's confectioners. But most of Briggate is devoted to less ephemeral things. Stay on the left-hand side of the street to admire the metalwork in the window of Croisdale and Sons, who are cutlers, but also athletic outfitters (a little incongruous, you admit). Next to them, number 37 has been subdivided to house Jessie Brotherton's Café Royale, along with Walker's bookshop. Jennings the printer advertises as being 'over Walker's' and there's also a tailor in the same building.

Many of the shops have other businesses over them, advertised with large wooden hoardings fixed on to the fronts of the buildings, or painted signs, or posters, or all three. This has been the main drag since the medieval period, and the plots are still those of centuries before: long, narrow and not very practical.

One solution is to buy up several neighbouring plots. Numbers 40 to 41 are occupied by Waller & Richardson, a draper and silk mercer. Divided from them only by a narrow ginnel is the Leeds branch of Samuel Hyam & Co. They also have shops in London, Wolverhampton and Birmingham, and are keen advertisers in the *Mercury*. Their departments include hats and caps, hosiery, ready-made clothing, trunks and travelling goods, 'gentleman's cycling requisites' and 'school, sea and colonial outfits'. They are particularly keen to promote their boyswear when it is time to return to school.

Drapers and clothiers are well represented here, for Kendall & Co are at number 49, and directly opposite them on the right is one of the rare large plots. It's currently covered with scaffolding, much to the chagrin of the residents of the Grand Central Hotel next door. In December the scaffolding will come down to reveal 'the newest thing in Leeds': Broadbent's Great Drapery Store. To help get people through the door it's putting on a 'great exhibition and toy bazaar', which promises to be 'Switzerland in Leeds' for only 6d.[74] You are, undeniably, tempted.

Thoughts of the winter may persuade you to stop at number 50, Thornton & Co, rubber manufacturers. They make excellent wellington boots, plus waterproof leggings, overcoats and a lot more. You can't miss any of it, for in addition to the wooden signboards attached to every bit of blank wall on the building, the sill of the main window declares 'India Rubber Depots'. But they have competition, for the North British Rubber Co is further down the street. Based in Edinburgh, they're best known for inventing the pneumatic tyre, but they also do a fine line in hot water bottles. Next to Thornton's is the only shop on Briggate without plate glass: Green's the grocer has small-paned bow windows, which cast square shadows on to the packets in the window. There's a giant tea canister the size of one of the windows, with three golden sugar cones hanging from it above the door.

Boot and shoemakers are everywhere. Across on the right now is Stead & Simpson, founded in Leeds as leatherworkers, though they have since moved manufacturing to Leicester and expanded to be one of the biggest shoemakers in the country. To your left, divided from Thornton's by the archway leading to Turk's Head Yard, is the shopfront of Manfield & Sons, all gilt below and curved windows above. Before you look at the display of footwear, peep between advert-encrusted walls down the opening on your left.

One of the features of Briggate is the variety of ginnels, which lead either to narrow through passages or enclosed yards. Some contain housing, others allow access to the workshops behind some of the shops. Others still contain pubs. Turk's Head Yard holds Whitelock's First City Luncheon Rooms, which has expanded from a small site to take over a row of Georgian cottages just next door. It was heavily refurbished seventeen years ago, which was when it got its current name, and is resplendent with decorative tiles, engraved mirrors, stained glass and gleaming brass (120 years later it will still exist to surprise the unwary ginnel-explorer).

You may prefer a more obvious drinking place. Just ahead, where Briggate meets Kirkgate, the Buck Inn occupies a huge corner site, beyond which is another option, for Barnsbee Ephraim's drapery has its own central smoking café and billiard saloon (no prizes for guessing which gender is most welcome there – although apparently the store itself is most fitted for 'lovely, cute, bargain-hunting' women).[75] Stay on the left-hand side though, and cross Commercial Street – you might remember the giant bread arch which was built here nine years ago to mark a royal visit. The bread came from a bakery in one of Briggate's yards, and was supposed to be distributed to the deserving poor, except rain scuppered the whole thing.[76]

This part of the street has changed beyond recognition in the last few years. A few older buildings still exist on the left – number 56 is another multi-use address, with a hairdresser, tailor, glover and watchmaker operating on its several floors. But more typical is the single-use shop opposite, newly occupied by the Walk Over Shoe company – 'the boots which have made American boots famous in England'. They've got multiple branches including in Glasgow, Edinburgh, Belfast and Liverpool, and promise that 'no foot is too difficult to fit'.[77] Then again, John Cooper and his solid leather boots are moving into number 60 in October as part of the construction of a whole new street just ahead of you: Albion Place. It's the (current) culmination of building works, which seem to have been going on for a decade and which have resulted in two new streets on the right as well. That side is brand new, and very uniform, all pink and fawn striped brickwork, with turrets and columns, and swags and all sorts of vaguely baroque stuff. It makes for larger buildings: a pianoforte dealer takes up three units, and Boots Cash Chemists have a corner site complete with the season's decoration *du jour*, a large clock. Between them is the Empire Theatre, whose swish electric lights and minarets would probably stand out more if the shops to either side didn't have even bigger lit-up signs fixed to their fronts. It's a vast improvement on the shambles that still occupied the site until the 1890s, with open drains and streetside butchery – along with the Briggate Bazaar.

Bazaars are old news. Leeds is all about the arcades. Ahead of you on the left is Queen's Arcade, with another large clock outside it. Inside is all colour and light, with ground-floor shops and then a second storey with shops on one side and a

Fig. 4.6. Briggate, 1904. This view is from halfway up, where the Empire Theatre and Albion Place have just been finished. The space between the domes was glazed over in the 1990s and now forms the Victoria Quarter – the Empire theatre was converted to a Harvey Nichols.

hotel on the other. A few paces further on is Thornton's Arcade. It has an indoor clock featuring Robin Hood and his gang in dangerously short tunics. Between the two, on the other side of the road, is the County Arcade, still so new that most of the shops are unoccupied. However, the Ceylon Café is opening in October with a full orchestra. It promises to be 'the most magnificent café in the provinces'.[78] In the meantime, you could pop into Durham's fancy goods shop, which starts advertising Christmas cards in October (too soon).

As you reach the top end of the street, look to the right and shade your eyes. Even by the standards of this street, the Cash Clothing Company's signage is large. It apparently has a 'slaughtering sale' on. You can see why Bishop Eveleigh is moving his stationery, fancy goods and silverware shop from opposite down to the corner of Albion Place – he's bought a whopping five plots. On both sides now is Hilton and Goodrick, musical instrument dealers, with a window full of gramophones to 'make your evenings enjoyable'.[79] Unconvinced? You'll find the City Varieties Hall just down Swan Street to the left.

As you come to the junction with Upperhead and Lowerhead Row, look left towards the town hall. This street, which will be heavily altered, widened and renamed in the 1920s, also has shops, but for now you're exhausted. Turn back to Briggate and head for number 77. It's one of the four branches of Lockharts you've seen on this walk, and the most upmarket. Give in, and order a soothing cup of cocoa.[80]

Chapter Five

1870–1914

Husband: why do your clothes cost you twenty pounds more this year than last? Aren't things cheaper? Wife: yes, dear, that's just it. There are so many more bargains.[1]

– *TitBits* (1893)

Shopping list: A pair of boots, a watch chain, a piece of cheese, an outfit for a small boy

This chapter's shopping list could be that of almost anyone with a bit of disposable income. Let's assume you're at the border of working and middle class: the main wage earner may be a clerk or a policeman, a gamekeeper or a boarding-house keeper. You may well have help at home, but this is likely to be a casual char or the teenage daughter of a friend practising for going into service. As a woman, you may well work, perhaps as a teacher or, if single, a shop assistant or waitress. Our list today mixes business with pleasure, for while every element might be regarded as necessary, each might also be superfluous to actual need. In the brave new shopping world of the late nineteenth century, it's your choice.

The closing decades of the nineteenth century are known for glitz and glamour, bustles, wasp-waists and impressive facial hair. For the French, it was the Belle Époque, in America, the Gilded Age. The rich installed central heating and electric lighting, and altered their coach houses to fit motor cars. But two-thirds of the British population were classed as poor, with a third living below the nominal poverty line.

Social reformers such as Seebohm Rowntree and William Booth spearheaded campaigns to highlight the enormous social inequality and lobbied government to change it. In Manchester, a movement to provide free school meals started and spread, while at a national level, old age pensions and a plethora of Acts to legislate on working conditions and food and drug safety were ushered into law. The population continued to grow, standing at 36 million by 1911 (slightly over half that of today).

The old Queen died in 1901, succeeded by the surprisingly successful Edward VII. With his accession came an era of increased royal pomp and ceremony. From now on high streets across the country would be festooned in banners and bunting in honour of any and every royal event, while shop windows were awarded prizes for their patriotic displays. The retail environment was tough, and prices were kept low through a combination of continued technological advances, terrible conditions and low pay for workers. The era is often loosely termed that of the second industrial revolution – though the benefits and drawbacks were as hotly debated and as patchily distributed as they had been during the first.

By the early twentieth century, shopping for fun was recognised as a truly universal pastime, with the delineation between 'shopping' (fun) and 'marketing' (tedious) now applying to all.[2] The wider function of the high street as a focus for leisure was fully established and was something in which everyone could participate, according to their own criteria. But not everyone was keen on the opening up of what had once been a relatively exclusive exercise, and the expansion of shopping areas was accompanied by a resurgence in moralising grumbles over luxury, waste and unrealistic aspirations. Gender tensions continued to lurk, with female shoppers portrayed alternately as silly geese off to the slaughter, or cunning spendthrifts intent upon ruining their husbands. Female shop assistants were infantilised by the widespread habit of calling them shopgirls (their male equivalent were never shopboys), while still suffering from the age-old problem of sexual objectification. Working conditions for shop assistants were frequently dire, sparking sporadic attempts at collective action or top-down lobbying, which included exhorting individual shoppers to engage with ethical questions, while useful legislation moved at a glacial pace.

This era has traditionally been seen as the crucial period for the development of the high street as most of us know it. Both a side effect and then a driver of the high street's expansion was the growth of what would become known as chain stores. To contemporaries, they were known as multiples. Familiar names crop up in trade directories of even smaller towns, as businesses expanded from having just one or two shops to several hundred, and a small number of shops in larger cities became what the Americans called department stores. But still, new shops co-existed with the old, and the developments we'll see in this chapter were all built on existing practice. Don't get too excited by the businesses which appear either – nearly all of them will later be taken over or go bust, if not in the period covered by the main part of this book, then shortly thereafter. It's entirely likely that some of you will exclaim at something familiar, while others, through age or geography, will have no recollection of the shop at all.

Most people still shopped at markets as well as shops. Everyday shopping for anyone without servants was price-driven, and while it could be pleasurable, it was mainly just a chore, for 'we had to go to numerous different shops, which made shopping a lengthy business. This was especially so because being served took quite a time, as social chit-chat was expected and many of the goods had to be weighed out specially for each customer.'[3] Molly Hughes, living near Bayswater in the 1890s, had a middle-class background, but living with her husband in a small flat with limited help did all of her own shopping. She quickly learnt to eschew the prestige shops her peers shopped at for a small row of local 'shops and stalls catering for those who have no money to waste and mean to get the utmost value for their outlay. They were not to be put off with stale vegetables or doubtful fish – such as I had encountered in the "better-class shops".[4]

The gap continued to grow between large, regional urban centres with a range of shops catering to every budget and the tiny, locally focused retail hubs of suburbs or small towns. Take Arnold Bennett's *Old Wives' Tale*, where 'the Square really had changed for the worse . . . as a centre of commerce it had assuredly approached very near to death'. The cause was the shift of business to 'arrogant and pushing Hanbridge, with its electric light and its theatres and its big, advertising shops'.[5] Though fictional, this represents a real trend. In East Anglia, Ely's High Street was typical of a small market town in the 1880s. There were insurance companies, banks, six drapers/milliners, a confectioner, and a couple of chemists, one of which sold both foreign wine and 'Pate's celebrated sheep-dipping preparation for scabs etc'. The short street opened directly on to the market square, with its food shops and saddler (and a ladies' seminary). A resident would easily find everything they needed, and there were ample places to eat and sleep. But it was far from a retail paradise, and with Cambridge now merely twenty-five minutes away by train, anyone wanting a full day out and not needing sheep-dip need only head to the station.

Another reason for the stagnation of some towns was the prevalence of mail order, which had been given a boost by better transport and communication networks. Shopping from catalogues was well-established and enjoyable – who doesn't like to browse through pictures and enjoy lavish descriptions of things for sale? Take, for example, Silber and Flemming's 1883 bewitchingly named *Illustrated Catalogue of Furniture and Household Requisites*, with pages of line drawings showing everything from the 'standard' tree pruner ('the most effective pruner yet introduced'), to the pannier luncheon basket ('may be carried on a man's back, or in pairs over a pony or horse, one fitted for luncheon . . . the other, without fittings, to hold game').[6] Gamage's 1914 *General Catalogue* had a special feature on its 'featherweight' cycles – 'we feel sure this model will especially appeal to ladies, many of whom are physically incapable of propelling the ordinary heavy cycle', and a whole page of wirecutters, an item with which so many men were to become intimately familiar as the Great War engulfed Europe just a few months after the catalogue's release.[7]

Shopping by post was not without its issues though. In addition to the obvious perils of items not being entirely as described, some people already recognised that by increasing the reach of big companies, smaller businesses – and by extension small high streets – might suffer. One Tunbridge Wells vicar exhorted his flock to buy local in 1888, for 'the weight of goods arriving at our local stations for private people far exceeds that for the tradesmen'.[8] Big-city-dwellers were even better positioned, with John Maynard Keynes airily stating that 'the inhabitant of London could order by telephone, sipping his morning tea in bed, the various products of the whole earth, in such quantity as he may see fit, and reasonably expect their early delivery upon their doorstep'.[9] Sometimes mail order was a means by which a high street store could extend its customer base, but eventually, the catalogues of bricks-and-mortar stores would be outshone by those of mail order specialists such as Freemans, founded in 1905, or Grattan, which started as a jewellery business in Bradford (both were bought out in the 1980s but still exist as online stores).[10]

Let's assume that the post has already arrived, and head to town. Perhaps hop on a tram from the suburbs, admiring the way in which the streets have been reconfigured to soften sharp corners and allow for access. When tramways are put in, the rest of the street gets sparkly new paving by law. Many trams are horse-drawn, a few are powered by steam and, by the 1890s, electric trams are coming in. If you're brave, head for the top deck, which is open, and from which you can look down on the bustle below. Be warned, though – it gets quite dirty up there, though in all honesty it's probably still better than the fug of a rainy day when everyone crams inside. Before we reach the main streets, let's have a quick wander up the latest addition to the most up-and-coming of towns, the covered arcade.

The arcade

Arcades are one part of the Victorian shopping landscape which has survived in reasonable numbers across Britain. The first few were built during the Regency, inspired by the French. Back in 1783, the then resident of the Palais-Royale, Louis-Philippe d'Orléans, had presided over the reconstruction of the Palais and its enclosed garden, building galleries of shops, two theatres and housing. In, too, went the Cirque du Palais-Royale, a top-lit, half-subterranean space with stalls, food outlets and the potential for horse racing. At the southern end of the gardens were more shops, proper ones, built of stone and in rows which were covered with an arching frame and skylights. They opened as the Galleries du Bois in 1786. Seven years later, Louis-Philippe was guillotined, and five years after that the Cirque burnt down. But the galleries survived, and even while the Revolution raged on, inspired a host of others. Many still exist today, and a walk around the galleries of the *première arrondissement* is a gentle pleasure. London's first iteration was the Royal Opera Arcade, opened in 1817, with the Burlington Arcade next up in 1818. Others followed, including the Corridor in Bath (1825), the Argyle in Glasgow (1827) and the Royal Arcade in Newcastle (1832).

For the upper classes, the early arcades were an upmarket alternative to the bazaars. The Burlington was probably the most successful, combining a West End location with careful attention to the needs of its desired clientele. It was very strictly regulated and only open to vendors of 'hardware, wearing apparel and articles not offensive in appearance or smell'. Pushchairs, bulky parcels and open umbrellas were banned and no whistling, singing or playing of musical instruments was allowed, making it a remarkably calm space. It also closed at 8pm, mindful, like the bazaars, that it was vital to avoid any accusations of late-night dodginess. There were still rumours that one particular bonnet shop had a back room wherein sex workers could take clients, but for once the dirt didn't stick.[11] George Sala visited in the 1850s, summing up its wares with typical snark:

> I don't think there is a shop in its *enceinte* where they sell anything that we could not do without. Boots and shoes are sold there, to be sure, but what boots and shoes? Varnished and embroidered and be-ribboned figments, fitter for a fancy ball or a lady's chamber, there to caper to the jingling melody of a lute, than for serious pedestrianism. Paintings and lithographs for gilded boudoirs, collars for puppy dogs, and silver-mounted whips for spaniels, pocket handkerchiefs, in which an islet of cambric is surrounded by an ocean of lace, embroidered garters and braces, filagree flounces, firework-looking bonnets, scent bottles, sword-knots, brocaded sashes, worked dressing-gowns, inlaid snuff-boxes, and falbalas of all descriptions; these form the stock-in-trade of the merchants who have here their tiny boutiques.[12]

A few more arcades were built during the 1830s and 1840s, but while they were admired by some architects, who saw them as both beautiful and fulfilling a need (Joseph Paxton suggested building one around the whole of central London), it wasn't until the 1870s that arcades really took off.

The new wave was led by the north, where civic authorities were desperate to create more space for retailers who wanted to take advantage of the burgeoning wealth of industrial towns. Between 1870 and 1900 sixty-one new arcades were built, twenty-seven of which were in Yorkshire or Lancashire. Newcastle had two, Manchester got five, as did Leeds, where the County Arcade of the turn of the century remains one of the most stunning examples of the form.[13] Most were built over existing streets, or, rather, as replacements for them. This had the huge advantage of maintaining the mental map residents had of the streetscape. In Norwich, when the Royal Arcade replaced the Royal Hotel in 1899, the building even retained much of the fairly austere hotel facade on the Gentleman's Walk side. The architect made up for it at the rear entrance, with a colourful cacophony of tiles and art nouveau decoration. In Leeds, Queens and Thornton's Arcades also replaced former inns and narrow alleyways, while the County Arcade was part of a complex that included two new streets and opened up access to Kirkgate Market.

Many arcades incorporated what would later become known as anchor tenants: entertainment venues, cafés or hotels. Most were double-storeyed, with shops below and rooms above, which were initially intended as living quarters, but quickly became storerooms or offices – nobody wanted to live over the shop any more. Manchester's Barton Arcade had two floors of shops and a further two with offices, providing space for 143 different tenants. A few examples ventured beyond the corridor concept, with atriums providing space for entertainment beyond retail. In Southport, the Wayfarer Arcade had a central atrium containing a bandstand along with that late Victorian cliché, the potted palm tree.[14]

Fig. 5.1. The Royal Arcade, Norwich, in 1978. Built on the site of the Royal Hotel in 1899, this is the back entrance, off the evocatively named Back of the Inns. It is a riot of colourful tiles and stained glass, very much art nouveau meets arts-and-crafts.

Fig. 5.2. Interior of the Royal Arcade, with its bowed shopfronts and light-filled walkway. The front is quite boring, in comparison.

The shops themselves were varied, though rarely sold food, apart from the pleasant-smelling, attractively arrayed confectioner. Shop turnover was fast, for the units were small, and not all arcades were successful. Some types of shop were stalwarts. Not for nothing was the original arcade – the Royal Opera – known as 'the arcade of the melancholy-mad bootmakers'.[15] While we're here, therefore, let's think about the first item on our list, for it is frankly hard to imagine a late Victorian arcade without at least one shoe shop.

The shoe shop

Boots and shoes were a staple product, and, although the very poor could not always afford them, most people put their feet into something, even if it was the second-hand shoes of others. Those who could afford it did as they had always done, buying bespoke shoes from a small maker who would make a wooden last as a model to work from for each individual foot. Mechanisation was slow to catch on, making shoes expensive and, inevitably therefore, a mark of wealth. Lower down the social scale, ready-made shoes had been around since the medieval period, with demand especially high during periods of war, when thousands of soldiers suddenly needed shoeing, fast.

By the early nineteenth century some of the processes involved had been brought under a proto-factory system, with many workers supervised in one place. This gradually developed into a fuller factory system, especially once sewing machines made their appearance in the 1850s, followed by other machinery. By the 1870s even upmarket footwear was being produced in factories, with Northampton, Leicester, Norwich and Yorkshire leading the charge.[16]

The rise of big shoe manufacturers inevitably meant the decline of the local shoemaker. The rich continued to buy

bespoke, of course, with shoemakers coming to them for fittings. But on the high street the normal model was now simply
a retailer, no workshop needed. Shoe shops were able to stock
a wide range of models, drawn from makers across the country,
each promising the fit of a bespoke shoe thanks to sizes which
came in fractions, and with different width fittings. C. & J. Clark
of Street in Somerset made a 'hygienic' boot and shoe (hygiene
still being a magic word), which promised not to 'deform the
feet or cause corns or bunions'. Children, they promised, would
especially benefit. The models came in 'four fittings of every size
and half size', and would-be purchasers were assured that they
were 'manufactured on anatomical principles' but that 'the
shapes are not carried to such an extreme as to appear conspicuous or unsightly'. The fear of an orthopaedic-looking shoe was
already alive and well.[17]

Window-dressers for shoe shops went fully to town. Plate
glass was now the preferred choice even for small shops, and
although older sashes and paned windows were still present
on every street, the shoe trade was sufficiently competitive that
any retailer who could adopted it as soon as possible. A large
window with a looming sign and lettering plastered across the
building was simply the start. Gone, for the most modern of
shops, were simple stacks of shoes, to be replaced with exuberant and eye-catching displays, which prioritised care and
attention to detail over just showing what they'd got.

Some shops opted for boards with shoes attached to them
in whirls or concentric circles: others went for horizontal
displays with a pyramid or cascade in the centre. More shoes
hung around the door, across the front of the shop and down
the divides between the windows. Each was priced, with signs
declaring further offers or proclaiming the particular virtues
of particular shoes, along with assurances that 'same prices
inside the shop as ticketed at the doors and in the windows'.[18]
Gas, and by the end of the century, electric lighting was used to

enhance the display, flickering off buckles and patent leather to catch the eye of the potentially oblivious passer-by.

One reason for the level of display was that inside, the shops still tended to be dark, dingy and lined with stacked shoe boxes. The smell of leather was masked by that of polish, for wares didn't always arrive in a fit state for display, and in the hours before and after closing time shop assistants, both male and female, had to unwrap and polish wares from the factories, which would then be stuffed with paper and boxed ready for sale. Despite the claims of the manufacturers, even in the 1900s, there was still a hint of the cheapskate about ready-made shoes, with ease of production prioritised over ease of wear. One (wealthy) shopper bemoaned that 'shoes were made to fit "lasts", not feet, and the exact sizes of these lasts were "stock sizes", handed down from the reign of the Georges'.[19] Barratts of Northampton launched the 'footshape' brand, a mail order gimmick whereby people could draw round their feet and send the picture with their order to ensure the right size.[20] You could always try one of the American shoe companies, which included 'Walkover', 'Sirosis', and 'Signet', for 'if an American attends to you, you may spend each afternoon trying on his wares, and you are likely to uphold his brand of shoes for ever'.[21]

By the 1890s there was change afoot(!). Some of the larger makers already had their own shops, and now, with production increasing and demand rising, they started to open multiple branches. This was not a new idea. Remember William Stout, back in the 1670s, dealing with his annoying nephew and the exploding shop? The grocer he'd trained under had operated two separate outlets. William Ablett, the draper who'd been busy burning the edges of sheets to pass them off as damaged stock in the 1810s, also did time in a smaller branch of his drapers' firm. But these were small fry compared to the new breed of retailer.

Let's head to Leicester in 1879, home of Freeman, Hardy & Willis, a name which will be familiar to anyone born before

1980 (the chain collapsed in 1996). Early branches were opened in Leamington Spa, Lincoln and Leeds, which did so well that by 1887 they had 130 shops, rising to 200 by 1894. At this point, with the idea of multiple shops – chains – established in the public's mind, the company started buying up small competitors and rebranding them, meaning that by 1914 they operated 460 shops and claimed to be 'the largest boot and shoe dealers in the world'.[22] Competition for that title came from Leeds-based Stead & Simpson, who had around 100 shops in 1889, and Northampton's Manfield & Sons who grew from twenty-one shops in 1895 to seventy by 1910. By this point the multiples controlled just over 20 per cent of total footwear sales – not bad considering they'd barely existed just a generation before.[23]

An advantage of shopping at a multiple was consistency. The same shopping guide that recommended American shoes praised multiples for having 'the same shop windows, the same neat shelves, the same adaptable ladders, the same up-to-date trying-on appliances'.[24] While the majority of shops continued to have dreary artificially lit spaces filled with walls of boxes, some of the more enterprising shop fitters turned to interior design, fitting stands upon which to display shoes in the shop itself, or in one case, in Portsmouth, installing an aquarium complete with goldfish and South African lobsters in which to tastefully display waterproof items.[25]

You're probably hungry by now (maybe the lobster has put ideas into your head). Perhaps you've arranged to meet a friend for a catch-up or to get a second opinion as you shop. Budget is an issue, but there's a great deal of choice now, and it's not all drinking dens or terrible food in a quasi-charitable concern. You could stick to the arcade, or head out to the open street. Either way, it won't be long before you find an inviting glass door and hear the clatter of cutlery from a suitably set-up establishment.

The luncheon rooms

For a long time, eating out was largely restricted to men, although some wealthy women ignored the risk of social opprobrium and found places willing to cater to them. In the late 1820s Jane Carlyle enjoyed a mutton chop and glass of bitter ale at Verrey's on London's Regent Street, writing to her husband that 'I see single women besides myself at Verrey's – not improper – governesses and the like.'[26] This started to change properly in the 1870s, with the advent both of French-style high-end restaurants led by the Savoy, and mass market cafés aiming squarely at shoppers and workers. Very quickly the rules of eating in public changed. There were still a lot of eating houses aiming predominantly at men, including the perennially popular chophouses and taverns. If your shopping street was near the financial and business district, you'd have been well advised to avoid both these and the cheaper cafés around midday, for they would have been rammed. P. G. Wodehouse pointed out with feeling that that 'few workers in the City do regard lunch as a trivial affair. It is the keynote of the day. It is an oasis in a desert of ink and ledgers. Conversation in a city office deals, in the morning, with what one is going to have for lunch, and in the afternoon with what one has had for lunch.'[27]

However, with women entering the office-based workforce, as well as being increasingly visible on the high street, there was profit to be made by welcoming everyone. One tourist guide to London in the 1890s made a point of including a chapter specifically for ladies, pointing out that 'there are, as most of us know, two kinds of luncheon, the substantial and the light. The first appeals rather to the robuster appetites of men than the fastidious tastes of women, and belongs more to the London restaurant and club than the modest refreshment place to which the daintier sex ordinarily resort.' The guide included an advertisement for Verrey's, still going strong, and proudly offering 'luncheons for ladies shopping'.[28]

Women were out there. In 1899 *The Lady* magazine published an article entitled 'Should Women Dine in Restaurants?', the latest in a salvo of scribblings from authors who generally hated the idea that women might dare to do something their husbands had been doing for centuries. Think, cried the author, of the poor neglected children, fleetingly seeing their mother 'as she rushed in with not a moment to spare: a hasty kiss and she is off again for a luncheon party at the Berkeley'.[29] The whole thing was very tedious, and not at all original.

For over twenty years the trade press and papers had joined enthusiastically in sniping about women eating and drinking on the high street. Squabbles over liquor licences (licensees could serve both men and women) were particularly unedifying. On one side were hoteliers such as Emma Shickle in Bayswater, testifying that 'families of good position and great responsibility' found it a great 'inconvenience' to have to seek their wine elsewhere. Even Gatti's, a café-restaurant, caterer and entertainment venue of some repute on the Strand, had to beg to obtain a licence 'in conformity with the wishes of the frequenters of the gallery'. Ranged against them were local councils and middle-class letter-writers (who might, perhaps, today be called NIMBYS), claiming that women would become drunk, sexually incontinent and morally debased by their habit of going out to eat. It was even worse when shops themselves proposed opening refreshment rooms. One contributor to *The Graphic* must have been positively frothing at the mouth while writing:

> They [women] have lunches which might serve them for dinners. They acquire such things as soups, cutlets, omelettes, macaroni, fritters, and so forth; they revel in the accompaniments of cruets full of sherry or claret, or lilliputian bottles of champagne. What is the effect? They have

not left the halls of temptation; the voice of the charmer still rings in their ears, and it is not very gently that he charms . . . 'Reinvigorated', they return once more to the slaughter, and we are not exaggerating when we say that in the wild and reckless period that follows things are done in a financial way which would make the angels weep.[30]

Such attacks simultaneously denied women agency and yet portrayed them as ravening beasts, both far from the truth. They also didn't work. The architects of arcades and purpose-built shops made deliberate provision for café facilities, including a designated café-restaurant in Leeds's County Arcade. Initially occupied by the Ceylon Café, a Liverpool-based concern with several outlets in Liverpool and Leeds, in 1909 the site was converted into a Lyons as the latter group expanded into full-service eating rooms, as well as its more basic teashops. Joseph Lyon explained his rationale in 1904: 'I found that not only were the so-called restaurants dirty, but the tablecloths were soiled and greasy and the waiters wore unclean shirts and aprons and their general appearance was slovenly, with a suggestion of prolonged interviews with Bacchus the previous night. There was no quick service, and there were no joints or dishes ready except the eternal "roast and boiled with veg", and college pudding to follow . . . and oh, the teas and coffees I have suffered from!'[31]

Standards certainly varied, and the food was plain. A nicely done chop, some chipped potatoes and a glass of claret was the suggestion of one guide, and that same menu crops up with alarming frequency. But even when other choices were available, they weren't always quite allowed. In *Howard's End* (1910), Margaret Schlegel attempts to order fish pie for lunch at Simpson's, only to be admonished by her male companion, who insists upon the mutton with a bit of Stilton cheese instead. She retaliates by taking him to a vegetarian restaurant, a popular choice for customers who preferred not to be patronised or preyed upon, for they were heavily associated with women. Unfortunately, the menus could be equally monotonous and you really did have to like macaroni cheese. But they were cheap, safe and increasing in number: thirty-four in London by 1889, and eighteen in the provinces.[32]

Eat up, and take advantage of the facilities to 'arrange the toilet' as the contemporary wording would have it. Toilet provision is still woeful, and the subject of many hundreds of official words, which never seem to result in anything concrete. It's recognised that there's a real gender imbalance, with one 1879 report stating baldly that 'there are periods and conditions peculiar to the sex, when latrine accommodation would be specially convenient; and as at such times the requirements of nature are apt to be more urgent and more frequent, women would be spared much unnecessary mental and physical distress, were the accommodation provided.'[33] And yet . . . apparently it'll encourage prostitutes (yawn) and even men's urinals are viewed in some quarters as suspiciously foreign, called out as being 'German abominations'. The current vogue is to conceal them underground.[34]

The jeweller

Next up is the jewellery shop. Jewellers were mainstays of the high street and were one of the earliest types of specialist shop. The 1880s purveyors of costume jewellery and mourning rings set with hair were direct descendants of the goldsmiths and swordsmiths of London's Cheapside 200 years before, and even the cheapest jewellers retained a certain cachet as a result. Of course, there was a scale. At the bottom end, some also acted as pawnbrokers, though their shops were usually to be found on the edge of the main shopping area, or in places with high levels of poverty. You could spot them by the three balls outside the shops – one of few remaining purely visual signs of a specific trader (the red and white striped pole of the barber – previously barber-surgeon, hence blood and bandages – being another).

Jewellery wasn't an everyday purchase, and shopkeepers recognised the need to encourage people to window-shop (a new term introduced from America) before they entered. Some shopkeepers even took out adverts asking potential customers to 'see the display in the window in the shop'.[35] Like shoe-makers, leading jewellers invested in plate glass windows and fabric-covered display boards to make the most of the available space. In this case, the privacy afforded by a blocked-out window was also a boon. Some redesigned their shopfronts, installing mini arcades, with a deeply recessed door and long shallow displays leading to it.[36] There were angled boards showing off necklaces, bracelets and things that would lie flat, and vertical boards with items pinned on, including earrings and precious stones. Then came dangling watch chains and watches, thicker necklaces and anything that would drop heavily and add bling. Plate glass windows usually had a horizontal divide about two-thirds of the way up, behind which a jeweller might conceal a shelf displaying heavier items: tableware, clocks, vases, candelabra and so forth. It was overwhelming enough that one London shop was described as 'a hollow square of glittering plate'.[37]

Jewellers – at least outside London – were rarely just jewel sellers, but also makers, menders and sellers of a variety of wares, anything from candlesticks to chamber pots. Many were clock and watch makers, and by the end of the century it was common to install a clock above the shop. Most were plain, perhaps attached to a turret or sticking out of the building. In Norwich, Bullen's floor-to-ceiling glass curved around a narrow corner site, and incorporated a clock above the door from 1898, while just around the corner Dipples made use of a swan sign from a former pub and installed a clock just below.[38]

Some jewellers, like John Dyson of Leeds, decided that a statement was necessary. Dyson installed an electric time ball and a projecting clock complete with Father Time wielding an hourglass and a scythe, which was perhaps not the most reassuring message for shoppers, but became a local landmark. Over in Hull, Scott's had a gas-powered time ball, while in Gloucester 'practical watchmaker' (and jeweller and optician) G. A. Baker erected five mechanised figures representing Father Time along with England, Ireland, Scotland and Wales, each of which rang different bells.[39]

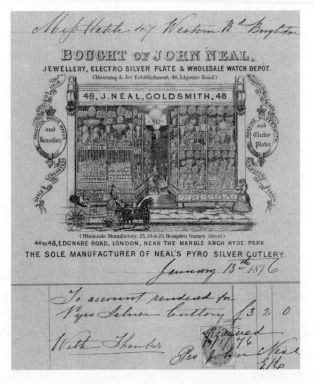

Fig. 5.3. Receipt from J. Neal, Goldsmith, on London's Edgware Road in 1876. The shop window is absolutely crammed, and the shopowner has taken full advantage of plate glass, including installing a short arcade up to the entrance.

Jewellers were obvious targets for thieves, and as such had some of the best security going. The interior was designed to awe and impress – and safeguard. Think mirrored glass cabinets and display cases, mirrored walls, decent lighting, and an insistence on personal service. On entry you'd already have been eyeballed, a long entry arcade being ideal for watching would-be customers. You could expect to be pounced upon, seated and served from the counter, with nothing to browse, turn over or otherwise fondle without being carefully watched. The plush chairs and individual attention which still accompany many jewellery transactions today reflect this very necessary need for theft prevention. Overnight, windows were protected by sturdy shutters either lined with metal or made entirely of iron. Anything of value was removed entirely. Some jewellers invested in hatches in the floor through which baskets of plate might be lowered into the basement and put in a safe. Dyson's went one better, with a hydraulic mechanism to lower the entire window display into the ground.

Most jewellers were independent. There were a couple of exceptions. In Manchester Harriet Samuel opened a shop with a mail order business after the death of her clockmaker husband in 1877, expanding to Preston through her son in 1890. By 1914 H. Samuel had around fifty branches, with competition from 1905 from Sanders & Co (with whom they later merged).[40]

Assuming you've found a suitable watch chain, let's move on. Your next item is a piece of cheese. If you're feeling flush, or want to impress, you might be here for a piece of Parmesan or some Stilton, but they're hardly everyday cheeses. A more practical option is a wedge of Cheddar or some Cheshire, ideal for cooking as well as eating. Choose your shop carefully, for prices can be alarming. In the late nineteenth century the working class spent around 75 per cent of their household income on food, dropping to around 35–45 per cent for the middle classes. In 1901 Cornhill Magazine published a series of ideal budgets. Their lower-middle-class family, on around £150 to £250 a year, was one which 'cannot spend much on luxuries', and looked for bargains where they could. Above £250 p.a., however, the picture changed, and it was made clear that everyday food shopping was to be left to servants, with a nice budget set aside for 'teas in town' and titbits from a high-class grocer whose aim in business was to woo the wealthy and keep that still-important carriage trade.[41] *You should be so lucky.*

The provision merchant

Grocer, Italian warehouse or provision merchant: food stores were still a big part of the high street. There was a shop for everyone, though with definite demarcations. In Tonbridge, Albert Headey's grocery shop was at the upmarket north end of town. His wealthy clientele still expected him to do the rounds with his pony and trap, all dressed up in morning coat and top hat to visit his customers at home. He'd meet with housekeepers to go through the food order, and coachmen to organise leather cleaning equipment. These clients were still kept on a credit model, paying quarterly or even yearly, for 'no well-thought-of firm ever demanded or expected more than a yearly payment of their debts'.[42] There was a rhythm to dealing with the wealthy, and 'when they paid the accounts they had the carriage out and came round to all the tradesmen at once – butcher, baker, grocer – and made a day of it. That was all you really saw of the lady when she came to pay up. If she was a really good client she was generally invited into the office and out would come the port or sherry or whisky as the case may be.'[43]

It was accepted that shopkeepers would offer kickbacks to cooks and other senior members of staff – as well as to decision-makers in clubs, hotels and other catering establishments – who would, in turn, patronise those suppliers who built the best relationships. Twinings, a tea dealership with a shop on the Strand and a network of aristocratic clients, sent their contacts carefully recorded presents every Christmas. The system was always implicit and rarely realised by the actual bill payer. It could go wrong: celebrated chef and grandfather of French cuisine Auguste Escoffier was sacked from the Savoy in 1898 based on cooked-up charges based of taking bribes (shocked, he promptly banned such kickbacks in his future jobs).

For the middle classes, a visit to the grocer was a treat to be savoured in person. The shops could be just as resplendent as any jeweller, with carved woodwork, glass display cabinets and

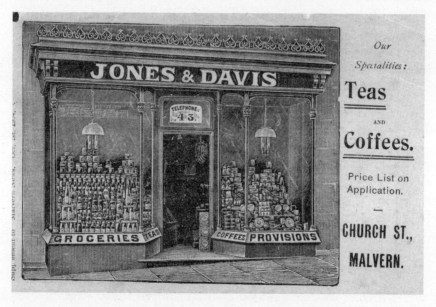

Fig. 5.4. Jones & Davis of Church Street, Malvern, in Worcestershire, described themselves as high-class grocers and provision merchants, and this is a typical shopfront for such a business at the start of the twentieth century. Gone are the small panes and hidden shelving of previous eras, replaced, now, with plate glass, careful lighting and a display of branded goods and packets. The art of window dressing was well covered by trade manuals of the time.

excitingly exotic smells and sights. They were 'a real delight. There were mounds of dried fruit, chests of romantic Oriental appearance, with strange black marks on them in some Eastern language, lined with foil and crammed with tea of all qualities. Tea mingled its aroma in the mixture of scents which went to make up the particularly rich smell of the grocer's shop.'[44] On London's Piccadilly, Morel Brothers, Cobbett & Son occupied two basements, the ground and mezzanine floor, with the interior rich in decorative paintwork proclaiming such things as 'Périgord Truffles', 'Spanish Hams', and 'Cailles Farcies', because as nice as stuffed quail is, it sounds even better in French.[45] Just down the road was the ever-expanding tea dealer and grocer Fortnum & Mason, founded in the eighteenth century by a royal footman and by now the holder of several royal warrants.[46] In 1886 they became the first stockist for Heinz baked beans, then an interesting foreign novelty, quite in keeping with their reputation for the highest possible order of goods.

Inside a grocer of this type, you'd expect to be offered a seat. Service was efficient and highly personal, and assistants were almost always men. They were expected to serve a full apprenticeship still, although this now took the form of on-the-job training with pay. It was a skilled job, for the stock of the average grocer was wide and growing ever wider. Much was bought in bulk from wholesalers and needed to be packaged up ready for sale. Tea was a staple, and was usually still blended in-house. Coffee needed roasting and grinding, dried fruit and nuts had to be sorted, washed and weighed, and then there were cheeses to mature and cut, meats to be smoked and rolled or dried and hung, and butter to be made. Spices needed grinding, flour drying, sugar pounding and ice, which was imported from North America, had to be broken up both for refrigeration in the shop – if present – and for selling to customers.

Some grocers sold fresh fruit, others wines, beer and/or spirits, which arrived in barrels and needed bottling. Then there were seasonal lines including Christmas cakes, biscuits and puddings as well as crates full of imports in jars and bottles and cans and boxes. Assistants were also expected to know what to do with the products they sold: 'if a man was a real grocer he knew everything from A to Z. He wasn't classed as a grocer unless he did . . . they could tell them what sauces to use with various things and, of course, where you had a shop like we did with a licence, they could advise on wines to go with a meal.'[47]

At least mechanisation meant that processes like stoning fruit could now be done by machine, and the customer duly charged for it. Served and server played a delicate dance. The eye-wateringly snobbish Walter MacQueen-Pope was one of the former, enjoying the 'civility and respect' and happily accepting obsequiousness as sincerity: '"And the next thing?" he kept asking, politely. You simply could not order enough to please him. He would draw your attention to new lines, he would give you a biscuit to taste. He was very anxious to please.'[48] Seen from the other side of the counter it was a little different: 'You always offered the lady a chair and if she'd got a dog you gave them a biscuit. Then you started the treatment! You sold the stuff YOU wanted to get rid of, what you were making the best halfpenny out of. The old man might say to the men, "We've got this to sell. There's a penny a tin for every one you sell." These blokes would push the stuff.' Where personal service met inexperienced wives wanting to put on a show the assistant was in his element: 'perhaps she'd only come in for a few items, but when she went out you'd got an order book as long as your arm. Very often they would come in and say "I'd like your advice. I'm giving a dinner party on Friday. What would you suggest?" That left the door wide open! We'd got tongues in . . . [glass] dishes . . . jars of prawns and capers, stuffed olives and I don't know what.'[49]

Even at the posh end of provisioning, sealed jars were a draw. They were convenient, safe and reliable. Sharp practices were common: adding water to milk, beer and butter, short weights and all the age-old ways to bump up profit just a little bit. The 1850s had seen a sudden upsurge in public awareness of food adulteration, with Arthur Hill Hassell's articles in *The Lancet* starting a wave of outrage at the abuses he proved to be rampant within the food industry. Not a single loaf of bread in his tests proved free of adulterants, which ranged through chalk to alum (though he did not find evidence of the human bone rumoured to be present in some cases). Then in 1858 a Bradford market stall holder added arsenic to his humbugs instead of the gypsum he intended to adulterate them with and killed twenty-one people, adding to the growing fear and pressure on the government to do something about it. Naturally, they prevaricated, seeking voluntary agreements from manufacturers, which did little to address the fact that most adulteration happened at shopkeeping level. Eventually various Drug and Food Acts were passed, meaning that by the end of the century things had improved – but it left a legacy of mistrust, especially when (as I can testify) Hassell's suggested easy tests for adulteration didn't work.

Trusting your grocer was one way to avoid accidentally dying in hideous pain (or, more realistically, having a mild stomach upset, or a meal lacking a bit of flavour). At the lower end of the grocery market, though, this wasn't always feasible, especially if you were in the habit of buying up the broken biscuits or slightly rancid butter left at the end of the day. It was one reason for the growth of branded goods, sold with a maker's mark on the packet, and whose advertising emphasised trust and purity. Fry's registered their Pure Concentrated Soluble Cocoa as a trademark in 1885, while Norwich-based Colman's put out adverts advising 'to insure getting the best quality of mustard & the same as supplied to the royal table, ask for Colman's Double Superfine and see that the tin bears a yellow label similar to this illustration'.

Some provision dealers now saw a clear opportunity for growth based on winning the trust of the lower classes. In Southampton Misselbrook and Weston expanded from one shop in 1885 to eleven branches seventeen years later.[50] More nationally recognised names included David Grieg's, which emerged from a Hornsey shop run by David's mother, Mary, to have over 150 branches by the 1920s, and Home & Colonial, which had an astonishing 500 branches by 1903. Its owner, Julius Drewe, built Britain's last castle (Castle Drogo) with the profits. Both of these, along with rivals such as the Star Tea Company, had corporate branding, ranging from thistles (David Grieg) to stained glass (Home & Colonial).[51]

Most multiple provision dealers dealt, at least initially, in a limited range of stock. The Maypole Dairy Company started in Birmingham in 1891 and had over 200 shops by 1900, plus its own butter factories. Inside, the shops had lavish green tiles and pictures of cows. There were marble slabs to keep produce cool and for many years they sold only butter and margarine, plus eggs, tea and condensed milk – very much working-class staples.[52] John and Mary Ann Sainsbury's early stores also specialised in dairy, advertising the 'best butter in London' as well as 'railway milk', brought in by train.

By the 1880s the Sainsburys had their own warehouse for smoking ham and bacon, and in 1900 they expanded outside London, also now selling tea and tinned goods. As with their competitors, the shops were tiled inside with a mixture of gleaming white and decorative tiles, stretching from floor to ceiling, and had marble counters faced with glass. The shop assistants were all men, with living quarters provided above the shops.[53] Mutterings over the inappropriateness of such glamour in nondescript towns was faced down, for 'the critics missed the point . . . that was to produce a shop to ensure perfect cleanliness and freedom from the menace of all food shops in those days – mice and rats'.[54]

Rats were a definite problem. At one shop in Newcastle, 'if we had any kind of a parcel in our hand, we threw it in first before we went in – we were dead scared, because there were rats in the shop . . . it was black dark.' They set traps which the local barber would then take down to a bit of scrap land to let his terrier finish them off.[55] Albert Headey tried cats (obvious) and a hedgehog (less so). Apparently, though, 'if you had a hedgehog, you'd never get rats. I most certainly never saw any. If, as was generally the case with hedgehogs, they got trod on, he used to get round some of his farmer friends and it wasn't long before he got another one.'[56]

There was profit to be made in grocery whichever level of society you served, but shopkeepers had to innovate or lose out. At this end of the social scale keen pricing was key. Pre-packed goods, branded items, cutting machines and centralised training schemes cut the time needed for training and enabled less skilled – and cheaper – assistants to be employed, allowing prices to be cut still further. *The Times* fulminated about de-skilling and forecast a time when 'a large proportion of the grocer's work of the present day could be accomplished almost equally well by an automatic machine delivering a packet of goods in exchange for a coin'.[57] Sainsbury's installed a 'mechanical cow': a vending machine which sold milk when the shop was closed.

One of the sector's undisputed leaders was Thomas Lipton. Lipton was a Scot, brought up in poverty before heading to the States. There, he worked in a variety of shops, returning to Glasgow emboldened by American selling techniques. His shops combined a decor calculated to woo the working class with a series of publicity stunts to attract attention. In 1878 residents of Glasgow Cross were treated to the sight and squeals of three piglets, driven by a man dressed up as a pantomime version of an Irishman, and sporting the words 'The Orphans, Home-Fed, Bound for Lipton's' emblazoned upon their haunches.

They stopped the traffic, leading to a formal caution for Lipton himself.

There were also the Christmas cheeses, the first of which was paraded from the Glasgow docks through the city and displayed in the shop window. The *Glasgow Evening Citizen* declared that 'an idea of its dimensions may be obtained when it is stated that it is about two feet in depth, over three feet in diameter, and weighs 13,751lbs'.[58] Gold coins were hidden inside, and the police ended up involved again. However, the force demurred when asked to provide an officer to maintain order, on the grounds that the man risked being a 'walking advertisement' (fair).[59] The cheese became a Christmas tradition throughout Lipton's empire – 254 shops by the end of 1898. By that stage he had taken to using elephants from local circuses to help with the cheese parade. Once at the store, 'the hissing fish-tail gas jets or oil-lamps lit up the heaped piles of eggs, the mountains of butter and margarine, the bacon, sugar and tea that customers were invited to purchase. The staff numbered two or three and the "outside man" in his white serving coat would be shouting the price, value and quality of the goods, enticing and attending to customers, and handing or throwing purchases or money back to the counter for weighing, wrapping, or putting in the till.'[60] It was fast, furious and very successful.

We shouldn't leave the provision merchant without a quick mention of the Co-op, a chain which started with grocery and eventually encompassed everything from clothing to funeral provision. The Co-operative movement was born out of various ventures in the north of England. It was especially influenced by the work of the Rochdale Pioneers, formed in the 1840s to pool resources to buy wholesale goods, which could then be sold on to members at affordable prices. By the 1870s the movement had spread and established a model by which members received profits directly related to their spend – the infamous 'divi' (dividend), which became an important source of income to many poorer households. A centrally organised wholesale division ensured that individual societies could offer goods at the best possible price.

The idea wasn't confined to the lower class, but spread up the social scale, most notably with the foundation of the Army and Navy Stores in 1871. The large, windowless Westminster store counted Winston and Clementine Churchill among its aficionados – though they did not shop there in person. There were 1,101 societies by 1881 – though 80 per cent of them had only one shop – and the next few decades saw a great deal of streamlining.[61] Like the other grocery multiples, they provided a clean, reliable and cheap service for the working class. But they also had utopian principles, and as such operated explicitly to improve the lot of the working class, running community halls, libraries and evening classes. With a few exceptions, their shops weren't showy, and until the 1920s tended to be situated off the high street, or in the cheaper and ever-expanding suburbs.

Where you buy your cheese – independent or a multiple – is up to you and your budget. But let's dip briefly into some of the Edwardian debates over where the high street is headed. Some say that the Co-ops are dangerously egalitarian – potential hotbeds of revolution. Chains are derided by the trade press as 'mere blood suckers making a profit out of a gullible public', and attempts to impose a corporate style on outlets is said to be eroding the individuality of towns, with 'every shop belonging to a particular company being a duplicate of every other shop'.[62] Do you care? Perhaps you have a suspicion it is all being overplayed. Even in 1915 only twelve chains have more than 100 branches, and while Lipton's is responsible for over 10 per cent of the nation's tea stash, and Maypole for over 30 per cent of its butter, they really don't (yet) sell a huge range of goods. Anyway, it's approaching late afternoon, but the shops won't shut for at least another four hours, so for now, put such questions aside and have a nice cup of tea.

The tea rooms

'Poor days when they had no tea rooms!' declared one guide to Edwardian shopping, before continuing, 'nowadays our shopping area is so extended, our time so limited, our comfort and health of so much more reasonable consideration than formally, that London is dotted with delightful luncheon and tea rooms which are daily crowded to the doors'.[63] The author went on to particularly praise the ABC tea rooms, which had emerged from the bakery business of the Aerated Bread Company in the 1880s to become a household name, at least in London. They

Fig. 5.5. Interior of an ABC tea rooms in London at lunchtime. The clientele is mainly businessmen after a cheap lunch, but there's a table of women, probably also office workers, to the right as well as a family with a child. The fug must have been immense.

were happily mass market, summed up by H. G. Wells in his *Tono-Bungay*, where the protagonist's aunt and uncle, a couple living 'dingy lives', take him on a tour of London complete with tea and buns: 'Sometimes we were walking, sometimes we were on the tops of great staggering horse omnibuses in a heaving jumble of traffic, and at one point we had tea in an Aerated Bread Shop.'[64]

Another chain was Lyons, whose first branch opened in 1894. In contrast to the ABC, Joseph Lyon harnessed the historical cachet of tea, and the association of it with the leisure rituals of the upper classes. At the Piccadilly branch 'red silk covered the walls and gas-lighted chandeliers hung from the ceiling. You sat in a red plush chair, and were served by a very smart waitress in a grey uniform with voluminous skirts down to the floor.'[65] It was an immediate success, and by 1914 there were branches in all the major commercial towns, including Manchester, Liverpool, Leeds, Brighton and Eastbourne – 180 in total. The initial tea rooms didn't have much in the way of kitchen facilities and concentrated on mutton pies, scones, custard and the occasional truffled foie gras sausage by way of (probably quite considerable) surprise. In 1909 Lyons opened the first Corner House, a new concept which was not only massive – seating 2,000 people – but contained a variety of different offerings under the same roof. There was a lot of marble, and a lot of gold, but it was nevertheless 'intensely middle class'.[66] It was very successful for a while, but not a concept to take beyond the capital.

The ABC and Lyons got a lot of praise and custom, but outside London their impact was limited. Both local chains and independent tea rooms flourished, catering to every type of person. Glasgow became home of the first dedicated tea rooms in the country in 1875, and by 1903 it was said that 'nowhere can one have so much for so little, and nowhere are such places more popular or frequented'.[67]

Fig. 5.6. A Lyons tea rooms at 14 North Street, Brighton, around 1910. The window is stacked with biscuits and cakes on stands, with the transom windows providing ventilation. The barber and hairdresser above shares the recessed entranceway.

The long-established link between tea and women became particularly important as the suffrage movement grew in force in the early twentieth century. You could buy tea in the colours of the WSPU (Women's Social and Political Union – the leading militant branch of the movement), and several tea rooms advertised in the various magazines associated with the cause. In London, the gorgeously appointed Criterion (stained glass, palm trees, a ballroom) was one of several tea rooms used to plan the suffragettes' infamous window-breaking campaign of 1912. Posing as shoppers, and escaping police questioning by claiming to have been looking at carpets, suffragettes smashed windows in the West End, raising awareness of the movement and expressing a burning anger. This was the high street as a theatre of war. And it was very confusing for the male owners of the businesses they targeted. Lasenby Liberty, founder of the eponymous shop off Regent Street, wrote to *The Times* seeking an explanation as to 'the mental process by which they deem the breaking of the very shrines at which they worship will advance their cause'.[68] Women were supposed to spend their money and shut up, not bite the very hand that laid out pretty fabric and furs to distract them.

Got your mettle up? Excellent. You might be drinking a bucket of good ordinary tea in the slightly damp atmosphere of a crowded ABC, shifting on your wooden chair and peering past the top hat of the man in front to attract the attention of the waitress rather than sipping orange pekoe from a delicate china cup, but it still feels like a well-deserved break. However, you're not yet at the end of your list, for you still need an outfit for a small boy. Something of the sailory persuasion, perhaps – always popular. As you leave the tea rooms, time to engage with another ethical row, this time around the size and ambition of a very few – but a very talked-about few – Big Shops.

The big shop

It's impossible to discuss the late-nineteenth-century high street without looking at the rise of the big shops. We've seen how some drapers were expanding into adjacent sectors such as millinery, tailoring and haberdashery. By now more than a few ambitious businessmen were taking over neighbouring properties, broadening their offering and creating a type of store that

Fig. 5.7. The Bon Marché store in Brixton. Built in 1877, and essentially unchanged for much of its life, despite several different owners, the building originally incorporated staff domitories as well as selling space. It folded in the 1970s, and is currently divided into office and retail units marketed as 'the department store'.

went far beyond mere drapery. By the 1880s they'd grown to the point that you might be calling them a universal provider, a 'monster store' or quite simply a big shop.

The biggest were in London, and started out in such varied sectors as grocery (Harrods), ribbons and fancy goods (Whiteleys), drapery (John Lewis, Debenham & Freebody, D. H. Evans and Liberty's), and mercery (Marshall & Snelgrove). One of the earliest, Bon Marché in Brixton, was purpose-built as a big shop in 1877, and was inspired directly by the Bon Marché in Paris, which was a sort of bazaar on steroids and hugely influential across the world. Big shop sounds a lot better in French, and *les grands magasins* is still the term applied to today's surviving iterations such as Paris's Printemps and Galeries Lafayette.

There's some argument over the birth of the big shops, for although they are very much a phenomenon of the late nineteenth century, one establishment briefly showed the way 100 years before. Harding, Howell & Co occupied Schomberg House on Pall Mall from 1789 until the 1830s, predating the Bon Marché by seventy years. Nominally drapers, the store also sold wall hangings, jewellery, millinery and accessories such that 'no article of female attire or decoration, but what may be here procured in the first style of elegance and fashion'. Importantly, it had a breakfast room and toilets and secured the first patent for a permanent green dye for chintz, which may or may not have influenced its series of royal warrants. But it didn't last, though various partners went on to set up similar stores, one of which, Howell & James, would accommodate your coachman with bread and cheese at a basement window.[69]

It's very hard to really define what separated a big shop from a big draper or furniture emporium. Part of it was sheer size – the visibility of such shops is one reason they were so talked about then (and remain so now). Another was variety. The *Birmingham Daily Gazette* summed it up: 'time back the grocer confined himself strictly to his speciality, the draper to drapery, the hosier and glover to hosiery, the hatter to hats, the umbrella maker to umbrellas, and so on through the whole list of retailers of various commodities, but by degrees persons specially conversant with one particular trade have found it easy and advantageous to themselves, and not inconvenient to the public, to dabble in wares dealt in by their neighbours, and for the last few years there has been even more complete obliteration of the old dividing lines in the establishment of huge stores conducted on the no-credit principle at which almost everything can be purchased at the lowest market price, from drugs to boots, and from a pound of butter to a hat and feathers.'[70] Each department had its own buyer, and operated almost like a mini shop within the shop, a crucial difference compared to the later department stores or American-influenced variety stores which we'll visit later on.

One well-known early example of the big shop was Whiteleys in Bayswater. William Whiteley opened his first outlet in 1863, and just four years later it had expanded across the neighbouring premises and had seventeen different departments. In the 1870s he opened a refreshment room, hairdressers, ironmongery department and finally a butcher. Much of this was (deliberately) provocative, pushing the boundaries in order to change the way shopping worked. In 1876 the local butchers burnt his effigy instead of that of Guy Fawkes, while the newspapers painted the store as little more than a knocking shop, encouraging unaccompanied women to meet their lovers and, even worse, populating Bayswater with pretty female and male shop workers who then appeared on the streets when the shop was shut.

It was all great advertising, though. By the 1880s he was claiming to supply everything from 'a pint of fleas to an elephant' (both were real orders, apparently, the fleas procured from the keeper of the monkeys at London Zoo). The actual experience of shopping there was not, perhaps, as glorious as the clever advertising suggested. Molly Hughes found the place bad value for money, and not at all able to supply all she wanted. Seeking a Valentine, she recalled 'even going to Whiteley's for the purpose, and reminding the shopwalker with some acerbity that they called themselves "universal providers". Upon this he became facetious and I thought it best to say no more.'[71] The shop was large, but despite its size, status and impressive facade was old-fashioned, still made up of tens of separate shops, all linked with a couple of internal corridors: not the easiest of spaces to make glamorous.[72] It wasn't until 1910 – after Whiteley himself had been shot dead by a man who may or may not have been his illegitimate son – that the building was properly rebuilt.

Fig. 5.8. The resplendent central staircase at the new Whiteleys store in Bayswater, London, built in 1911. This picture was taken in 1961.

By then, Whiteleys was losing its way. The next big thing in London was Selfridges, which opened on Oxford Street in 1909. Gordon Selfridge was a dynamic moderniser from Chicago. Arriving in Britain, he saw an opportunity in what he saw as a stuffy, backward, British retail environment. In New York and other American cities large shops and chains were more normal, and shopping was faster and less formal. Just as William Whiteley had lobbied for changes to licensing laws, Selfridge also came up against what he saw as antiquated English laws and set out to challenge them. First to fall under his influence were London building regulations, which limited store sizes. The result was a purpose-built behemoth, in a deliberately palatial style which echoed Hampton Court Palace. Unlike the majority of stores, which still insisted on live-in staff, the Selfridge assistants lived out, freeing up the top floors for luncheon halls, smoking rooms and a rooftop garden with views across London. By 1913 there was even a crèche. Like many American stores it had a bargain basement to maintain the illusion that it was open to all – but while channeling the less minted into their own, special, area. This was widely copied by other, regional, big shops seeking to maintain reputations for exclusivity while reaching the widest possible audience.

Selfridge also replaced shopwalkers with assistants who only spoke when asked – though this was perhaps not quite as innovative as Mr Selfridge liked to claim. One article reported that 'the . . . plan is to interest and entertain the potential customer, without asking him or her to buy, and this is nothing new in London, as most of the large houses no longer harass their customers with the attentions of a too officious shopwalker'.[73] The *Oxford Chronicle* dared to muse that personal service, in the shape of the assistant, might even be done away with altogether – or almost, for 'clearly one could not be permitted to handle clothes or personal ornaments quite as one does books'. Still, 'I do think that in the shop of the future he will be a less obtrusive personage than he is in the shop of today.'[74]

Like Thomas Lipton, Selfridge was fond of a good stunt to draw in the crowds. The architecture of the store was one thing, but he upped the ante with his window displays, another area where he felt the British lagged behind. Despite innovation in other areas, many window dressers still relied predominantly on cramming in a huge quantity of stock. Approaching the Bon Marché Christmas window in Liverpool in 1900 you'd have been greeted with a vertiginous display of absolutely everything the shop sold, neatly categorised and attached to vertical display boards. It was dramatic, but now seen as rather vulgar, dismissed as 'stocky', and by the early twentieth century shop-fitting firms had started manufacturing wares to display goods in a more muted form. This included mannequins mimicking the human body, but without heads. The reliably unpleasant

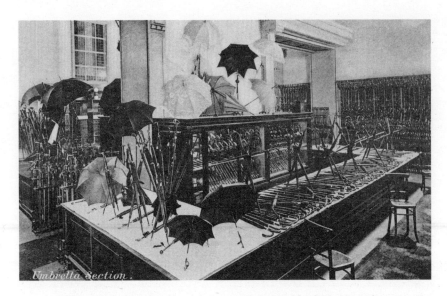

Fig. 5.9. The umbrella department at Selfridges, London, *c.* 1870–1910. Umbrellas were a big thing – and this vertiginous display is typical of the way in which big shops laid out the wares on offer.

G. K. Chesterton, no fan of the big shop (apparently it was 'exactly like hell'), described how 'the ladies who minister to the shoppers are made up exactly like the dress models that stand behind them. When you look at the dress model you think that some shop-girl has had her head cut off; when you look back at the real shop-girl you feel inclined to do the same to her.'[75]

Selfridge undeniably brought some American bling to the big shops, but his views of the British high street were jaundiced, and he was hardly responsible for changing the face of shopping on his own. Yes, he did display Blériot's monoplane the day after it crossed the channel, but Lewis's of Liverpool put the hand of a woman who'd been dug up at Pompeii in the window of their Manchester shop in 1881. Lewis's also flooded the basement to showcase the delights of Venice. Meanwhile a few years later the director of London's Swan & Edgar was threatened with prosecution for blocking the pavements with a mechanical display of moving mannequins lit by electric light, which attracted enormous crowds. Big stores – not just Selfridges – generally drove innovation. Harrods installed a moving walkway (not quite an escalator) in 1898, adding further theatre with an assistant armed with smelling salts and cognac at the top.

Lewis's Birmingham branch went one further, with an ornamental cage lift to convey shoppers up to the refreshment rooms and down to the basement grocery department.[76] The first lift had been installed back in 1855, at Glasgow's Wylie & Lochhead's, who advertised that 'parties who are old, fat, feeble, short-winded, or simply lazy, or who desire to have a bit of fun, have only to place themselves on an enclosed platform or flooring where they are elevated by a gentle and pleasing process to a height exceeding that of a country steeple'.[77] In, too, came the cash ball system (by which cash was removed from tills by being stuffed into balls which ran along rails suspended from the ceiling) and cash registers, while advances in electric lighting meant that shop windows were no longer habitually shuttered at closing but kept lit all night. Electricity was also employed for shop signs, which just got more and more lurid. *Punch* published a cartoon called 'Picturesque London, or Sky Signs of the Times', in which the advertisements for everything from hot lunches to umbrellas dwarf, not only the shops, but also the dome of St Paul's. The high street experience could easily be one of total sensory overload.

By 1914 the big shops were in every major urban centre and many of their names still lurk in popular memory. An entirely non-exhaustive list includes Bainbridges and Fenwicks, both in Newcastle, Footman, Pretty & Nicholson (Ipswich); Kendal, Milne & Faulkner (Manchester); Brown, Muff & Co (Bradford); David Evans (Swansea); Buntings (Norwich); Fraser Sons & Co (Glasgow); and Clerys in Dublin. (The names may be familiar

Fig. 5.10. Clery & Co, a big shop on Dublin's Sackville Street, *c.*1885. Clerys started out as McSwiney, Delaney & Co, housed in a purpose-built ambitious edifice which, after failing under its initial owners, was reborn and reopened in December 1884. The building was destroyed in the 1916 uprising, but quickly rebuilt even more magnificently. Clerys survived – just – until 2015.

to you with apostrophes in different places: shopping history is a riot of inconsistent possessive apostrophising.) The leading stores not only invested heavily in new technology, but also rebuilt their patchwork of premises to present a united front along with an interior that incorporated eclectic design elements drawn from cathedrals and country houses. Clerys was truly magnificent, with balconies and classical elements making it an attraction in its own right. Inside, 'the great front hall, which is entered from the central vestibule, is oval in shape, and is surrounded by shelved compartments, divided by fluted Corinthian columns, which sustain a gallery which runs round the entire apartment . . . ascending a few steps, we enter the central vestibule, which will be applied to French, German and Swiss products including fancy goods and "Berlin" needlework. From the vestibule, we enter the splendid middle hall, with its arched roof, graceful galleries, and grand staircases at either end.'[78]

Such glories weren't universal, though, and there were probably only a few hundred such stores across the country, accounting for about 3 per cent of total retail spend (this rises to 8–9 per cent if you only look at clothing and footwear).[79] That includes slightly smaller shops which still retained a certain specialism. Thus, Leak & Thorp on York's Coney Street was registered as a general drapers, silk mercers, milliners, dress and mantle makers, woollen drapers and tailors, carpet warehousemen and general furnishers when it became a private limited company in 1905, not branching out into china, luggage and other household requisites until after the Great War. In Bath, Jolly's underwent a massive expansion in 1912, adding furniture, carpet and an estate agency to its services, but, again, it wasn't the biggest of big shops until later.

The big shops inevitably attracted criticism, both from the same critics who foresaw the death of the small independent shop through the growth of the multiples, and from the growing trades union movement. The plight of the dressmaker, which had started to gain public attention in the 1860s, was now joined to that of the more general shop worker, especially women. By 1910 shopwork was the third biggest employer of women, after domestic service and factory work. It was highly discriminatory, for the most prestigious shops imposed a minimum height and actively recruited both men and women who were attractive and could pass as well-bred. Apparently 'no lady cares to be served in the showroom by a five-foot nothing'.[80]

Fig. 5.11. The tea rooms at Derry & Toms, Kensington, London, 1893.
Kensington High Street was a mecca for big shop afficionados:
in addition to Derrys, you could also find Pontings and Barkers.
By the 1920s all three were under the same ownership. Derrys was
rebuilt with a set of themed gardens on the rooftop. It closed in
1973, though part of the building is still in use for retail.

Conditions were often dreadful, with long hours spent standing up, and the usual indignities of dealing with the public. As
one assistant sighed, 'I sometimes hate women. When I read of
a woman being good and sympathetic, I want the writer of that
article to come and serve her with a bonnet. I wonder if it ever
strikes a customer that we, too, are alive?'[81]

In all but the most modern of big shops women lived in,
often in squalid conditions, while their male counterparts
progressively won the right to live out. It could be horrendous.

Margaret Bondfield, a shop assistant who later became the first female Cabinet minister, recalled the women's quarters at Hetherington's in Brighton. On Race Week a gang of young men 'knocked at our ground floor windows and tried to pull them down. The occupiers of the room facing the street were not that kind of girl, and after a slight struggle the window was shut and bolted. That experience did frighten me.'[82] Female assistants were portrayed either as innocents who could be easily abused or – in the case of George Gissing and other male authors – bored, degraded and looking for illicit pleasure. In the latter case they were also guilty of reading romance novels (of course).[83]

There were increasing calls for reform, centred often on the damage allegedly done to women's health, especially their delicate reproductive systems – in yet another demonstration of the class distinctions that so concerned Edwardian Britons, reformers held up the horrific idea that without reform sort-of genteel shopgirls would be unable to have children, while rough housemaids would be left to breed unchecked.[84] But although the government passed a series of Shop Acts enforcing a sixty-four-hour working week, and there was an early closing lobby, little really helped. At least the expansion of shops meant that space used for dormitories was increasingly wanted for stockrooms, and the living-in system declined in the decades after 1900 as the number of women employed continued to grow.

As a shopper, it's easy to ignore the potential pitfalls of the changing high street and concentrate only on the pleasure it brings you. Being treated with deference in a palace built to titillate and tantalise is, after all, quite a novel experience for most people. The big shops make it even easier to get ideas and find out the latest fashions, even if you don't plan to necessarily buy from them. They do make it easy though, for opening hours are still long, and even by 10pm the lights are all still blazing. The whole high street remains one where late shopping is normal, especially for the working classes, who don't finish work until early evening. On

Saturdays – payday for the salaried masses – Lipton's stays open until midnight, the better to compete with the markets.

By now, the cityscape has changed again. There's a telephone box on every street corner, and motor vehicles are starting to appear, although they remain rare. The summer of 1914 will be one of the hottest on record, the sun bleaching goods in shop windows as dusty shoppers walk slowly by.

In June 1914 an Austro-Hungarian duke will be assassinated, and a tangled web of treaties will result in a four-year-long world conflict. Global politics has rarely impinged directly or quickly upon the whole nation's shopping and leisure habits, but as the Edwardian age comes to an abrupt halt, that will start to change.

High Street, King's Lynn, 1933

King's Lynn is a little different to the other towns we've visited. It's smaller, for one thing, and its heyday is well gone. For much of the medieval period Lynn – then known as Bishop's Lynn until the Reformation necessitated a hasty name change – was one of the most important towns in Britain. It grew very rich off the back of trade with northern Europe, and was one of the Hanseatic ports, a network of routes between Scandinavia, Germany and the Low Countries. It was also a centre for salt production. The city is rich in medieval and early modern architecture, including the small, yet perfectly formed Customs House, on Purfleet Quay. However, from that point on the good times came to a slow end. Two hundred and fifty years later Lynn is still a significant port, but has other industry too. Many people will have ridden on a merry-go-round made by Savage's Ironworks, who until the Great War made nearly all the fairground rides in the country.

History weighs heavy here, and although the usual inter-war amenities are present, including a couple of ballroom-cinemas, alive in the evenings with stained glass, jazz and laughter, modern life sometimes seems to be happening elsewhere. The *Lynn News* recently carried an article quoting a former pastor, active in Lynn before the Great War but long since moved away. In answer to the question of what changes he'd seen in the town on a recent visit, he replied, 'Lynn has changed as little as any town I know. The names over the shops in High-St are about the only things that have changed noticeably. The multiple shops have taken the place of the private trader.'[85]

We're starting at the south end of the High Street, once known as Briggate. Behind you is the minster, also known as

St Margaret's Church, and the wide, flagged expanse of the Saturday Market Place. On Saturdays the striped awnings of various stalls cluster around the church, but if it's a weekday you are more likely to find a couple of parked cars and a collection of bicycles leaning against a lamppost in the middle. The chequered frontage of the medieval guildhall is along the street to your left, and a row of rather old-fashioned shops to your right. Ignore them and head up the main drag. On your left on the corner is number 123, which older people know as 'The Restaurant'. It was run by Lizzie Wenn until 1910 and it's been officially called Wenn's for as long as you can remember. It is now a tied pub, recently extended and made into a hotel by Greene King. Across the road (number 1) is the complete opposite, a small shop which keeps changing hands and names with it – for a long time it was Thew & Son, a major printer which also occupied the next few shops along, all in the same, brick-built building with a curved corner, but then there was Lowe the grocer who went bankrupt, then Gemmell's clothiers who moved from further up, and now it's a tobacconist. There are insurance offices above, along with the Kleen-e-ze Brush Company, one of several British companies taking an American approach to naming themselves.

The units on both sides of the road are small, the shops functional, and they frequently change hands. At number 2, Manchester-based Crook's tailors (known for the generous number of pockets in their suits) is about to be replaced by the Kettering & Leicester Boot Co, while at number 3 the dyer and dry cleaner will move out next year, leaving Hartley's ladies and children's outfitters a few doors down as their agent. There are three other dyer/cleaners on the street as well as a steam laundry at number 4. Opposite, carcasses cover the double frontage of one of the five butchers' shops run by Thomas and Elsie Andrews in the town. Another, at number 108, has only just opened and will close in 1936. Tragically, in moving the kit out,

Thomas will be crushed to death beneath a sausage-making machine.

Most of the buildings here are brick and of three storeys, though details vary wildly. Carry on past the florist-fruiterer, the hosier, and Cecil and Elsie Oxby's gift shop. There are workshops and yards tucked away behind the shops, and more businesses as well as apartments on the upper floors.

Ethel Letzer's ladies' clothing shop, home of Madame X's Reducing Girdle ('makes you look thin while getting thin') is at 115–117. Its fashionable recessed door and streamlined frontage belies a succession of pokey little rooms with different ceiling heights inside – it's all terribly Victorian. Now, though, the street widens out and things get much more ornate. This is partly due to fires which have ripped holes in the high street, the first in 1884 and the second in 1897, described as 'the most disastrous and extensive fire ever known to have occurred in King's Lynn'. Both started at Jermyn's, Lynn's biggest shop. As a result, this part of the street has resplendent red-brick late Victorian buildings: on the left the classical facade of Jermyn's staff accommodation, followed by a series of smaller units with arches and turrets, patterned brick and vaguely Flemish gables (a baker, a bootmaker, an optician and the deep green tiles and carved panelled door of Lipton's). The ornate frontage of the Lynn Drapery Emporium next door bears the date of 1898. Until a few months ago it was one of the many and confusing parts of the Trenowath empire, a local family which still runs a removals business among others. Now it's the home of the Fifty Shilling Tailors and Sterling's shoe shop, both multiples based in Yorkshire.

Look right though, to the local landmark that is Jermyn's. Watch out for traffic if you need to cross the street to have a better look: horses mingle with cars, and there are bicycles piled against the kerb. One complainant to the *Lynn News* moaned recently that they'd counted forty-nine cycles blocking the street, mainly laden with huge carriers and that 'opposite one large store were eleven, with no space between for people to pass through'.[86]

Jermyn's is nominally a draper and furnisher, but it has many other departments. Its huge glass windows are a real draw, and its advertisements carry lines such as 'Jermyn's for Seasonable Coats: a most attractive display will be found in the front windows'. A tasteful sign runs along the top of them and there are flags, and further signs on the chimneys, but it isn't garish. A few years ago, they took over the shops next door and opened a domed arcade with stained glass and prominently displayed town crests. Now, with the slum clearances announced, Jermyn's is also taking over Armes Yard, which runs up the right-hand side and is currently filled with tiny, substandard housing. The council report talks of 'serious dampness', 'insufficient lighting, air space and ventilation', and a total lack of plumbing. The absentee landlord is fighting their demolition, and despite the crumbling walls, the residents are worried that they won't be able to afford the rents in the new council flats being provided to rehouse them (they are assured that they will). By 1935 it'll be Jermyn's household linen and Manchester (cottons) department.

Go past – the road narrows again, with small units on the left and a few bigger ones where shops have been thrown together on the right. You've got three more multiple grocers here – Home & Colonial, the International Tea Stores and David Grieg – but also a children's outfitter and two sweet shops. There's a pawnbroker, Le Grice's clothing store and a few more shoe shops. Newsagent W. H. Smith is at number 23, also selling leather goods and stationery and so much more. It's a rather beautiful Georgian house with a wrought-iron balcony, though the upper windows have faux-Victorian bottle glass panes, making the shop instantly recognisable as a Smith's. Next door, and half the height, is a branch of Hepworths (apparently, they 'clothe more farmers and their sons than any other firm in Great Britain'). Over the narrow alleyway Hilton's shoe shop (another chain) is pretty shabby in comparison. There's a second branch up the other end of the street, the idea being presumably to catch trade from each marketplace.

There's a gap in the numbering after number 26, for when New Conduit Street was built over the Purfleet, the bridge which crossed it was demolished, along with its shops, and the numbers were never adjusted, just lost. On your left is the Corner House Tea Rooms, run by Mrs Roofe (with a promise of home-made cakes). Rumour has it that the site is about to be bought by Montague Burton and redeveloped into a Burton's, with a billiard room and a ballroom.

Cross the road and pass the impressively large furniture shop of Scott & Sons. They are Lynn-based, with a factory on the outskirts, but also sell things like carpet sweepers, cooking ranges, bedlinen and Pyrex. The shop is a 'huge pile of business buildings', with multiple entrances.[87]

This bit of the street is good for food: you've got the London Central Meat company, the Maypole Dairy and, at numbers 39–41, Ladyman's, Norfolk's own answer to the multiples, selling tea, coffee and other groceries. There's a branch in Norwich, but this one really stands out. It's a black and white mock-timber frame building, with a giant red teapot swinging above the door. The builders have even festooned the sides of the buildings sticking out to either side with fake timber framing. It's got a cash railway, which is quite an attraction to the local children, and it goes a very long way back from the front, opening out to encompass much of the block. Two doors down, to confuse the unwary, there's another, equally out-of-place Tudorbethan facade, built nearly a decade before Ladyman's. This one is Boots' Cash Chemist, and the black and white is very much their house style. (The latter survives, though is no longer a Boots, and is generally mistaken for Ladyman's, which closed in 1969, when the building was demolished to make way for a Littlewoods – later BHS and now a Primark.)

The left-hand side now is quite varied. There are two cycle dealers, though one of them, Curry's, no longer makes its own, but is branching out into toys and radios. There are three more cycle shops just on this street, including Halford's at number 68. You'll also find three jewellers, a hairdresser and two photographers – plus a dance studio. This is your last chance to nip into a pub, for the jettied front of the Queen's Head is just beyond Boots. It provides support for one of the four wrought-iron arches, two of which you've already passed. The arches have lights hanging from them – gas, for now, though there's murmurs of electricity replacing it one day.

Careful not to trip on the sudden step jutting on the right while looking ahead to Street's pianoforte warehouse, now run by the last Mr Street's ex-shop assistant, Daisy Regester. Just opposite you'll find one of the main draws of this end of the street, the American cheap bazaar and self-proclaimed department store, F. W. Woolworth, at numbers 73–4. When they moved in they rebuilt much of the store, which was in a 'very dilapidated and dangerous condition'.[88] They have competition from another bazaar, Marks & Spencer, who have been here since 1910, but three years ago expanded into the two shops next door, demolishing much of them to build a grand new shop, the better to counteract Woolworth's, opposite. Burtol's cleaners, right next door, must be eyeing their expansion with trepidation.

Past this point there are just a few more shops – another chemist, a stationer, a fancy goods (and fancy dress) shop which advertises 'Father Christmas in his ice cave' and 'Mickey Mouse' at Christmas, plus a wine merchant and yet more boot and shoe shops. Finally the street ends with two prestigious corner plots. On the left, the independent ladies' and gents' outfitters Jones & Dunn, and opposite, the unmistakable architecture of the

Midland Bank. Before you now lies the massive expanse of the Tuesday Market Place, very much the hub of the town. From here, you might catch your bus, head to the ferry, or retrieve your bicycle from a convenient kerb.[89]

Chapter Six

1914-65

When at last Barbara emerged from the shop she felt somewhat dizzy, and tremendously excited – she had never known until now that clothes could be exciting.[1]

– D. E. Stevenson, *Miss Buncle's Book* (1934)

Shopping list: *A loaf of bread, a roll of film, a new suit, some sweets*

A functional list for this chapter, reflecting your position as a member of what contemporary social commentators call the respectable working class. It really just means those with a steady salary. Whereas previously you did most of your shopping at the market plus the lower-end grocers, now, post-First World War, the range of shops in which you'll be welcomed is rapidly expanding. Look out for signs stating 'admission free', intended to reassure that you can browse without buying. Man or woman, you're almost certainly shopping on a Saturday, given that you work the rest of the week. You may be a manual labourer, a factory worker or a telephonist. If you're single, you probably can't afford even the tiny bedsits so common in towns now, and you still live at home and sometimes shop for your family, all while chafing at the bit to get out into the big wide world.

The year 1914 carries a huge resonance. It's indelibly associated with the start of the First World War, a four-year conflict which led to the death of around 15 million people worldwide. This figure includes civilians killed through disease and famine as well as soldiers. In the UK, 750,000 military personnel lost their lives, with a further 180,000 deaths among the thousands who joined up from the British Empire.[2] Military meant male, and in the decades after the war many thousands of women found that lives they'd expected to be occupied with marriage, children and domestic duties went in a different direction. Some embraced the opportunity to push against social expectations; others faced a daily struggle against grief and loneliness.

During the Great War, as it was known until the next one, shopping was thrown into sharp focus. Leisure shopping, so long a source of tension, was affected by the switch of manufacturers from cloth and pans to uniforms and munitions. The *Drapers' Record* declared that 'to keep calm, to preserve one's balance . . . is not only a patriotic duty; it is the policy dictated from the point of view of our business interests'.[3] Nobody told the public this, though, and as ever in a time of crisis, people – 'panicmongers' and 'poltroons', said the *Drapers' Record* – rushed to stock up. In one corner shop in Salford 'a rush of customers to the shop gave us the first alarm – sugar, flour, bread, butter, margarine, cheese, people began frantically to buy all the food they could find the money for. "Serve no strangers!" my mother ordered after the first hour. "Only 'regulars' from now on."'[4] The pattern was repeated across the country, as the government resisted rationing or price controls, instead exhorting people to eat less bread and share nicely. Add to this the internment of 'enemy aliens', the loss of most able-bodied male workers to the armed forces, and the struggle to retain female replacements because munitions work was better paid, and you have a perfect storm.

Inevitably, prices shot up, food costs rising by 87 per cent in the first two years of the war.[5] Many smaller shops closed for good as their customers and staff dwindled and their overheads increased. Some shops implemented their own rationing schemes, including making customers buy the widely loathed but readily available margarine if they wanted to obtain other goods. Eventually the government established a Ministry of Food, though its impact was limited. As late as 1918 in Abertillery in Wales, the grocer was mobbed, windows smashed, and police were forced to take charge. They promptly sold 'a quantity of dripping and condensed milk'.[6] Shop opening hours were regulated, restricted to 8pm four days a week, 9pm on Saturdays, and an obligatory half-day closing once a week. The twice-yearly annoyance of British Summer Time and a flurry of changing all the clocks came in.

The repercussions of war were long-lasting, although they can be overplayed – many of the social changes of the next few decades were well under way before 1914, and were simply hastened, or, in some cases, delayed before catching up, giving the impression of seismic change.

The interwar period was one of increasing living standards. The Depression certainly affected many people, especially those in industry in the north, but for those in a job, even a relatively low-paid one, wages rose, the price of consumer goods fell, and working conditions in general improved. The *Liverpool Echo* summed it up when considering the grocer, grumbling that the era of pre-war obeisance was over and 'perhaps the most signal example of his emancipation was the institution of a staff dinner hour'.[7] (How dare he give staff time to eat!) Meanwhile, the vote was extended, giving women an official political voice for the first time. Some women could vote from 1918, and a decade later women and men achieved voting parity. Eventually, in 1948, plural voting was eradicated – until then property holders could vote where they lived and where they held property, meaning that many shopkeepers – mainly men – who held the freehold of their shops but had a townhouse elsewhere merrily voted multiple times.

Society remained deeply unequal, though. Homosexuality was illegal in England and Wales until 1967 (and in Scotland until 1980). Most children left school at fifteen. Whole sections of society which are now heavily marketed to simply didn't – officially – exist. Poverty was widespread and living conditions frequently horrific. Slum clearance programmes seeking to tackle the issues of substandard housing were implemented from the 1930s, increasing in pace in the 1950s, when bomb damage from the Second World War saw whole areas disappear under rubble. Roads were widened (again) and towns redrawn with the aim of rehousing the homeless and improving conditions for the poor, as well as allowing the freer movement of the growing number of motor cars. Sometimes they worked; sometimes they destroyed communities, and left pockets of isolation.

The era is defined by war, for this chapter also covers the Second World War. Then, the issues of supply and the need for rationing were recognised well before the commencement of hostilities. Ration books were issued in the autumn of 1939 for use from January 1940 and slogans such as 'make do and mend' were plastered on posters. The high street went into limbo, forced, like the population, to adapt and survive by any means possible. Rationing continued until 1954, and restrictions on building materials until around the same time. However, by the early 1960s the high street was recognisably modern in very many ways.

The 'passing of the grocer'

In 1902 *The Times* published a series of back-and-forth letters arguing over the 'passing of the grocer'. Initially sparked by the expansion of the Co-operative movement, it eventually encompassed other 'mortal enemies' of the independent trader, including Home & Colonial, the International Tea Company and Lipton's.[8] Around the same time the social campaigner Charles Booth declared that 'it is now exceedingly difficult for the man with only one shop to make a living. In a few years' time the trade will probably be confined to large firms and a certain number of very small shops in poor districts where the master is on the same level as his customers.'[9]

Hand-wringing initially concentrated on the food trade, where the multiples were a very obvious threat – not just the like of Lipton's, but also butchers such as the River Plate Meat Company, James Nelson, Eastmans and Dewhurst's, all of which catered to a working-class clientele. Writing from within the trade, the *Grocer* magazine took a more phlegmatic view: 'the bankruptcy figures are not alarming . . . they . . . represent, we may be sure, the elimination of the unfit . . . the untrained adventurer or group of tinkers who think they can master its mysteries in a week.'[10]

Competition also came from the big shops, the latest addition to which were food halls. Size was an advantage, enabling them to buy in bulk. In 1917 potatoes were in short supply – they were unrationed and had to be sold at a fixed price, so were a mainstay of the country after three years of shortages. Bentalls of Kingston procured enough potatoes for 2,000 people, direct from the grower in Norfolk. By 8am, half an hour before the shop opened, 5,000 people, mainly women, were in the queue. They sold out by 10am, but the mixture of altruism and publicity was so successful that they did it again two weeks later, with even more success.[11]

Post-war, shops and shopping opportunities exploded. Freed from wartime constraints, yet bolstered by wartime contracts and investment, manufacturers produced ever more goods, at ever cheaper prices. The working classes were the great growth opportunity, with shops catering to a mass market springing up in town centres and in planned suburban shopping parades. It wasn't just multiples. As soldiers returned from France, some invested their demob money in shops, for small-scale shop-keeping remained an attractive means by which to try to earn a living, despite the competition. This included Jack Cohen, who invested in a grocery stall in 1919. In 1924 he decided to rename his expanding business, using a portmanteau of his tea supplier – T. E. Stockwell, and his own name. By 1939 Tesco had 100 grocery shops, expanding into supermarkets in 1958 off the back of 'a low-price trade in a high-class manner'.[12]

Shops such as confectioners and tobacconists were particularly easy to open, for by now they required little specialist knowledge, increasingly stocking proprietary (branded) goods for which the customer was likely to ask by name, having seen an advert. Cigarettes eclipsed loose tobacco in the 1920s, while in confectioners – now more often called sweet shops – the 1920s and 1930s saw the launch of a whole range of brand names which remain familiar today – from Quality Street to Kit Kat, and Chocolate Orange (and Apple) to Crunchie. And, of course, shops like this were everywhere, not just on obvious streets in urban areas. Across the country, just before the First World War it's estimated that there was one shop for every fifty-nine people (or 607,300 shops). Overall shop numbers peaked in the 1920s.[13]

It's hard to know exactly how many of these outlets were multiples. The most comprehensive survey of shop numbers suggested that in 1920 there were 24,713 branches of various chain stores, rising to 35,894 in 1930 and 44,800 by 1950. But this includes a lot of local chains with fewer than twenty-five branches. In 1920 only twenty-one firms had more than 200 outlets and there was a great deal of variation within trades and between regions.[14] However, the general trend was up, and by 1966 historian Dorothy Davis concluded that around 20 per cent of shops were owned by multiple traders, controlling around half the total spend. In addition, 'they are still expanding, they occupy the best sites in the main shopping streets, and they set the pace, the style, the standard for all the rest'.[15]

Davis had just completed a study of shopping, which encompassed around 300 years. She took a dim view of the high street of the early 1960s, lamenting that food shops were now around half the street, while traditional markets were in decline. Retailing was simpler and less skilled than it had been, while the organisation behind it – the stuff the consumer didn't see – was immensely more complicated. The idea that shop assistants were merely there to fetch goods and hand them over, rather than to give expert advice or act as an intermediary for uncertain consumers, was particularly irksome to her: 'A century ago a shopkeeper could say with conviction, "this is a sound article", where his descendant today only dares to say "we get asked for a lot of these"'.[16] It was also a rather rose-tinted view of the past, given that a century ago shopkeepers were selling sweets accidentally laced with arsenic and drapers were hard-selling unwanted hats in order to gain the maximum commission.

Multiples were very visible, especially on the high street. Many had house styles, specifying how shopfronts should be constructed, and window displays laid out. Nineteen-thirties King's Lynn was not unique in experiencing a modernising rush by both independent and multiple traders. Antiquated Victorian shopfronts were replaced by the deep lobbies – essentially mini-arcades – and full-length plate glass windows which had started to appear in the late Edwardian era and had now come to epitomise the modern, forward-looking retailer. Plans submitted for the Lynn branch of Hepworths, a leading multiple tailor, were typical, with the shopfront based on a low granite plinth upon which were pavement-to-ceiling display windows ending with a set of ornamental transom windows at the top (they're the small horizontal panes that run along the tops of the main windows). The wooden surrounds were mahogany and there were mosaic tiles spelling out the Hepworths logo in the entrance foyer, plus a shop sign with gold lettering on turquoise green.[17]

Repetition bred familiarity, which was good for sales but less good for retaining a town's individuality. Architectural historian James Richards admitted in 1938 that 'in many places the personal and local character of the shops is disappearing. This is because many shops are now only branches of the big multiple stores, which for convenience are made all the same, and because of the use of ready-made shop fronts and fittings.'

On the other hand, 'it is no use regretting the coming of the multiple store and the standardisation of shop fronts, as these are part of our modern way of organising business and do, on the whole, make better goods available for more people. Even if they do make towns look more alike, and therefore duller, it is a convenience when you are travelling to find branches of a shop you already know.'[18] Richards was overplaying it a bit, for above the standardised shopfronts the individual buildings were often still distinct, and each town retained a character very much of its own.

Some companies went further, though, replacing complete buildings, or, indeed, blocks, in their own house style. Woolworth's, Marks & Spencer, Burton's, W. H. Smith and Boots were the main retailers to invest in this approach. The first three all built large stores which were broadly consistent in style, although they often differed significantly from one another, and the style itself changed over time. They tended to be a mixture of neo-Georgian classicism blended with the strong horizontal and vertical lines characteristic of 1920s and 1930s modernism. They had regular frontages and carefully planned detailing including logos, crests, parapets and carvings, which meant that the shopper walking through a town new to them would be able to spot them at quite some distance. They could be quite lavish, occupying key sites on high streets and, while they didn't always fit exactly (or at all) with the rest of the high street, especially if it was built in a particularly distinctive local vernacular, the money spent on them, and the effect achieved, could enhance streets, as much as threaten their overall character. Certainly, local councils perceived them as a positive. Just as William Whiteley's fellow traders back in the 1850s had eventually come to recognise his mammoth store as a draw to the area, so too did the presence of a smart new 'superstore' act as an anchor for other shops. M&S made explicit the link between its house style and desired effect on a local townscape, stating that their stores should become 'a landmark in their respective towns'.[19]

Not every multiple with a house style opted for fancy columns or art deco details. W. H. Smith was a huge chain, having expanded rather suddenly into town centres after losing the contract for two of the major railway companies in 1905. Its branches played with nostalgia, with fake bottle glass inserted into the transom windows, black and white facades, and sometimes even faux-Georgian bow fronts with small paned windows. Shop signs featured a newsboy with a tray of papers, and some shops had literary quotes above the doors. They may have been partially inspired by Boots the Chemist, which had spent the decade prior to the First World War building fake timber-framed stores, complete with jetties and leaded windows in the upper floors. They were nominally intended for towns with history and prestige, nestling along with existing timber-framed buildings. However, inevitably they reflected the 1930s more than any earlier era, not least as on the main shopping streets, constant modernisation of shops and other buildings had left very little in the way of outdated medieval-style architecture, so theirs was sometimes the only timber-framed building there. King's Lynn's small, very early example was decidedly plain in comparison with that on York's Coney Street, the latter (both are still there) being ridiculously lavish, complete with gargoyles and town crests.[20]

Multiple shops were both liked and loathed. In addition to mourning the de-skilling of shopwork, some commentators also recoiled more generally from the idea of a mass market. Here's social historian Richard Hoggart on cheap furniture stores in 1957: 'at first glance these are surely the most hideously tasteless of all modern shops. Every known value in decoration has been discarded: there is no evident design or pattern; the colours fight with one another, anything new is thrown in simply because it is new. There is strip-lighting together with

Fig. 6.1. Woolworth's on Western Road, Brighton, in the early 1930s. The stacked windows and loud signs mean you can't miss the (apparent) bargains within.

imitation chandelier lighting; plastics, wood and glass are all glued and stuck together; notice after blazing notice winks, glows, or blushes luminously.' Hoggart's snobbishness went on, concluding dismissively that 'one buys the suggestion of education and elegance with the furniture'.[21] For some people, that was precisely the point, but it was a generalisation that failed to recognise the way in which any cultural group or class forged its own identity. The working classes who were the main target of the multiples didn't just want to sit on sofas or put on hats to look more middle-class, but wanted to show their own identity – and have a comfortable place to sit while looking good.

The snobbishness lasted quite a while (and is arguably still with us). Even in 1938, one article pointed to the 'peculiar form of class distinction in retail distribution', which saw even large chains attempt to pass off stores as independent for fear they'd otherwise 'lose caste with a "family-minded"public'.[22] All those modern coffee chains trying to look like cool indies are doing nothing new.

However, attitudes in general did change, not least as the Depression drove a more middle-class audience to look for savings in their shopping habits. As one trade manual put it, 'multiple trading, like mass production, has been blamed for many of the business troubles of our generation. Slowly, it is being learned, however, that standardisation of production, by reducing the price of goods, does not necessarily lower the quality. We are realising that "cheap" and "nasty" are not inevitably correlative terms, nor an inviolable example of cause and effect.'[23] The overall effect was to increase the variety of things on offer, and the numbers of places where you could buy them – at any price point you could afford. According to one big shop owner: 'Shopping today is a recreation as well as a duty; the thousands of people who come to town in the mid-week, mostly to see the shops, are a sure sign that is has become part of modern life.'[24]

Much as commentators moaned about homogenisation, older rhythms of life still remained important. In York, 'Saturday . . . is market day and a certain number of people come into the city from the neighbouring villages.'[25] Even where the market had declined, habit was hard to break. In Southport in 1939, Yvonne Stukey reported unexpected crowds as she shopped and 'I asked why. Years ago, it seems, there used to be a market on Wednesdays, and people still come here on that day because that is the day they used to come! What slaves to habit!'[26]

You're not a slave to habit. Look about you and enjoy the modern town. True, there are still a lot of ads and signs stuck to every surface, but there's a lot of chrome and pared-back design as well. It will take until 1948 for the government to enforce permissions for adverts, partly in an effort to stop them distracting motorists. The town is undeniably full of distractions. With electricity taking over, shops have enthusiastically embraced the possibilities. One 1928 shop manual advised solemnly that 'a flashing sign is preferable to any other sort'.[27]

Our first stop is on the periphery of the high street. You may well have a baker in your suburb or village, but since you're already here, reap the benefit of the bakers in town, which offer more choice, and have better buns.

The baker

It is a cliché that bread is the stuff of life, but it's certainly true that it's a longstanding mainstay of the British diet. Bread consumption was directly related to living standards: the poorer you were, the more bread you ate (and the richer you were, the more cake). The twentieth century has seen a gradual decline in the overall amount of bread consumed per person, but in the interwar years it was still eaten on a daily basis by the vast majority of people. As toast, it was a breakfast staple, eaten by over 80 per cent of the population, while half of the bottom 15 per cent of society also ate it for their evening meal (versus only 10 per cent of the top earners). The profit on each loaf might be small, but the quantity sold could make up for it, so baking was a competitive business.

Most bakers were independent, though by the 1930s not all of them baked on site. Space on the more desirable streets was costly, and separating the retail side from production made sense. Freed from the confines of small shops, some bakers expanded into wholesale, taking advantage of mechanisation, in the shape of vast mixers and automated biscuit breaks (to flatten and beat stiff doughs) to increase production, and supply either their own outlets or those of others. Not only did they sell to cafés and tea rooms, but also to grocers who wanted to stock bread or cakes – the slab cake was an easy sell – as well as to the institutional market, which included hospitals, schools and works canteens. There was a great deal of crossover between bakeries and caterers. In towns, many small bakeries had a café attached, while some chain cafés were offshoots of industrial-scale bakeries including the ABC and Lyons. Smaller copycat chains included Cadena and Zeeta. The Cadena Cafés were upmarket venues with dance floors and entertainment. The Oxford branch was on a (fairly short) list of 'approved hotels and restaurants' in which students at Oxford were permitted to dine in 1930. Zeeta, meanwhile, was an offshoot of Barkers, a big shop in Kensington. While both operated predominantly as cafés, customers could order baked goods or, in some cases, buy directly from a small shop counter.

Attracting customers who had an increasing range of options for buying their bread or baked goods could be a challenge. As one advisory manual put it: 'It is, of course, an admitted fact that the humblest housewife who wants to purchase a blouse or a hat will think no trouble or exertion too great. In fact, the expedition to the shopping centre to make a selection of such an article is the occasion for a jaunt. But when it comes to the weekly food supply, the same housewife will not take trouble to the same degree. She goes by force of habit to her usual shop. Now, this habit is quite a good one – provided that it is to your shop she goes.'[28] Trade manuals exhorted bakers to use any means at their disposal to attract customers to their shop and thereafter stay loyal. It was particularly hard in the face of grocers selling bread made by the wholesale bakeries, for 'the public is prone to give the preference to the large bakers, and to ascribe to their goods superior qualities to those of the goods made by men with whom they are familiar, and on that account local men have to meet this kind of competition at considerable disadvantage'.[29] But there were ways to fight back: small bakers could be more nimble, able to nip down to the grocer and buy ingredients at a slight discount and bake to immediate order. They knew their customers, and could arrange deliveries which might be eschewed by bigger concerns. Apparently 'even the poorest people expect now to have their bread delivered at their doors, and to get credit for a week or more'. No need for an expensive van, either: 'after a good deal of experiment, horses have been retained for private deliveries and for frequent stoppage rounds generally.'[30] In extremis, they could do away with the shop and become entirely delivery-based.

Assuming your baker still has a shop, he (rarely she) has probably adopted all the tiny changes possible. Good window displays were of course paramount, a chance to show hygiene and modernity, as well as the range of goods on offer. A baker who was mainly a confectioner (in the older sense) would place ornamented cakes in the main position. Bakers in the 1930s were very fond of novelty cakes, so you might find yourself admiring edible landscapes, sugarcraft fairy tales, or, in the case of Bettys in Bradford, a chocolate donkey cart driven by gnomes and flanked by cakes at exuberant angles. If the baker aimed at a more quotidian market, bread took centre stage, perhaps placed on a stand in the centre of the window and surrounded by draped fabric and brightly coloured small cakes on trays and stands. There was a logic to this, for 'bread needs to be made prominent and as enticing as possible because of its commonness, while those fond of confectionery will readily look for it'.[31]

The range of confectionery offered could be enormous. Around the same time as the donkey cart window, Betty's presented a fancy tray at one of the London trade fairs. It included marzipan potatoes, almond alps flavoured with rum, chocolate dipped kirsch cigars, hazelnut coffee boats, multi-coloured iced fancies, cake 'cauliflowers' and snowballs made with meringue and whisky buttercream.

Price was a crucial selling point in this fiercely competitive market. It was important to make sure prices were genuinely competitive, and that people knew this. Signs in the window were good, but printing ads on the back of receipts was even better – and easy to do now that cash tills were superseding the

Fig. 6.2. Shop window display from Betty's (later Bettys) café and
tea rooms in Bradford, *c.*1927. This won an award during Bradford
Shopping Week that year. Yes, those are chocolate gnomes riding on
a donkey cart, flanked by the classic 'my lady' cakes.

old pay desks. Suggestions from one manual included 'we use
no fat but butter in our confectionery. It does not pay you to
bake at home', and 'Our bread costs a farthing more than that
of some others, but its value is a halfpenny more than theirs.'[32]

Competing with grocers got even harder in the 1930s, when
'another Yankee idea!' was introduced in the form of sliced
bread.[33] It was marketed as more economical, more convenient,
more sanitary, neater for sandwiches, safer (as children wouldn't

be handling knives), more palatable, more digestible, and the highly dubious 'free of gases – slicing the loaf before wrapping it releases impounded gases, and keeps that fresh wholesome flavour'.[34] It was immediately successful, leading trade magazine *Shelf Appeal* to declare in 1933: 'We are all lazy buyers nowadays. Even the woman who used to pride herself on judging good flour by the feel of it now shops for bread by 'phone. Often she saves time for bridge or the movies – time she would have to spend picking out a particularly crusty loaf – by phoning for So-and-So's ready sliced, standard-baked bread, which has no "particular" variances within the bread.'[35] At least the sliced bread of this era had some texture: in 1961 the Chorleywood process was invented, a highly industrialised process that enabled a loaf of bread to be made – including slicing and packaging – in under four hours. Modern sliced bread is almost all made using this technique, which is fast and efficient, as well as enabling the use of low-protein British-grown wheat, but it is also unfortunately floppy and bland and, according to some studies, not brilliant for the bowels.

The bread you're buying will almost certainly be white: brown bread was still associated with poverty and lack of choice, although there was a small movement trying to promote wholegrains as healthy. During both wars, the government mandated a much higher extraction rate than usual – the higher the extraction rate the browner the loaf, and the less waste, as more of the bran is kept in the flour. Forewarned by the 1914-18 conflict, when National Bread was announced in 1942, 'women, protesting against the inevitable, are making a last-minute dash round the shops for white bread and flour. Most are now fairly resigned but determined to eat white bread until the last minute, although some have grumbled that the Government is trying to starve them and they will not eat brown bread for anyone.' It was all about the visual appeal. Kathleen Hey was a grocery assistant in Dewsbury, grumbling about the grumblers:

'It is a real grievance the colour. My remarks that the Greeks and others wouldn't care if bread was sky blue pink if they could get some are received lukewarmly. "Yes, it is awful for them – they're starving they say. But just think of having this to eat till the war ends."'[36] Her customers complained that it gave them indigestion and diarrhoea. And it got worse, for after the war, when American food aid ceased, even the National Loaf went on the ration and stayed there from 1946 to 1948. When white sliced came back to the shops in 1950, Britons rushed back to its soft embrace, and bakers went back to trying to persuade people to patronise them in the face of ever more convenient and larger grocery stores.

Let's talk about the Second World War. Rationing was imposed in 1940, eventually covering food, clothing and fuel. People had to register with one supplier for rationed items – one butcher, one grocer, etc., though they could shop around for unrationed things. Both multiples and big stores leapt on the opportunity to persuade people to register with them, with Sainsbury's advertising, 'you can obtain all rationed, registered and "free" provisions, groceries and meat under one roof. No rushing about in black-outs and winter weather.'[37] They also took full advantage of their enhanced buying power, with one small draper darkly prophesying that 'their grip on trade is apparently not realised by most people, but one . . . day we shall wake up to the fact that they are the real bosses of this country'.[38] Smaller food shops suffered particularly badly, especially after the imposition of a minimum registration rule of twenty-five customers.[39] As with the previous conflict, shortage of shipping space for imports, the conversion of factories to war industry and a government-led emphasis on frugality led to shortages, and, despite the imposition of an excess profits tax to stop profiteering, prices rose. Some shops simply couldn't compete. Twenty-five per cent of the independent shops in Leeds closed in the first two years of rationing.[40]

The enforced diet of brown bread may have your gut grumbling. It's good that your next stop is to somewhere you can buy something to remedy it. Pharmacy shops are surprisingly colourful. It's true that pills and potions are not the most conducive items to a jazzy window display, so pharmacists have long since taken a different approach. As you approach, you'll find a window full of carboys (glass flagons) containing different coloured liquids, perhaps backlit for added effect. Pharmacies are one of the few remaining trades to habitually incorporate one of the age-old signs of the trade into their shop design. Look out for a snake twined round a staff (from Asclepius, the Greek god of medicine) or a unicorn (the horn was supposed to be an antidote to poison).[41]

The chemist and pharmacist

The world of pharmacy was a confusing one for a long time, with a number of different names for professions largely defined by whether they could dispense or prescribe, or whether they made up medical mixtures. In the nineteenth century the apothecary shop disappeared, sadly taking with it its ceilings, invariably hung with crocodiles in contemporary prints. The profession merged with surgeons and doctors. Then came a series of regulatory changes, bringing in qualifications and a statutory register. The trade became steadily more professional, and more tightly controlled. In 1908 a fierce internal fight culminated in the Poisons and Pharmacy Act, which allowed any qualified chemist to dispense. This meant that as long as a qualified chemist was employed in the shop for dispensing, the owner and counter staff need not have industry qualifications. This was a game-changer, especially for the multiple chemists, all of whom promised cheap ready-made drugs as well as a wide range of auxiliary services such as dentistry and opticians. The term druggist declined in favour of pharmacist.

These included Jesse Boot, who operated 560 branches of

Boots by 1914, competing mainly with Timothy White's along with Taylors of Leeds (these would merge in 1935 and in turn be taken over by Boots in the 1960s). All these, as well as the many thousands of independent shops or small chains, were then given a further boost by the National Health Insurance Act of 1911, the first of several Acts that introduced compulsory insurance, fixed doctors' fees, and stopped doctors from prescribing and then selling the drugs they'd just prescribed. All prescriptions now had to go through a pharmacy: it was 'a new era', as the *Pharmaceutical Journal* declared.[42] Refinement of the National Health programme between the years eventually culminated in the 1946 National Health Service Act. Prescriptions rose from 70 million in 1947 to 250 million in 1949.[43]

Dispensing National Health prescriptions wasn't lucrative, but it brought people through the doors; alluring window displays and the sheer range of products on offer inside did the rest. Out went the carboys, in came slightly 'stocky' but exuberantly stacked shelves showing exactly how many things were on offer inside. Chemists had never sold purely medical concoctions, habitually offering make-up, soap, hair products, sanitary wear and technology such as photographic equipment and film processing. If you were a would-be murderer or, more prosaically, were plagued by a moth infestation, you could buy poisons, though the purchase of them had to be recorded carefully in the poison book. Artists' supplies were another source of income, as the old oilmen folded or retreated to the side streets. Then there were perfumes – Boots' 'jockey club' perfume was 'most realistic, so much so that you could smell the stables'.[44] Larger Boots stores had lending libraries until they were phased out in 1966, and the really big sites even had tea rooms.

Boots was present on every high street by the 1950s, but it was never the only option. Smaller chemists could not compete on price for branded drugs, nor, indeed, for the in-house alternatives with the same formulation, which Boots made at

Fig. 6.3. Queuing for the sale at Boots Cash Chemist, Western Road, Brighton, *c.* 1920. This building was replaced in 1927 by a neo-classical edifice which looked more like a church.

their own factory. But the nature of the business meant that they could still sell through personal service, and long-standing relationships with local customers. Stiff competition meant that even small shops had to keep up to date, though. One 1959 retrospective in the trade journal *The Chemist and Druggist* diplomatically suggested that the multiples were useful in 'prodding the private chemist to brighten up his shop, improve his window displays, and generally adopt more systematic business methods'.[45] This meant installing the usual large plate glass windows, with display stands through which, in the most cutting edge of outlets, you might now see through to the shop interior. Inside, you could expect a mixture of brisk modernity and a determined reminder that the profession was old, trustworthy and ever-so-slightly mystical. Where they had them, many chemists retained Victorian mahogany fittings, stuffing them full of a mixture of cardboard boxes containing proprietary medicines and the carboys relegated from the shop window. The latter were finally outlawed for actual use in the 1950s due to hygiene concerns. Other shops swept away the old entirely and went for wipe-clean surfaces, electric refrigerators, glass display cabinets with only a hint of wood, and free-standing cases for specific ranges – including the photographic film you've come in for.

Space was at a premium, for service was still almost all via the counter. By the 1960s the range of goods was even more immense, and some shops were experimenting with partial self-service for non-pharmaceutical goods. Adverts from 1959, aimed at the buyers for chemists, range from the obvious (nylon support stockings, trusses, shavers, nerve powder and disinfectant) to the more intriguing (dog biscuits, slippery elm food – made from actual slippery elms – egg-nog shampoo and 'kumfy kiddy wear'). Contraceptive tablets were also now available, though the NHS only allowed them on prescription from 1961. Rubber condoms (some of which were reusable) and diaphragms had been around for decades, but the Pharmaceutical Society banned its members from selling them without a prescription until 1953, and Boots refused to sell them until 1965. This was an area where smaller traders could capitalise, though it was a fraught one, as barrier methods had been used primarily to avoid STDs for centuries, and so contraception was associated with extra-marital sex and promiscuity, both still frowned upon. Some chemists invested in vending machines with 'surgical rubber ware' outside, others stocked them on demand, and a few had them on open display. But the stigma remained, and most people preferred to use mail order catalogues offering caps disguised as powder compacts, and condoms concealed in fake cigars. Women might seek out a birth control clinic, while men had the options of garages, barbers and tobacconists.[46]

Got your film? Anything you wanted to pick up for the weekend? Pop it all in your bag, and head off for lunch. Every shop seems to have its own café now, as do cinemas, and there are dining rooms and luncheon rooms and teashops on every side street. However, you're after a cheap thrill as well as a pudding, so it's off to the departmental store.

The department store café

Big shops were still big business. Slowly the American term departmental or department store came into use for them, though as late as 1974 the Ladybird children's series 'People at Work' published a volume called *In a Big Store*. The term 'department store' was certainly accurate, in that the shops it described were still made up of different departments which operated semi-autonomously until the 1960s, but it was also a little pejorative. In 1910 H. G. Wells had sniffily referred to 'one of those large, rather low-class establishments which sell everything from pianos and furniture to books and millinery—a department store', and the majority of the shops we'd now call department stores preferred to style themselves as something else until well after the Second World War. Most remained independent, though there were some small chains – Binns in the north-east, Bobby's and Plummer Rodis along the south coast, Featherstones in Kent, and Lewis's, which from its base in Liverpool went on a buying spree that eventually included Selfridges in 1951.[47] (Don't confuse it with John Lewis, which emerged from Peter Jones in London, scooping up Waitrose in 1936 and going on from there.) Meanwhile the United Drapery Stores were quietly buying up department stores and drapers, as were Debenhams, Selfridges and, a little later, the Glasgow-based House of Fraser. The shops they bought retained their names and identities for now, though, and, as a shopper, you'd

Fig. 6.4. The central atrium of Fraser's on Buchanan Steet, Glasgow, 1972. Founded in 1849, Fraser's expanded to fill much of Buchanan Street, with a central store including this multi-storeyed gallery (built in 1883), used for everything from Christmas trees to catwalk shows. As House of Fraser, Fraser's went on to be a major department store chain, before retrenching furiously in the 2010s and rebranding as Frasers from 2023.

almost certainly refer to your local big shop/department store by name rather than type.

Inside, you'd expect to find the catering outlets on the upper floors, keeping smells away from shoppers, and taking advantage of views, if any were on offer. Some shops added roof gardens, though few matched that at Derry & Toms in Kensington, which included a Spanish garden with an 'authentic mission bell', a Tudor garden and an English water garden 'where pigeons and sheldrakes waddle across a brilliant stretch of green lawn . . . and apples ripen on the bough'.[48] The other advantage (for sales staff) was that you had to go through the entire store to get there. Escalators were the new thing, enclosed in their own halls due to buildings regulations. D. H. Evans's escalator hall was a triumph of modernist beauty, painted pale pink, with silver and copper bronze metalwork. The illustration of it in the store's 1937 Coronation brochure also shows free-standing glass cases, palm trees around a piano in the atrium and plenty of elegantly dressed women – with very few men – browsing the items on display.[49]

Departmental stores really did offer everything under one roof, though they were far from homogeneous. Debenhams categorised its shops by type, depending on the audience. Others simply took stock of their clientele and priced their wares accordingly. In Finchley, Prior's new store was opened by actress Marie Lohr, who declared it had 'everything everybody needed at reasonable prices. If a woman did leave this district to do her shopping she could not understand why.' They were one of eighty-five stores listed as suppliers of materials to make the patterns offered as part of the *Daily Mirror*'s 'Film Star Week' in 1936.[50] Further up the social scale, Selfridges had a wart removal service, while Bentalls of Kingston produced prefabricated houses.[51] The rise of branded goods meant big stores had to fight hard to differentiate their offering from the big shop up the street, which led both to in-house brands and individual shops within the shop. Early examples were the Men's Shops – Bainbridge's of Newcastle advertised theirs as having 'a separate entrance for the nervous male', recognition that such stores were overwhelmingly seen as female-oriented.[52] There were also 'Junior Miss' departments aimed at the youth market, with brighter colours and less formal layouts.

Another way to get people through the door was a large-scale stunt. This is really why you've come – the sandwiches and omelettes on offer for lunch will be excellently prepared, and

Fig. 6.5. Bentalls, Kingston-upon-Thames, just after a major refurbishment in 1935. Quite what the Personality Shop sold is unclear, but it was one of Bentalls' attempts to compete with more specialised retailers. In 1948 they became one of the earliest big shops to open a 'Junior Miss' department.

well-priced, and the cakes are all made in-house, and the decor is tasteful, and it all feels like a very good restaurant but without the worry over the bill or the etiquette or whether the other people will be quite like you – but secretly it's all about the elephants. In Kingston, Bentalls had elephants from the 1930s until the 1960s, as part of its Christmas circus.[53] One pooed comprehensively in the doorway of a neighbouring shop, causing it to be closed for forty-five minutes at peak shopping time. There were lions, too, which were kept in the lift shaft after hours, terrifying the office staff. The theatrics weren't confined to Christmas. In 1939 the summer fair featured Anita Kittner, a Swedish diver known for 'her blonde beauty, her charming personality and above all, her daring 70ft dive from the roof of

Bentalls escalator hall into a shallow 5ft tank of water'. The act involved a 'blood-curdling scream' as she leapt from the board and plunged down to the (reinforced) ground floor. Such was the force involved that on one occasion her swimming costume split, though she was saved from public indecency by a quick-witted electrician and a towel.[54]

If you've quite finished, it's time to get serious. You need a new outfit. If you're a man, that means a suit, at least until the 1950s when dress becomes a little less formal. If you're a woman, a dress or a skirt and blouse will do – and a hat, of course. Now, you might choose to stay in the big store, for the shopwalkers and assistants working on commission are long gone, and you can browse freely. There's certainly plenty of choice, and this now includes decent-quality ready-to-wear. Selfridges advertised 'ready-for-service' menswear in 1910 (garments were merely tweaked to fit and delivered to you the same evening). But it's in this era that it really takes off. By 1960 the (male) author of a book on Derry & Toms happily claimed that the size ranges were so comprehensive that 'most women can expect to buy clothes that fit perfectly'.[55] More realistically, they also had a large alterations room.

However, there are other options. There are the penny bazaars, which are cheap and cheerful, there are markets, and there are advantages, still, to the small independent shop. As the Drapers' Record *pointed out in 1930, 'The independent shop keeper, because he offers a "friendly, personal service and satisfies the individual tastes of each of his customers, whom he knows and who know him through long and intimate service" will continue to hold his place in the system of distribution for many a year to come'.[56] Where you go will depend on what kind of person you are, so let's have a closer look at the options around.*

The tailor

The cachet of a tailor was entrenched into male society. As one trader in Kingston-upon-Thames put it, 'the youth starting out in life and buying his own clothes for the first time likes the idea of "my tailor", and will a thousand times prefer a real man's shop to the place where his mother used to take him'.[57] There were, of course, suits and suits, at least according to those who could afford an expensive one from an independent tailor offering a truly bespoke service. At the top end were those who offered fittings at home, or had shops with an atmosphere redolent of a gentleman's club, all leather and dark wood. In Sheffield Lew Harbour had a 'baronial lounge' complete with oak panelling and tiger skins on the floor.[58]

Next came the 'ordinary middle-class tailor', self-described by one trade writer as 'we are engaged in business today to make a living; we are bound to make ourselves felt or perish. We cater for the great majority, but, because the market is a large one (far greater than at either extreme), competition is fierce, hence our belief in the adventitious aids of advertising and window-dressing.' He went on, stating that while they would not sell a suit at 12 guineas, 'we do not touch the level of the fifty shilling man'.[59]

These tailors were in fierce competition with the big shops, and you'd be able to spot them by their aggressively modern facades, all marble and shiny bronze lettering, and frequently changed window displays. These windows were backed with cloth, completely blocking the view to the shop within (if you needed to peer in, you weren't the right person to be entering), and with a few artfully displayed items on dummies and the usual printed or handwritten signs proclaiming price, quality and service all to be had within.

The visual cues, as might be expected, were all about cool masculinity, the aim being to 'possess a certain severity both inside and out, just as a man's club or the smoke-room of an hotel is designed on severe lines'.[60] Alternatively, the shop might be dressed inside and out to suggest tradition and longevity – bales of cloth, measuring tapes and all the tropes of the trade. These were spaces where men could participate in all the same pleasures of shopping, which women were still sometimes criticised for liking quite so much: the discussions on size and fit, the fondling of fabric, the anticipation of a finished garment, and the admiration of the dapper results in a hopefully flattering mirror.

Today, we're shopping for a cheaper suit, though it still needs to be fashionable, as well as reasonably well cut. That really means a multiple. Multiple tailors were derided for promoting the 'cult of shabbiness', being just one very short step away from the ready-to-wear, of which one trade journal declared that 'the average Englishman' would be aghast at the thought of 'having his clothes reached down off the shelf, however attractively they may be got up'.[61] Even if Selfridges did sell it, ready-to-wear was still associated with army uniforms – especially so after the experiences of so many men in the First World War – and with poor quality and fit. But it underwent a real revolution in the inter-war years. Factories based largely in London's East End prided themselves on being agile and responsive, able to harness modern technology to produce garments designed to appeal to a mass market well versed in the latest looks, not just through magazines or fashion displays, but through cinema and newsreels. The wholesale trade was dominated by Jewish entrepreneurs, and some of the criticism of ready-to-wear was driven by anti-Semitism. Jewish tailors brought much-needed skills to Britain – as well as expertise in sizing, especially in womenswear, which had previously relied on such descriptive categories as 'maid' and 'matron', and now changed slowly to offer SW, W and WX.[62] No wonder men preferred the semi or fully bespoke services of a tailor.

It took until the 1950s for ready-to-wear to become truly acceptable in menswear, and, even then, shops continued to offer basic alterations for things like length of trouser or cuff. In the 1930s, the standard garb for a respectable working man was a semi-tailored suit, an area in which multiple tailors flourished. Overall, they supplied around a third of all tailored menswear between the wars, with the biggest players being Burton's, Hepworths and Price's Fifty Shilling Tailors.[63] As the name of the latter suggests, their suits came in around the 50 shilling mark (Burton's charged 55 shillings, to show they were just that little bit better without actually pricing themselves out of their intended market).

What could you expect when you visited? First, a sense of familiarity. All the multiples had clear branding, and you'd find it hard to miss them. In the late 1930s Hepworths' 313 shops were 'situated in the best positions in the most important towns in the country', while Price's 270 outlets had the words 'fifty shillings' plastered all over them, including a main shop sign in sleek neon lettering on a black background. Windows featured little and large shop dummies and had signs promising 'no extra charge'. In Sevenoaks they were accused of leading the 'vulgarisation of the high street'.[64]

Dwarfing all its rivals was Burton's, with nearly 600 stores by the start of the Second World War. Heading it up was Montague Burton, the 'tailor of taste'. Born as Meshe David Osinsky in what is now Lithuania, Burton fled increasing anti-Semitism and persecution, arriving in England in 1900. He started trading in men's suits before the First World War, operating fourteen shops and a small factory in Leeds by 1914. Like many other retailers who also operated factories, he benefited from war contracts, in this case for uniforms, followed by huge demand for demob suits. By the 1920s Burton's was one of the biggest employers in Leeds, and its shops were some of the most resplendent buildings on the high street.

Fig. 6.6. Burton's in Coney Street, *c.*mid-1930s. A classic corner site, with Market Street branching off to the right. The store was built in 1931 and has since lost its parapets.

Fig. 6.7. Interior of a Burton's, *c.*1933. You can almost smell the wood polish.

Burton's bought prestige sites, on corners if possible, and rebuilt the premises so that, while often quite different, they were nevertheless all recognisably Burton's. Like so many others, they tended to be classical-meets-unmistakably-1930s, with stone cladding and dramatic columns. They included the logo, in stone on the front, and shopfronts that sometimes had the names of other store locations in lozenge-shaped frames across the transom windows, or sometimes the bywords of 'elegance', 'taste', 'courtesy' and 'economy'. Windows were 'tastefully arranged without too much in it'.[65] Inside, the shops were surprisingly small, with no need for stockrooms, because after choosing a suit from a catalogue, and choosing cloth from the bolts on offer, in discussion, of course, with 'your' tailor, measurements would be taken, you'd pay a cashier at a separate desk, and the suit would then be made off-site. You'd collect it a week or so later, with a final chance to try it on and settle up. If you looked up as you left and wondered quite why the building was so large, it was because ownership of the whole site gave the company extra assets. Burton himself was a teetotaller who believed in quiet promotion of alternatives to drunken rowdiness, and the upper floors often contained temperance billiard halls, along with offices and staff flats.[66] In an industry renowned for poor working conditions, Burton also promoted employee welfare, providing medical and leisure facilities for his factory staff, and encouraging unionisation. He prided himself on paying the highest wages in Europe – and given his Leeds base was now the biggest clothing factory in Europe, this was quite an impressive statement.

The idea that men's tailoring might virtually disappear from the high street would have been unthinkable in the 1930s. Burton's did, it's true, introduce ready-to-wear in some shops towards the end of the decade, including taking over two whole floors of its New Oxford Street branch. But on the other hand, shirtmaker Austin Reed, hitherto a ready-to-wear specialist, announced it would open a made-to-measure department at its Regent Street flagship store in 1935. The chain's 1933 Christmas catalogue promised '100 ways to please a man – from 1/- to £5' and included 'golfiacs' (anoraks for golfing enthusiasts), as well as whangee umbrellas (they're the ones with the knobbly cane handles). They also had a barber in the basement – all a man could possibly want.

But perhaps you aren't a man. Working and lower middle-class womenswear was much less reliant on the multiples, although there were a few chains. These included former hosiery specialist Dorothy Perkins, named after a rose, and whose shops featured a slightly odd cottage roof, all very bucolic; and Jaeger, who despite selling ready-to-wear by the late 1930s claimed not to 'sell clothes': rather, they 'dressed women' (whatever that meant).[67] Another alternative was Cresta Silks, though this is probably above your price bracket as a working-class woman. How about the Co-op? Very limited choice though, so not ideal. Or there's the Dutch firm C&A Modes, which opened in 1922 (universally known in Britain as Coats 'n' Ats, though the initials were actually that of its founders). It catered for middle-aged, middle-ish income women, selling 'fashion goods at low prices', and did well out of the move towards ready-to-wear during the 1930s when rapidly changing fashion met a drop in income for some of its new clientele.

There's also Marks & Spencer, which we'll visit properly later. They've recently started concentrating far more on clothing, and since they're present in a lot of towns, they're hard to miss. But they are a bit boring. One Mass Observation respondent explained that they were 'good value, good quality compared with prices. Unfortunately, when you have bought a frock and come into the street, you see a lot of people who have the same frock. And nobody likes that.'[68] So after getting some ideas from their windows, we'll try somewhere a bit more interesting, in the shape of what's usually called a 'madam shop'.

Of course, if you were very wealthy, you'd still employ your own dress-maker, but let's set that idea firmly aside. At the opposite end of the spectrum (and this includes M&S) you might encounter what's known as a 'walkaround shop'. As the name suggests, here you can walk the store, examining goods without being accosted by an assistant until you decide to make a purchase or wish for a fitting. The concept has spread from the big shops. Some love that it is very impersonal: others still crave a bit more personal attention.

Madam shops

Madam shops bridged the gap between dressmakers and walkaround ready-to-wear outlets. They were small, with con-notations of exclusivity, and aimed at specific market segments, working hard to appeal to a small group of people who would be loyal to them, rather than the mass market which had been lost to the multiples.

If you're not sure what a madam shop looks like, fear not, for all you need do is look for the French name. Brighton has Melanie, Madame Helene and Madame Bloom. Some advertise as 'Guinea Gown' shops, stocking catalogue dresses that you can order to the shop and have altered to fit, cheap stockings and a few more expensive party dresses.[69] (If you're still stuck looking for elephants in the department store, you can find them there too. Beatties of Wolverhampton opened a dedicated Guinea Gown Department in 1934 advertising such wonders as a 'Matron's' Charming Gown' and 'Really Smart Crinkled Crepe Frocks'.[70])

If you're willing to splash out, though, you might head for the kind of shop Marjorie Gardiner worked in in London in 1925: 'a small, very exclusive shop . . . where the window had silk drapes and was dressed with one gown, one hat and a vase of real flowers, beautifully arranged. All was changed every

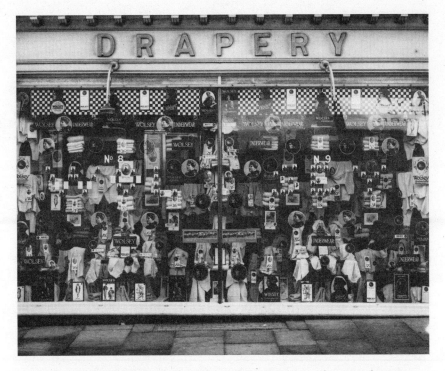

Fig. 6.8. Alongside specialist shops for women and men, the more generalist drapers still held sway. This is Woodward's Drapery in Leamington Spa, with a shop window full of Wolsey underwear in the 1930s. Not the most fashionable of window displays for the time, but the Cardinal would surely have been proud.

few days and everything had to be of the very best.'[71] Later she moved to Brighton, selling hats at a milliner on Western Road. Stock came from wholesalers, to be titivated in house, though there was a small workroom for making. The shopgirls all wore black, with satin high heels, and, in an indication of how little conditions had changed since the seventeenth century, the door stayed open all the time, 'no matter how bitter the weather. The girls suffered acutely from the cold and most of them had chilblains for which mittens did little or nothing. Occasionally they tried to sneak a moment in which to warm their frozen fingers on the one tiny radiator which was all that the shop possessed. Incredibly, this was not allowed.'[72] Wages were low, supplemented sometimes by hostessing at the dance halls, but the camaraderie was fierce, especially since Madam, who arrived in a chauffeur-driven car, could dismiss any assistant with no references, so covering for each other became second nature. Far from the walkaround shops of the working class, this was a shop which prioritised customer service, attending to their every whim.

Along with class, ageism was embedded in shopping for womenswear. It was assumed that older women – matrons – would wear bigger sizes and want higher necklines. Littlewoods, a penny bazaar turned catalogue retailer with some high street shops, carried dresses aimed at 'young ladies in your teens', advising, 'don't adopt styles that are meant for women nearer thirty than twenty. Yours is the fresh charm of youth.'[73] They only sold them in small sizes. Sizing was a nightmare, for despite the advent of letter-based codes to give a general idea of fit, so much depended on whether a woman still wore corsets, had adapted to girdles, or – daringly – was moving towards a brassiere and basic shape garments. It was hardly surprising that when successful one-fits-all garments were launched, they did well. Wholesale clothier Mansfield's supplied coats in a 'magic measure', one size only and 'this was a tremendous success commercially. We capitalised on the fact that garments were very big – full coats rather than fitted coats. The amazing thing was that even if it felt tight on a woman she convinced herself it fitted.'[74]

The advantage of a good madam shop was the illusion, at least, of personal service, which remained desirable, especially when purchasing expensive items such as clothing. Recommendation remained important, both for the shopkeeper and the customer. In D. E. Stevenson's *Miss Buncle's Book*, the heroine is recommended to a 'little shop for hats and frocks in Kensington

High Street', by a friend who writes to 'tell her not to rook you'. It's sufficiently high end that is has just 'one small hat in the window and the name above the door in black letters'. Once inside, Barbara Buncle finds merely 'a few fragile-looking gilt chairs and long mirrors which showed Barbara her form at several distressing angles', and is left terrified by the supercilious assistant. However, the personal letter does the trick, Barbara is whisked into a back toom full of clothes and hats, and after a bit of small talk about their mutual acquaintance she and the owner spend three hours trying on clothes with Barbara's own, somewhat frumpy, views on sensible attire mown down. She emerges, thrilled, with the clothes to be sent on after alteration. In this case the shop has also furnished her with slips, stockings, shoes and a hat to match.[75]

The landscape of shopping changed drastically during the Second World War. Like food, clothes were rationed, and 'make

Fig. 6.9. New Malden High Street, following German bombing raids on 16 August 1940.

do and mend' threw renewed emphasis on domestic skills such as sewing and knitting. Physically, too, town centres were changed, sometimes beyond recognition, by bomb damage. Even if you had the coupons, you could never entirely predict whether a shop would still be standing following an air raid. After a night spent scrambling to put out fires and aid the efforts of the rescue services and home defence, shopworkers frequently found themselves clearing rubble or setting up temporary shops in the morning.

Not all bombs fell during the night, either. At Debenhams in 1942 Celia Coomber recalled staff and shopper alike dropping behind the counters 'when a bomb shook the foundations, hurling merchandise and plaster in all directions. After what seemed ages, it was all over. I looked round, no-one was hurt. The silence was heavy as I got to my feet and peered through a cloud of dust mingled with the acid smell of explosive. I looked towards the open door, and heard the steady clopping of footsteps approaching along the arcade to the store entrance. The customer entered, stepped over a mound of debris, spotted me behind the haberdashery counter, and said: "good afternoon, may I have two yards of white baby ribbon please."'[76]

Post-war, it was difficult to get materials or personnel to rebuild. Walking the streets in the 1950s, you'd still pass by fenced-off craters and condemned buildings. Where shops were rebuilt, it was in a utilitarian style with minimal decoration because that was your only choice. However, the dust did settle, and after fourteen years of rationing you will understandably be eager to shake off the drabness of the immediate post-war world and embrace a bright new future. That included a new type of clothing shop.

Boutiques

By the 1950s ready-to-wear had triumphed, and clothing retailers had to work harder than ever, seeking new audiences or ways to spark interest in what were increasingly standardised items. Market segmentation was now recognised as vital, and marketing techniques and market research became increasingly sophisticated and integrated into the business of retail. The forefront of change was no longer on the high street though, where multiples jostled for attention and fought each other on price. In local shopping areas or in back streets, a new wave of design-led outlets started up aimed squarely at the burgeoning youth market, using all the tried-and-tested techniques of shop design and window display to create a buzz and get people to stop and look. Mary Quant's Bazaar on London's King's Road was one of the first and best known of what became known as boutiques. It opened in 1955, followed quickly by the equally iconic (to a certain generation) Biba. This was also the era of Terance Conran's Habitat, which opened in 1964. It was a genuinely new movement, though it had roots in earlier trends.

Wholesalers had sold clothing for teenagers since the 1930s, and, as we've seen, big shops had created departments for them. They were pretty staid, though, assuming the average teen shopped with his or her parent, and wasn't looking to dress in a massively different way. Now the new boutiques both recognised and helped to develop new markets, recognising that older teens and people in their early twenties wanted to look (and act) differently to their parents. The desire itself was not exactly new. However, the new wave of designers harnessed mass media to promote their goods – the popular young women's magazine *Jackie* had a regular column on local boutiques as they spread rapidly outside London – and their very visibility helped create the market they intended to sell to.

Fig. 6.10. Biba, Kensington Church Street, London, in 1965.
Reminiscences of boutique shoppers frequently dwell on the smell
of damp and condensation up the windows as customers crammed
themselves into tiny spaces clad in fully synthetic dresses. Hopefully
the incredible wallpaper and oh-so-cool clothing made up for it.

The emphasis of the boutiques was on transgression. Buzz
came through such things as paper dresses, drastically high
hemlines and flamboyant outfits for men. Vince's Man's Shop
in Carnaby Street emerged from a photography studio specialising in attractive men in cut-down M&S briefs. The briefs
proved so popular people started asking for them, and selling
underwear was less likely to attract police attention than the
photographs, which were intended for the gay scene, still officially illegal.[77] These were not working-class stores, despite their
emphasis on back-street locations, dismal changing-rooms and
reputation as actually selling quite low-quality goods. Bazaar's
dresses featured in *Vogue* and one pinafore cost more than three
weeks' wages for the average office worker.

Fig. 6.11. The make up counter at 'Big Biba', 1975, after its move into the former Derry & Toms on Kensington High Street with a complete refit in 1970s-meets-art-deco-kitsch. Despite attracting over a million customers (or, at least, visitors) a week, the venture, which was on a grand scale, very much a department store, lasted only three years before financial collapse.

However, the boutiques didn't stay small and edgy. By the 1960s Quant was manufacturing in large quantities, focused more on design than shops, and Biba opened its own big shop (known colloquially as 'Big Biba') in the former Derry & Toms in 1973 (it failed). More successful was Lewis Separates, a chain of womenswear shops which had come out of a wool shop in 1948. In 1965 they rebranded as Chelsea Girl, booming off the back of mini-dresses. The big shops quickly responded to the sales opportunities created by the boutiques as well, with their own, more mass-market iterations. Peter Robinson (by now owned by Burton's) launched Top Shop in 1964, and Selfridges countered with Miss Selfridge in 1966.[78] The model for boutique owners became one of emerge, expand – and in most cases sell out and retire.[79]

If the damp from a dank basement fitting room is making you wince, perhaps it's time for a pause. Let's assume you are young and have a bit of cash in your pocket. Maybe you want to meet a friend to discuss whether you should splash out on a dress or be wise and buy a sewing pattern and fabric instead. Maybe you're meeting a potential boyfriend or girlfriend away from the prying eyes of your parents. Let's head to one of the newer refreshment venues on the high street, for a frothy, flavoured milkshake, or, if you prefer, a continental-style coffee.

The milk bar

Milk bars started to appear on British high streets in the early 1930s. They were inspired by an Australian concept, itself part of a concerted effort to market milk to the masses. In the UK, they were promoted by the Milk Marketing Board, but were run independently. In Wales, farmer Robert Griffiths started a chain called the National Milk Bars, while in London Australian entrepreneur Hugh McIntosh borrowed the name of an Australian chain to found Black and White. They took off very quickly, partly because they built on the existing craze for soda fountains, an American import of the early twentieth century, but which was starting to lose steam. Some milk bars were the epitome of art deco cool: the show bar at the Milk Marketing Board's Ideal Home stand in Belfast was 'decorated in pastel blue and of contemporary design'.[80] This was deliberately at odds with much of the sensory overload of the rest of the high street. Others were less startling, often by necessity. In Diss, Norfolk, the former Star Inn on the Market Place became a milk bar in 1951, the proprietors simply moving into an existing pub.[81] Northern iterations seemed to specialise in 'gritty'. In

milk-cum-snack-bar Ron's in Manchester, 'there was no atmosphere in there at all other than a bit of steam that came out
of the tea and coffee making machines. But we thought it was
wonderful.'[82]

While in their purest form milk bars sold milk and milk-
shakes, most offered other things, especially during the milk
restrictions of the Second World War. In Black and White you
could buy soup, while in the newly opened Ulster milk bar in
1959 'you can also buy your cakes and home-made bread' (further competition for the poor bakers).[83] Other milk bars shared
premises with cafés or other catering outlets. In 1953 Hazel's
milk bar in Leominster advertised 'a good cup of tea', along
with light refreshments and ice cream, and shared an address
with Nell's fish café. It also did lunches, rather strongly suggesting it was really a tea room, rebranded to appeal to a wider
market. One of its selling points was an adjacent car park.[84]

The main market for milk bars was the under-25s. In the
1930s they flocked to milk bars, driving the number of outlets
up from around 530 in 1936 to 1,475 in 1938.[85] After a pause
during the war, openings resumed in the 1950s, with late-night
closing times attracting people coming back from the cinema
or off to a dance. Milk bars were recognised as providing a
much-needed venue for young people to meet and 'feel their
own way toward adult life', in a relatively safe environment
which, importantly, did not sell alcohol.[86]

High streets were already established locations for the young
to meet. York's Coney Street was one of many, particularly
northern, high streets which became renowned for its 'monkey
runs' on a Sunday when shops were closed, and smartly dressed
youngsters gathered to parade, flirt and generally show off and
have fun. Milk bars were a natural extension of this, and rather
more practical in inclement weather. However, for a minority
they became associated with another side of the sudden upsurge
in youth culture, which was the rivalry between gangs charac-

terised by the much-publicised mods and rockers fighting of the 1960s. In 1958 one correspondent to the *Arbroath Guide* complained of 'the incessant use of the main streets of the town, especially between the hours of 9.30pm and midnight, by the Milk Bar Cowboys, who ride up and down on noisy, evil-smelling, spluttering construction of bedlam to the tune of "no-one will sleep tonight".'[87] Around the same time, two new trends hit the high street: Italian coffee and American fast food.

By the early 1960s, milk bars were adding espressos to their menus and converting into coffee bars. Out went transom windows and tiles, in came asymmetry and huge, all-glass fronts, revealing monster Gaggia coffee machines (or, more often, smaller, cheaper models), and bright, plastic-covered everything. In Leeds, Bettys of Harrogate (it lost its apostrophe

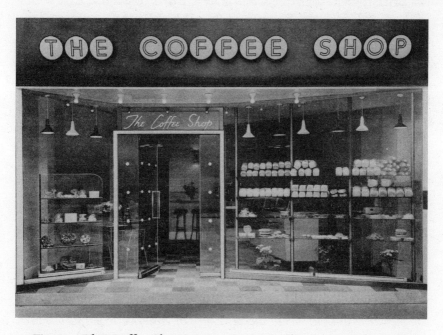

Fig. 6.12. The Coffee Shop, Street Lane, Leeds, 1955. Inside was a gleaming Italian coffee machine, along with colourful floor tiles and jazzy wallpaper.

in the early 1960s) opened an (unbranded) modern coffee shop on a suburban arcade in Roundhay, with owner Victor Wild forecasting that rising rates would push all but the highest turnover businesses off high streets, and that small towns and suburbs would be the next big thing. Down in Southsea, the Savoy holiday camp hedged its bets, advertising a milk bar, espresso bar and a Wimpy Hamburger Bar. The latter, the first branch of which had been opened in a Lyons Corner House in 1954, was an American franchise that became synonymous with fast food in Britain during the 1960s.

America was cool, America was full of meat (1954 was the last year of meat rationing in the UK) and its influence was everywhere on the high street – Wimpy was just the most obvious sign of it for British consumers. That said, it can be overplayed, for British teenagers freely adapted the bits of America they fancied, and disregarded those which didn't fit. An alternative to Wimpy was the Spaghetti House, with its unforgettable slogan 'spaghetti, but not on toast', which tells you as much about the state of British food at the time as it does about the menu in its many outlets.

Had your milky beverage? Feeling fortified? Let's go and buy an item sorely missed for much of the war. Sweets came off the ration in 1949 – only to go on again four months later as pent-up demand caused a buying frenzy. In 1953 restrictions finally fully ended. Whether you're after chocolate confectionery or simple boiled sweets, the obvious place to go is a sweet shop, but the choice, as with so much of your shopping list, is very broad now.

Since we've smelt the burgers at the hamburger bar, let's consider another type of shop where the influence of America is paramount. In retail speak, they're known by the American term 'variety store', but it's hardly a term in everyday use in Britain. Instead, you might once have called them penny bazaars, though by now they much prefer you to say 'superstore'. Realistically, like your local big store, you probably know them by their actual name. Let's just name them then: Woolworth's and Marks & Spencer.

The superstore

Walking down the high street in the 1950s you'd have a choice of shops falling into the category of variety store. Woolworth's (invariably shortened to Woolies) was dominant in numerical terms, mainly because its business strategy involved much smaller towns than its competitors, and so you'd find its shops anywhere with a population of more than 3,000 people.[88] It was an American chain, founded by F. W. Woolworth in 1879 and by now operating several hundred five-and-dime stores. When the first British iteration opened in Liverpool in 1909, it was as a shop offering goods only at 3d and 6d. The chain came with an established way of doing business, an established look and feel, and a red and gold colour scheme which it retained for nearly the next hundred years. Its success fed into a fascination with American ways of organising retail which would see many of the owners and managers of leading British shops head off on fact-finding tours of the States, bringing the latest American trends back with them. Some worked, leading to efficiencies on the shop floor and comfort for the customer: others failed to fully account for the very different geography and social culture of the UK, and were slower to take off.

Woolworth's was emphatically not a department store, for it had centralised buying and its stores were open plan, the different sales areas marked out by numbers or signs for both customer and shelf-stacking convenience. Nor was its great home-grown rival, Marks & Spencer, which worked on a similar model. We've met M&S before, first as a stall on Leeds Kirkgate market and then as a chain of successful penny bazaars spilling out of their fixed premises. By the 1920s their bazaars had windows and doors and counters and all the other things that made shops into shops. A green and gold colour scheme was introduced in 1924, and the St Michael label for their own-brand goods appeared in 1928.

Competition for both chains came from the Domestic Bazaar Company until their demise in 1935, then Littlewoods when they started opening shops from 1937, as well as British Home Stores (BHS), founded in 1928 with the explicit purpose of becoming a mass market multiple.[89] Additionally, there were smaller local independent shops, selling all sorts of things, to all sorts of people – as long as their primary motivation was price.

All these stores were marked out by their approach to buying, their shopfloor layout, and their determination to sell to the working classes based on value for money. M&S shifted its focus slightly up the social scale in reaction to the spread of Woolies, appealing more to the lower middle class. It also became slightly more specialist, known increasingly for food and clothing. It dropped the pre-Great War 'don't ask the price – it's a penny' slogan, expanding its range both in terms of goods and price. Nevertheless, the owners remained focused on maintaining a broad appeal. Israel Sieff, chair of M&S from 1964, commented, 'we answered the people's prayer. The prayer for goods at prices which even in their days of impoverishment they could just about afford to buy. Not all of them, God knows. But what we had to offer was within reach of most of them. To the others, beyond the pale of purchasing power, we held out what we could.'[90]

As costs went up, M&S's strategy was less hobbling: Woolies found itself in the awkward position of having to sell single socks and pans separately to lids in order to stay under its self-set fixed price limit.[91] On the other hand, it was so ubiquitous that it became a synonym for a particular type of shopper. In one of the most poignant scenes in Nevil Shute's *Ruined City* (1938), in an echo of numerous recessions to come, the protagonist, recovering from a nervous breakdown, walks down the main street of the fictitious town of Sharples where 'the shops were mostly small and unpretentious; a great number of them were unoccupied, with windows boarded up. He passed by two closed banks. On a fine corner site an extensive store was shuttered and deserted. On the facade above the windows he traced the outline letters of the sign that had been taken down, and realised he was standing in a town that could no longer support Woolworth's.'[92]

You'd feel a sense of recognition as you approached both M&S and Woolies. Both went in for a house style, though Woolies was more inclined towards a bit of art deco stonework and lots of red brick, while M&S was more often grey or beige stone and stripped-back regularity. Both had ground-floor windows with blocked-out transoms, or sometimes a solid pelmet curtain, which disguised the electric lighting used to light up the windows. Pictures of 1930s Woolies show windows not that far removed from the more daring displays of the previous century. Handkerchiefs dangle invitingly from boards, arrayed like folded chessboard squares, while stockings are splayed on dismembered legs or wooden shapes, forming a sun's rays in silk and, later, nylon. Many shops had cafés, or even American-style cafeterias. In Bristol the Woolworth's 'self-service restaurant' seated 1,000 people. Puff pieces in the local press extolled the employment of local firms for building work and the jobs created in store.[93] This was a time when pro-British sentiment ran high, and all the cheaper superstores made much of their patriotism, sourcing around 80–90 per cent of their goods from Britain.[94]

Inside, shops were open plan. Before you get properly inside, if it's a Woolworth's, look for the weighing machine in the lobby – scales were rare in homes, so this was not only useful but fun, and very popular. You might have gone in for one thing, but it was easy to get distracted: the layout facilitated it. From the sweet counter, you'd be able to see right across the store – it's why they were known as 'superstores'.

Even in 1913 the Derby Woolworth's stocked 'sweets, toilet goods, haberdashery, stationery, ironmongery, as well as mantles, burners, and globes and all articles in connection with incandescent gas lighting. Other special lines are ewers, basins, large jardinieres, umbrellas, ladies' velvet slippers, vases, a choice compartment of pictures and electroplated goods; jewellery, celluloid goods, and all kind of fancy and useful articles too numerous to classify.'[95] You could also buy pets (tortoises were apparently 'good for killing beetles and insects'), toys, photography equipment, gramophone records, gardening supplies, cosmetics and food.[96] Competition was thus set up with the grocers, the pharmacists, the fancy goods shops, the furnishing shops, the stationers, ironmongers, jewellers – you name it. From 1935, Woolies competed directly with bookshops, stocking books from the newly launched Penguin imprint, which was launched explicitly to sell good books at cheap prices, enabling the working classes to afford education and entertainment without relying on a library. Proving that some people hadn't moved on from the 1750s, one commentator declared that 'novel reading is now largely a drug habit'.[97]

Concentrate on the sweets you came in for, which you'll find displayed on a horseshoe or rectangular counter with space in the middle enclosing the shop assistant. Unlike most things in the store, they were sold loose. In Sunderland in 1931 you could choose from 'buttered brazils, chocolate-covered dates, Pontefract cakes, marshmallows, assorted toffees, mint imperials, marzipan, teacakes, orange and lemon slices, nougat, Fry's chocolate cream bars, and all kinds of liquorice, the pipes were particularly popular. One end of the counter was devoted to salted nuts and raisins. Everything had to be weighed out on small brass scales and most people bought in 2oz or 4oz categories [55g or 115g].'[98] You'd then expect the woman behind the counter to tot it all up using pen and paper before ringing it into the tills.

Woolies staff were smartly turned out, wearing uniform from the 1940s – maroon for most of the staff, hygienic-looking white overalls for confectionery. They had to be alert, for casual pilfering was rampant, despite the low glass barrier on the customer side of the counter. One of the key selling points of variety stores was the encouragement of actual handling, not merely asking for goods and having them taken out and arranged for your viewing pleasure. It was novel, exciting and led to massive crowds. When the Southend Woolworth's opened in 1932, 'at nine o'clock, with fast beating hearts and eyes wide open, we watched the big swing doors swung aside. In rushed customers, sightseers and competitors, all intent on finding out . . . what we had to offer in this new wonder which had taken place before their eyes.' Half the population of York went through the doors of either Woolies, M&S or BHS over one busy weekend in 1936, with Seebohm Rowntree commenting that such shops offered 'a range of goods far wider than was available to them before, and sold in many cases at prices noticeably lower than those charged elsewhere'.[99] It was fast and furious. Assistants didn't proffer help unless asked.

By the 1950s, shop layouts were changing. The latest American import was self-service, which was born back in 1916 in the American grocery chain Piggly Wiggly. In Britain, fresh from a trip to the States, David Grieg tried the concept in one of his multiple grocery stores. One-way turnstiles enforced a customer route through the store, with high shelving units and counters holding goods to be picked up and paid for at a staffed checkout at the end. It wasn't unsuccessful, but was hardly the gamechanger it proved to be in America.[100] Other stores dipped in and out over the next couple of decades, most notably several

Fig. 6.13. Marks & Spencer, Southampton, 1952. Instantly recognisable as an M&S due to the company's established house style, stores like this were present on every major British high street by the 1950s. Unusually, and despite some ups and downs, the chain is still going.

branches of the Co-op. M&S introduced it in their Wood Green store in 1948. At Bentalls, another of the stunts to pique the public interest in the 1930s had been the 'packeteria – the shop of 1950'. It was all self-service, with a woman taking the money at the end and dispensing change via a machine.[101] But 1950 came and went, and self-service remained rare. Even by 1959 Woolworth's only had sixty-two self-service stores. The then chair damned it with faint praise: 'whilst many shoppers do not take readily to this mode of selling, they seem to accept it after a while.'[102]

Other types of shop, however, were determined to press forward with self-service, most notably the grocers, some of whom, by the late 1950s, were also operating super-sized shops. In their case, the name was slightly different, not 'superstore', but 'supermarket', for that, along with small high street grocers and specialised food shops, was the main thing they replaced.

But even they struggled to persuade people that self-service was the next big thing. In 1950 a woman threw her wire basket back at Alan Sainsbury, then managing director of the family firm, when he offered it to her as she entered the store. Despite celebrations over the demise of the pushy shopwalkers a mere thirty years ago, a lot of people still wanted personal service: they just wanted it on their terms.

Agatha Christie spoke for more than a few people when she set out the changing high street in the fictional town of St Mary Mead in 1962, describing the fishmonger with his 'new super windows behind which the refrigerated fish gleamed', and the relief with which the lady shoppers entered the small grocer, 'so *obliging*, comfortable chairs to sit in by the counter, and cosy discussions as to cuts of bacon, and varieties of cheese'. But there was also 'a glittering new supermarket – anathema to the elderly ladies of St Mary Mead'. Its wares included 'packets

Fig. 6.14. An early venture into self-service at Woolworth's in Cobham, Surrey, in 1955. This was a new store, designed specifically for the new concept.

of things one's never even heard of', such as breakfast cereal, while 'you're expected to take a basket yourself and go round looking for things – it takes quarter of an hour sometimes to find all one wants – and usually made up in inconvenient sizes, too much or too little, and then a long queue waiting to pay as you go out'.[103] Jane Marple's friends associated this kind of depersonalised shopping with the working classes and looked down upon it. Slowly, though, the supermarkets (including the Co-op) forced a change: from 6,000 self-service stores in 1960, to over 20,000 in 1966.[104]

Today, the meaning of self-service has changed again: from simply picking your own goods, to scanning and paying for them as well. Introduced in the late 1990s, self-scan tills of various types were enthusiastically seized upon as a cost-cutting measure by many supermarkets (and other chain retailers) in the 2010s and 2020s, with around 27,000 installed between 2019 and 2023 alone. Like the first iteration of self-service, they are divisive – around two-thirds of shoppers say they loathe them – and in 2023 upmarket supermarket Booths announced they were rolling back on their use. Others, however, continue to install them.[105]

By the mid-1960s all the pieces were in place for the modern high street. Chain stores, which increasingly included the larger department stores, rubbed shoulders with independent traders, both big and large. The more ambitious shopkeepers aimed to open a boutique, become fashionable, expand and sell the concept, which would then be replicated across the country. At a street level in the busiest of areas, the names on the shopfronts, and the designs of the shops, became ever less locally unique. The goods within them could be equally identikit, meaning a person in Inverness could buy the same frock, and eat the same tinned mock turtle soup, off the same dinner service, as their counterpart in Truro, in Swansea or in Colchester. Additionally, while the casual shopper barely noticed, a few companies were starting to buy up multiple multiples, chopping and changing them to suit their changing audiences.

In the next chapter we'll move away from individual types of shop, for there's just too much choice now when it comes to buying any one item. The time of high street shopping has peaked, for, although it will take time for people to desert their butchers and bakers for self-service in a supermarket, or come to enjoy meeting friends in shopping centres off a grid-locked outer ring road, those changes are already upon us. Very soon we'll be in the townscapes we call home.

For now, though, don't think about the futuristic shopping precinct being constructed on top of a once-favoured shop or café. Dawdle a little, watching the lights flicker on as the shops are locked from within. Few now have shutters across the whole shopfront, though you'll hear a series of rattles as the metal roller blinds over the entry points clank into place. The shops are all shut by 6pm, apart from one permitted late night a week. Opening hours were once more restricted during the Second World War, despite the howls of dismay from the men's tailoring shops, whose clientele largely came in on weekdays and after work, and they've never really gone back. For now, Sundays remain sacrosanct, along with an early closing day once a week. Thursday night late opening will stay until the 2010s, when falling demand will see it quietly disappear.

Western Road, Brighton, 1971 [106]

Like so many towns in this book, Brighton has ancient origins, with its status recognised by its market charter in 1313. For centuries it was little more than a busy hub for fishing and farming, though Canon Place, at the town end of Western Road, hints at its time as part of the defence network against invasion from France.

In the eighteenth century it became a leisure resort, its reputation boosted by the Prince of Wales (later George IV) who commissioned the Royal Pavilion, which has been a tourist attraction since the mid-nineteenth century. Brighton is full of late Georgian and early Victorian terraces and squares, once highly exclusive but long since divided into flats. In 1971 the town's economy is based on tourism. However, it's got a reputation for boisterousness, to say the least. In the 1930s it was gangs, and more recently the mods and rockers hit the headlines fighting on the seafront. Keith Waterhouse says, 'Brighton looks like a town that is constantly helping police with its enquiries.' But the town also has a reputation for openness and youth, despite the high proportion of retirees. The University of Sussex has been here since 1961, and the number of students has tripled in the last decade. While some might mutter that they are all dope-smoking hippies, they've brought a vibrancy to the streets – look out for Rag Week parades if you're walking up this street at the start of the academic year. You might also have been drawn here by the town's gay scene for in 'no other European city is homosexuality so open and apparently so tolerated'.[107]

Let's start at the Hove end of Western Road. The street was once full of houses with gardens backing on to the road, and you can clearly see the way in which the gardens were infilled

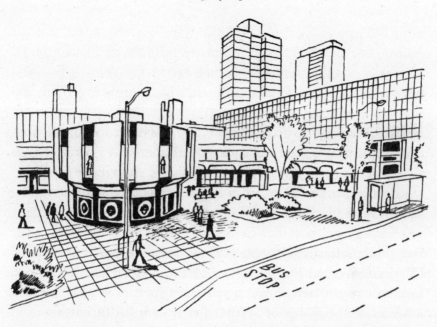

in the late nineteenth century. This part of the road is narrow and busy with buses and cars, though restrictions on the latter will be introduced in just a few years' time.

From where you're standing, the different sides of the road seem to sum up 1970s Brighton. On the right, numbers 95–99, is department store Plummer Roddis, known for 'Vogue, Value and Variety'. It's a bizarre set of buildings, part Regency-terrace, part-Gothic extravaganza, with one end housing an orangerie-esque first-floor restaurant which hosts mannequin parades every day at 3pm. Despite having a strong regional reputation, it's actually owned by Debenhams and will be rebranded as such next year. Opposite at no 130 is the Curzon cinema, its art deco front recently updated in a more modern style. Then comes Waitrose, opened in 1966 as 'Brighton's biggest food store'. In total contrast to the crenellations and carefully styled displays opposite, Waitrose has a totally blank wall above its shopfront, and its windows are open to the store. It keeps expanding, and there's not much hope for the carpet and furniture shop next door. Wimpy might hold out, though – it's very popular, with its burgers and benders ('the meaty frankfurter') – combined with proper table service. Further up on the same side you'll find various clothing shops, including Southwind's for 'ski and sea wear', plus a chemist, tobacconist/newsagent and a dry cleaner. There's also a tea dealer – and the entrance to Codrington Mansion, a typical Georgian townhouse now converted into flats. On the right, shoe shops and a fabric shop jostle for attention with Coxhead Rentals and Lyon & Hall, both advertising electrical goods for sale and hire-purchase.

Keep going, past the twin banks with their classical stone fronts (actually 1920s) facing off against each other at number 86 (National Westminster) and 142 (Barclays). Both have additional branches in the new shopping precinct further up. There's also a Midland at number 80 – you can't miss it because it, too, has columns and rusticated stonework, plus some slightly baroque flourishes. Banks are always obvious. Before you get there, yet more shoes (this street has so many shoe shops). Norvic Foot Fitters are particularly good for kids and give out 'fitter feet' badges to those who've gone through their rigorous width and length measuring process.

As you pass Preston Street on the right (you can see the sea at the bottom), the street widens out, thanks to various initiatives of the 1930s. It's this bit which was described in 1953 as 'Oxford Street-by-the-sea'. The buildings reflect the era in which they were (purpose) built. On the left, number 143 is about as art deco as it gets. It's been a wine and beer shop for ages. At only three storeys high, it's stuck rather strangely on to the enormous bulk of Mitre House, a block of flats built in the mid-1930s for the International Tea Stores. They're still there, but now share the ground-floor shop space with Timothy White's, which since being taken over by Boots three years ago now seems to mainly sell housewares. There's also Kendall's rainwear specialists, relocated from the top of the street in 1968.

Pause and admire the Jaguars, Triumphs and Rolls Royces in Moore's of Brighton's showroom before coming to the more mundane surrounds of W. H. Smith. Just before Spring Street you'll find your first boutiques, Richard Sport and Diversion. If you prefer something more mainstream, Peter Robinson used to have most of the block opposite, but half of it is now Burton's, which they own. The shop is shortly to include 'Mr Burt,' a range of 'high fashion menswear'. Bet you can't wait.

If you failed to get something to eat earlier, thank goodness for Lyons and the Long John Eating House, some of the rare catering outlets not inside bigger shops. Lyons has a lovely bay window on the first floor – good for people-watching. The buildings here are quite monotonous, so concentrate on the floral prints in the window at Dorothy Perkins or the flares further down at Snob, another of the six boutiques on the street. You've got another electrical hire shop, two shoe shops and a jeweller here as well. However, the left-hand side of the road is more interesting, for it is a vast Boots, built in a neo-classical style in 1927 and looking more like a temple than a chemist shop. The library, café and post office it used to have closed a few years ago.

Past Dean Street on the left and there's Bewlay's tobacconist, with its smoking lounge interior fully visible past the paraphernalia displayed on elegant shelves in the window. Another footwear shop is next to it and then Fine Wear, proudly declaring itself a 'departmental store' in that year's trade directory. All three shops occupy a slightly fussy building which used to be Stafford's hardware emporium. The right side still has S monograms on the decorative stone shields at the top. Opposite lies the bulk of the Times Furnishing store and then the ILA (Irish Linen Association) Man's Shop. By next year it will be the more prosaic Just Pants. This side of the street is now mainly smaller units, and a mix of chains and independent traders, some of which have been here for decades: a furrier,

Maynards sweet shop and then Baxter's clothing shop on the corner of Clarence Gardens. A sign in the window proclaims, 'big men, we can fit you'. Try not to be alarmed by the floating male pelvises clad in Y-fronts up the arcaded entryway.

The left-hand side is quite a contrast. Last year C&A replaced BHS in a big, American-influenced store which still has a winged crest and the BHS logo in stone on the front. Over the side street from them is Johnson's, a department store specialising in household goods. Another 1930s-built big shop, it will be gutted by fire in November following what is rumoured to be an unfortunate firework-related incident. Rebuilding won't be complete for another year, when it will reopen in what could kindly be called a flamboyant statement of modern architecture. It'll be a bit out of place (to say the least), but on the other hand, the 1930s buildings were probably shockingly modern at the time. Pass on quickly, to see what bargains are being advertised in the window of Woolworth's. Then you've got a couple of gown shops, Brighton being very much a place for eveningwear. One used to be an M&S, but it was just too small.

Cross Regent Hill, and you've yet another large 1930s department store, Wades. You can't miss it, for it has a vertical sign, cinema-style, on the outside. It's best known for its Christmas grotto. Then – how many shoe shops does a single street need?! – Freeman Hardy & Willis and Saxone, plus the Singer sewing machine outlet.

At this point you have a choice. You can head to the safety and predictability of Marks & Spencer, now calling themselves a departmental store, in their enormous building on the left. Four years ago its 1930s front was reclad in prefabricated cement squares. Brutal, but it sort of works. Dolcis shoes, H. Samuel jewellers and a couple of other clothing shops are beyond it. Or you can take a left into the Imperial Arcade, built in – you've guessed it – the 1930s, and which holds a toyshop, a baker and a florist, among others. If you keep going through and then look back, the end fronting North Street looks a bit like a ship. Your alternative is to cross the road and enter Brighton's latest, rather controversial, development, Churchill Square.

Back in 1935 the Corporation decided it needed a new shopping area, conveniently coinciding with the first wave of slum clearances. War and squabbling over the scale of the plans put the thing on hold, but the first phase was finally opened in 1968.

It's got lots of good things including a multi-storey car park, civic centre and a leisure venue which is currently called the Brighton Top Rank Centre and has bowling lanes and an ice rink. It is very much of the now, but by 2008 its aluminium roof and entirely windowless exterior (on the seafront – what were they thinking?) will be described as 'intrusively aggressive'.[108]

On the Western Road side there's a space-age round building with a café, and lots of well-used benches. Buskers and beggars come here too. The shopping centre is, of course, concrete, with an arched canopy providing shelter. You'll find BHS here now, as well as Habitat. It is nearly all chains. However, the real draw is Tesco and J. Sainsbury. The former has a dedicated following for its hot pies. There's also a 30ft (9m) sculpture called the 'Spirit of Brighton'. It's a concrete nightmare, conceived of as a 'piece of fun' that was supposed to be covered in plants but never quite got there. Mainly it serves as a dare for enterprising children, who like to climb it.

It's worth spending some time here, enjoying the precinct in its heyday. Give it eighteen years, and the local press will call the development a 'disgrace to the town', describing the end of a shopping trip in robust terms: 'The stench of urine hits you smack in the face as you descend the graffiti-scrawled stairwell. Even in daytime the dimly-lit car park is dank and menacing, full of black corners and shadows.'[109] The last shop will close in 1993 and the whole thing will be replaced by an indoor mall a few years later.

Chapter Seven

Beyond the 1960s

Shopping in this country, as no doubt in many others, is not for many women one of those chores to be done as quickly and easily as possibly. Shopping is more than buying an article, and it is difficult to see any substantial alteration in this state of affairs even though, as a nation, we are becoming more scientific in the house as well as the factory.[1]

– Wilfred Burns, *British Shopping Centres* (1959)

This book is concerned primarily with the period between the 1650s and the 1960s, during which, as we've seen, the idea of a shopping-focused high street as a place for leisure and pleasure emerged, developed, and reached its apogee. By the middle of the 1960s the mixed-use high street that had slowly developed over the previous three centuries was not only fully established, but fully embraced. Seventy-eight per cent of Britain's 55 million population lived in urban areas, a figure that would rise to around 85 per cent – of 67 million people – by 2020.[2]

So what happened next? How did we move from what seems to be a time of busy, thriving high streets to today, when the phrase high street is hardly uttered without being attached to ominous words like 'death' and 'decline'?

Some or all the decades covered in this chapter will be ones you have lived through. We'll start as the late 1960s turn to the 1970s, when an era of political stability and relative affluence turned to a time best known for industrial action in Britain, along with a global oil crisis, the combination of which led to a three-day working week, as power was rationed. Bin bags piled up in previously tidy town squares as refuse collectors joined the strikes, and inflation was such that, in Yorkshire, Bettys' staff took to writing the changing prices on the menus instead of having them constantly reprinted. Britain became known as 'the sick man of Europe'.

If the 1970s seems ridiculously far away, how about the 1980s? Known for Thatcherism, more strikes, and the ongoing Irish Troubles, which spilled out to include an IRA bomb attack at Harrods. Culturally this was the time when consumerism was celebrated, ushering in big, bright fashion in the form of shoulder pads and gravity-defying hairdos, plus yuppies on big phones, and people in leotards and legwarmers stepping up to the beat of an aerobics class.

In 1997, eighteen years of Tory government collapsed in one of the biggest landslides ever, and 'Cool Britannia' was ushered in on a wave of optimism as the new millennium approached. London was reborn as a major fashion destination, the Union Jack was printed on cushions and doormats, and the UK won the Eurovision Song Contest for the first time since 1981. The internet slowly took off, and DVDs were launched, just one of a burgeoning range of must-have consumer goods which, after the Millennium Bug failed to wipe out anything, grew to encompass mobile phones, laptops and, by the 2010s, personal fitness trackers.

However, amid the explosion in things to buy (and much cleverer ways to sell them), came the first inklings of the impact all of this was having on the planet. Some people had been shouting about it for decades: the first Earth Day was held in 1970, and environmentalists had been trying to point out the problems in agriculture for years. In 1997 the Great Pacific Garbage Patch was discovered, a massive area of ocean filled with plastic, both large and microscopic, which won't break down, and for which nobody will take responsibility (it isn't in any country's coastal waters – though there is a clean-up effort, directed by an international not-for-profit foundation).[3] Plastics were a very obvious issue, and by the 2000s some countries were starting to restrict the use of plastic bags – but this was the tip of the iceberg. By the 2010s the ethics of shopping were once more a hot topic, from packaging to production methods. Food and fashion – the mainstays of the high street – came under particular scrutiny, though even in 2023 only 53 per cent of fashion shoppers said they saw sustainability as important, skewed, unsurprisingly, towards younger people whose lives will be lived in the shadow of what is now recognised as a major climate crisis.[4]

We don't have a shopping list in this chapter, because most of the elements we're looking at aren't really on the high street. Our imagined shopper is very real – it's you. And if you did have a list, it would be personal, though I can make some suggestions. Depending on the decade, you might be in the market for an electric hostess trolley or a fondue set; a bum bag or a scrunchie (whether this is the 1980s or the 2020s I leave to your imagination). Perhaps you want a Sony Walkman, a discman, an iPod, or the latest in bone conduction headphones; or maybe you're seeking avocados, a French stick, plantain, baklava, or an organic poke bowl.

The changing town

Changes to planning laws were one of the key factors in the shifting high street. Retail was seen by authorities as a way to raise revenue through local rates, and so more shops were to be encouraged. Where previously it was left to multiple traders to weigh up the benefits of opening an outlet within a certain distance of an existing one, now councils started to work with retailers as they vied with each other to transform their town into a serious shopping centre. With the growth of motor cars, the catchment area for each urban centre grew, and competition between towns inevitably led to smaller high streets losing out as every town of any size seemed to sprout a new purpose-built shopping centre and ring road. Most shoppers were as unaware of the underlying processes affecting the physical surroundings of the high street as their ancestors, but the rebuilding of town centres in an effort to attract more shops was hard to miss.

The brutalist architecture of the 1960s and 1970s gets a harsh press, but at the time designers were determined to move away from the mistakes of the past – the slums, the lack of amenities, the tiny rooms, the grandstanding. Architect Basil Spence admitted, 'not all this newness will succeed. But it is far better that some of it should fail and people should try than we should continue copying past styles paradoxically called traditional. Modern architecture is as exciting as any adventure in history for it looks straight into the future, not backwards.'[5] The results could be breathtaking: Plymouth's Armada Way remains a triumph of post-war architecture (though it's not to everyone's taste). However, it's fair to say that the enthusiasm for opening up cities to cars and capitalising on the rebuilding opportunities opened up by bomb damage did go too far. In Blackburn, one journalist lamented that 'the bulldozers will cut out its heart and replace [it with] a supermarket, tear out its soul and substitute escalators'.[6]

The process was hotly debated, with those in favour of preserving old buildings and safeguarding communities pitted against others who adored living in their newly constructed suburbs, and accused their opponents of wanting to hamper the economy and force living standards to remain squalid. Some of the developments that resulted from the shift in emphasis from individual traders to local authorities were truly awful. In King's Lynn the Vancouver Centre was described by *Private Eye* as follows:

> Everything that the shopper could want lends itself in this tasteful development – rubbish spirals daintily across the windy expanses of concrete pavement – small bricked pig troughs display miniature shrubs at a convenient height for dogs and a set of gay flag poles pierce the Norfolk sky to give a yacht-club ambience. White plastic purpose-built interlocking fencing is supposed to surround the car park

but most of it lies splintered on the ground due to fierce sea breezes and runaway supermarket trolleys.[7]

More problematically for the established high street, the demolition of historic streets erased centuries of established ways of navigating the urban environment. While on the face of things any subsequent disorientation might only last at most a single generation, the redrawing of maps could easily leave established businesses or facilities isolated and inadvertently cause the decline, not merely of businesses, but of the areas around them.

Other 1960s experiments in town planning were more welcome. Over in Norwich, a collapsed sewer led to the closure of London Street for six weeks in 1965. Initial outcry from the shopkeepers who traded from the street quickly turned to pressure to keep it shut to cars. London Street was narrow, winding, and full of shops with lavish window displays that required stopping and looking at to fully appreciate. In 1966 it was pedestrianised for good, one of the earliest shopping streets to be closed to traffic. Every street we've walked down thus far is now partially or fully pedestrianised (though Bath and Brighton are open to buses all day).

Supermarkets

We've seen how supermarkets developed out of the multiple grocers' shops, expanding their range of products along with the size of their stores and slowly adopting self-service. Throughout the 1960s and 1970s they were still mainly situated on high streets, and even after the move to out-of-town locations, most town centres retained one or more supermarkets. As with other stores that focused on everyday goods, they were rarely in the most prestigious part of the main shopping area, but to one side, where there was space to build a bigger shop, with a car park. Space was a real issue, and while it was possible in some cases to adapt an existing building – in Maldon Tesco took over a former cinema – the need for parking and potential for expansion posed problems.[8] They were often anchor tenants in the new shopping precincts, or, especially in smaller towns, were built at one end of a small arcade joining parking facilities to the more established high street. Unlike the elegant edifices of the interwar multiples, intent upon beautifying the townscape while also declaring their own grand ambitions, these were deliberately utilitarian, reflecting the major selling points of the new breed of big grocer: price and convenience. Hence the blank upper walls, the stripped-back design features, and a new approach to convincing customers to stop, look and enter.

Walking past a supermarket (or a Woolworth's or an M&S) in the late 1960s, you'd have been struck by the sheer level of shop on display. All those solid-backed windows with exuberant shows of bread and stockings and saucepans, draped tastefully in swathes of brightly coloured fabric, were now just so pre-war. Even by the early 1960s some shopkeepers were taking down the backing boards, so that you could look through displays and see inside the shops. Now, with the introduction of toughened glass, it was possible to have true pavement-to-ceiling windows. For those stores that were pushing self-service, seeing inside was a crucial way to demystify the concept. For a population used to being served at a counter, showing a brightly lit, attractive shop interior full of exciting goods placed so that they could leisurely examine them was a vital way to overcome resistance to this new way of shopping. The idea that you could take a box from a shelf, read its ingredients and then put it back if you didn't want it was still novel, and the etiquette of self-selection uncertain. Those chains that had introduced it produced helpful pamphlets explaining the process to curious housewives, while TV

Fig. 7.1. Counter service at Sainsbury's in Golders Green, 1958.

Fig. 7.2. Sainsbury in Pinner, 1966. To the left of the door is the new self-service extension, with a view directly into the store, while to the right is the old shop with more conventional window displays. The sign advertises vacancies for women cashiers and display assistants.

adverts featured reassuring male assistants in clinically efficient brown or white coats.

The new-build supermarkets of the 1960s onwards were almost all self-service and, as the days of counter service waned, shoppers did, indeed, grow used to it. According to a Gallup poll in 1968, 60 per cent of the entire grocery market was now in self-service shops (not all of them multiples). But old habits died hard. The last Sainsbury's with counter service didn't close until in 1982 – the same year checkout scanning came in.[9]

The 1970s were a key decade for the rise of the supermarkets. It was driven in part by a grudging acceptance that this was the new way of shopping, and in part by a genuine enthusiasm for it. It is very easy to imbue older ways of shopping with nostalgia, and to consider a morning spent buying foodstuffs selected to order as time well spent, but for millions of women the hours spent trudging round the shops, week in, week out, were simply a chore to be dealt with. It's a simple fact that shopping for everything on the high street – as was the case for the majority of households prior to the 1970s – took time and effort, and was only possible through the unpaid labour of women or the delegation of shopping to paid servants.

Self-service promised liberation, and everything under one roof promised to free up time. One promotional film showed women frolicking in meadows, picnicking with their families, and dancing on feet that were neither worn out nor bunion-ridden from all of that tramping of pavements in ill-fitting shoes.[10] More and more women worked, but they were still expected to bear all the domestic burdens as well, including shopping. One woman explained in the late 1960s, 'when I did go back to work, that was when the supermarket was really handy. 'Cos I just didn't have time to do the cooking, because everything had to be made . . . from scratch. And you accepted it, that was what homemaking was about. But when you were at work you thought "can I have something quick".[11] And for every shopper who lamented the death of personal service, there was another who embraced the depersonalisation of buying flour and milk and greengrocer's goods, along with the enhanced agency open to the individual shopper. Journalist and restaurant critic Jay Rayner tells the tale of his father going to buy apples from a Soho market stall only to be fobbed off with dull fruit from under the display, rather than the beautiful examples upon it. Daring to query a decidedly sharp practice, he ended up in a brief verbal altercation and he walked off to the cry of 'suit yourself, you black-bearded, bollock-faced bastard' echoing in his ears.[12]

It isn't hard to see why the high street supermarket became popular. It wasn't (yet) the place to buy everything, though. Spend per head in 1968 remained low – 14 shillings on average (about £10 today). The first credit card was launched in 1966, but cash remained key for a long time to come. Most shoppers came on foot, shopping only for what they could carry, and did so several times a week.[13] All this changed over the next decade, as car ownership rose, along with things like fridges in homes. In the 1950s, fewer than 5 per cent of homes had had an electric fridge and Britain was described as a nation that 'regarded ice as only an inconvenience of wintertime and cold drinks as an American mistake'. Aggressive marketing on health and hygiene lines, emphasising that fridges (and freezers) weren't just for the wealthy to make trifle and ice cream, meant that by 1960, 50 per cent of homes had one and it steadily grew to over 90 per cent in the next few decades.[14] Now, not only could more people shop in larger quantities, but they could also store what they bought. Trolleys were introduced to cater for those who wanted to shop in bulk, complete from 1973 with baby seats after a spate of baby-nappings from the prams left under the characteristic canopies that indicated the entrance to the

Fig. 7.3. The first out-of-town supermarket in West Bridgford, Nottingham opened in 1964, and was almost the size of Trafalgar Square. Around 30,000 people visited on the opening weekend.

featureless front of the store. Plastic bags were introduced to enable the easier carrying of groceries from newly decimalised tills to the car.

The weekly grocery shop started to replace the not-quite daily one, and with it came out-of-town supermarkets, initially seen as a solution for getting car traffic out of congested town centres. The first to open, in 1964, was a branch of the American chain Gem, on the outskirts of Nottingham (it later became an Asda). Planning laws meant that companies had to get government permission for very large stores (over 50,000 ft² / 4645m², or about the size of four tennis courts). Most, therefore, hovered just under this size, until the bonfire of regulations which characterised the early 1980s. This was emphatically not the high street. It's been argued that the removal of food shopping from city centres was one of the most fundamental changes to the cityscape we've ever seen, and that supermarkets are at odds, not just with local high streets, but with the very concept of what a city is.[15] But concepts change.

Supermarkets are often blamed for killing high streets, and they undeniably had a hugely detrimental effect on some parts of it. By replacing markets, they drew would-be shoppers away from town centres, ending the age-old link between market day and the busiest day on the high street. When Morrisons started to expand from 1961 they made this link explicit with their 'market street' concept, where a vaguely high-street-esque format was applied to the in-store counters.[16] Those grocers that did not join the push to expand in size and number but opted to stay as smaller stores on the high street struggled. Lipton's had already merged with Home & Colonial, and now Maypole Dairies joined the group, rebranded as Allied Suppliers in a nod to the collapse of the British Empire. Most of their shops were rebranded or closed; others were opened as small supermarkets under the Presto brand. In the 1980s the group was swallowed up by Safeway (itself later taken over by Morrisons). Meanwhile the number of Co-ops halved.

Specialist food shops also suffered from supermarket competition. In 1998 one DEFRA report found that an out-of-town superstore reduced market share for town centre food shops by 75 per cent.[17] With higher rates and rents, they certainly couldn't compete on price, especially since the end of Retail Price Maintenance (RPM) in 1964. Up to that point, manufacturers had been able to set a minimum price for their wares. Retailers, in particular Tesco, argued that this was unfair, for it kept prices artificially high, penalising consumers who wanted cheaper food, as well as the businesses whose model was to compete on price. Manufacturers retorted that it maintained a balance of power and enabled them to pay decent wages and ensure reasonable profits along the whole supply chain. Throughout the 1950s and 1960s debate raged over whether RPM stifled competition or stopped exploitation of producers.

In 1964 RPM was dropped, triggering a price war between the supermarkets. Food prices dropped immediately: in the 1950s the average household spent around a third of their income on food. By 1985 this figure had dropped to 20 per cent, and by 2020 it stood at 10.8 per cent.[18]

The flipside, of course, was that as their control of the grocery market grew, the largest supermarket chains came to wield enormous power over the supply chain. Notoriously, by 2015 the average price paid for a pint of milk was below the cost of producing it.[19] It has become increasingly clear that reliance on supermarkets has far-reaching impacts on national food security, health, the environment and the conditions of workers across the globe. However, as has always been the case, the extent to which any individual shopper on the high street (or now, the internet) chooses to engage with such issues remains a question of both personal choice and economic capacity.

By the late 1990s the regulatory regime was changing again. Belated recognition that supermarkets were one factor in the closure of many town centre shops, along with planning concerns around the development of greenfield sites, meant that out-of-town stores were less likely to gain planning approval. The supermarkets therefore returned to the high street, now in the shape of smaller stores such as Tesco Metro and Sainsbury's Local. Any food shops that had survived now found themselves facing renewed competition from big brands with prices that were hard to match. Between 1997 and 2002 specialist stores such as bakers and butchers closed at a rate of fifty a week.[20] The high street became less centred on food and household goods, and more on clothing – and services such as hairdressing, finance and travel which were not (generally) offered in an out-of-town superstore. The centre of the high street had long been focused around leisure shopping, and this was even more the case now that so much quotidian shopping could simply be picked up by car from a giant warehouse.

Precincts and malls

Supermarkets weren't the only physical threat to the established high street. In addition to the replanning of bomb-damaged city centres, and the construction of dedicated modern shopping squares, which had at least some relation to the main shopping streets, some councils decided that what was really needed was a whole new building dedicated entirely to shopping.

From the mid-1960s, open-air planned shopping precincts were therefore joined by the latest iteration of the enclosed, private shopping area concept. Where previously we've seen selds, exchanges and market halls, now came the mall. Malls, like self-service, were an American concept, though Victor Gruen, the designer of the first mall, was an Austrian. In Minnesota, his Southdale Mall was intended to take the idea of European high streets but reinvent them for a car-dependent society that wanted to avoid bad weather.[21] Gruen was convinced that traditional town centres were over, and the idea of a climate-controlled, deliberately designed shopping and leisure space accessible to anyone with a car was the future. His initial concept also included a designed community set around the mall – a total reinvention of the town itself. However, it was in the form of the shopping mall that his ideas spread.

In the UK, less car-dependent and lacking in free space, the first malls – usually called shopping centres – were built in town centres. There was a lot of crossover, with open-air precincts converted to closed malls in some cases – Leeds's Merrion Centre, built in 1964 and roofed a decade later, being a good example. The bigger malls were purpose-built, with parking and separate access for deliveries. They were like the high street, but were not the high street. They contained shops, and sometimes other facilities such as catering outlets and cinemas. But they were privately owned, and, like the arcades and bazaars that preceded them, came with rules and private enforcers. The earliest iterations weren't always successful. The standard designs were inspired by the utopian ideas of continental architects such as Le Corbusier, but failed to fully acknowledge the very different weather in Britain versus southern France. Concrete blackened in the rain, and brutalist blocks sat uneasily next to the regular proportions of converted Victorian terraces or neo-Georgian department stores. The issues which had dogged previous attempts at enclosed shopping areas also applied: a lack of public thoroughfare meant that malls had to attract anchor tenants guaranteed to get people through the doors, and those who felt excluded showed their feelings in graphic form. In Manchester the Arndale Centre was called 'the longest toilet wall in Britain'.[22] Meanwhile in Brighton by the late 1970s the Churchill Centre (part-precinct, part-mall) was 'a horrible concrete mess . . . you only went downstairs as a dare to see if you got away without being knifed or approached by a child molester'.[23]

Malls could also be innovative spaces, though, using the latest technology to create spaces centred on shopping to the exclusion of all else. In 1964 Birmingham's Bull Ring was the first to install air curtains – a system by which hot air was circulated across an open doorway – removing yet another barrier between would-be customers and their potential purchases.[24] By the 1970s malls rarely featured natural light, but did have carefully designed soundscapes, magnifying footsteps, creating a feeling of bustle and movement.[25] And they were popular.

We've seen before that the introduction of new types of shopping experience led to cries that small traders would be put out of business, and the same was true here. But, as with pop-up shops and department stores, urban malls were both a threat, and a motivator for people to make the journey into towns. They had food courts and fountains and benches and loos. Competition worked to make existing traders spruce up

Fig. 7.4. Birmingham's Bull Ring was completed in 1964, a heady mix of shopping mall, market and car parking, all on the site of a long-established market along with several bomb-damaged streets. As with many such shopping centres, twenty years later it was regarded as a concrete carbuncle.

Fig. 7.5. Protesters at the Bull Ring in 1988 after plans had been released for redevelopment. It took a further sixteen years for a solution to be found, and the result remains controversial.

their shops, and, while many of the shops within them were multiples, there were plenty of independent retailers as well. The need for anchor tenants meant that many towns now gained supermarkets and department stores such as John Lewis, which were highly desirable. The apogee of the urban mall was perhaps 1979, when planners for the new town of Milton Keynes opted not to even try to build a traditional high street, but to install a giant mall instead.

Behind the Milton Keynes mall lay a genuine desire to rethink the high street. The Centre, as it was then called, was supposedly inspired by European arcades rather than American malls, and was intended as a corrective to what the chief architect called 'the prison-camp exterior/seedy nightclub interior mode of many recent commercial ventures in France and England'.[26] It was supposed to act as a civic centre, a hub for the dispersed communities who lived in the various parts of the town, and a declaration that Milton Keynes was proud to have arrived. But it was still a mall, and there wasn't a real high street, open to all. Once the open doorways had been filled in and twenty-four-hour access curtailed due to anti-social behaviour, it was hard to argue with those who accused planners of commodifying the normal patterns of urban living.

You know where this is going. If your primary aim in heading to the high street was to shop, as it ostensibly was for most of the people on it, then you would head to where the shops were, and while you might feel a vague sense of discombobulation, you'd soon get over it in the soothing surrounds of a building devoted to helping you achieve your aim.

You might also ask whether there was really any need for them to be in town centres, with all that nasty congestion and lack of space to expand? In 1975 the first out-of-town mall opened outside Northampton, followed by Brent Cross in north London the year after. In a slightly bizarre twist, next came open-air shopping 'villages' including discount designer outlets, full of faux-historic styling and devoted to big brands. Even further removed from the experience of a town-centre high street, they offered a stripped-back way to shop, divorced from the inconvenience of wind and rain, pigeons and dog pee, as well as from street performance, protest, obvious poverty, and anything else which might detract from the desire to spend money.

Need a pause? We're about to move even further away from the physical landscape of shopping to look at the wider economic context. Before we do, let's quickly consider how your eating and drinking options have changed. Both malls and big supermarkets provided places to eat, but if you did venture back out on to the street, your choices would be wider. Increasingly, though, like the retailers surrounding them, many of the outlets at the heart of the high street would be chains. Perhaps the most obvious, and certainly the most long-lived, were the American-style fast-food joints. We've mentioned Wimpy, but from 1965 you might also find KFC, followed by McDonald's in 1974. Or how about pizza? The British chain Pizzaland opened in 1970, fighting American rival Pizza Hut from 1973 until 1996, when 'the hut' took it over. Slightly more upmarket, Pizza Express started in 1965 and by the 1990s was known for renovating historic retail premises whose occupiers had moved out.

Other names, and concepts, came and went, and you may well have eaten in a Kardomah café (a survival from the nineteenth century), a Bella Pasta, or a Café Rouge. There were pubs, too, though their number dwindled fast over the years covered in this chapter. Of 69,000 pubs in 1980, by 2021 there were just 46,359 left.[27] In the 1990s many converted to quasi-restaurants under the newly coined descriptor 'gastropub', as would-be chefs opted out of the traditional restaurant industry – and traditional landlords gave up.

For lighter fare, don't forget cafés and tea rooms, many of which remained independent and included everything from old-style workers' venues (the term greasy spoon had been around since the 1920s), to chintzy tourist traps. As with fast food and pizza, the Americans moved in, when Starbucks bought out an existing British chain. Again, they faced home-grown competition from the (just) established Costa, among others. All sold nominally Seattle-style coffee (remarkably similar to the terrible brews of the seventeenth century). By the 2010s Australasia had brought us the flat white. You'd still find, of course, itinerant sellers, which included old and new style coffee vendors, as well as late-night kebab vans for those on the street after the shops had shut, and perhaps, by the late 2010s, an area painted up with faux graffiti and operating as a street food market.

Boom and bust

Behind the scenes, there were other changes, less physically obvious but just as far-reaching. In 1994, Sunday trading was legalised, albeit with restrictions on larger shops thanks to a determined campaign by Sabbatarians and shopworkers' unions. Proponents pointed out that the law that governed opening hours dated to 1950, when society was very different, and that it was simply not fit for purpose in a secular society, where the majority of people worked five days a week, and shopped at the weekend. Saturdays were the busiest day on the high street now, regardless of historical market days. Many shops had been opening on Sundays and foregoing half-day closures for years, and there had already been twenty-six attempts to reform the law. The following year licensed premises (pubs and off-licences) were allowed to open for all of Sunday afternoon, a recognition that it wasn't just about the shopping.[28]

Meanwhile, behind closed doors, mergers and takeovers meant that many of the names that now appeared on every major high street were owned by just a few companies. Burton's Group was now Arcadia, and included not just Burton's, but also Dorothy Perkins, Evans (a plus-size ready-to-wear clothing retailer founded in 1930), Top Shop, Miss Selfridge, and, from 1985, Debenhams. Debenhams itself had continued its buying spree of the 1960s, as had Scottish department store chain House of Fraser, whose holdings now included Dingle's of Plymouth, which in turn had bought Jolly's of Bath in 1970. Meanwhile the John Lewis chain, which also included multiple grocer-turned-supermarket chain Waitrose, had quietly taken over several other regional big shops, including Bainbridge's in Newcastle and Bonds in Norwich.

Walking down the high street in the 1990s most shoppers would have been oblivious to the complicated ownership patterns of the shops around them, not least as many of the former big shops retained their regionally resonant original names until John Lewis and House of Fraser rebranded them all. In the early 2000s you might have picked up on Arcadia's growth by noticing the conversion of some Burton's shops to hold one of their sibling brands as well (mainly Dorothy Perkins), or seen the new joint stores opening in smaller towns. It was hard to ignore the increasing homogenisation of the high street. In the early noughties the term 'Clone Town' entered popular consciousness as realisation hit that major high streets were increasingly filled with the same retailers, offering little real choice to the populations that depended on them.[29]

Architecturally, too, the high street entered a phase of shop design that was no longer locally relevant, but consisted of bland glass and steel buildings without provision for residential use or wider leisure. The idea that high streets were not purely about shopping seemed to have been lost.

Another factor came into play as the millennium passed. The growth of online shopping was a new way to access goods and services, but, like malls, was based on a much older concept. All the eager mail order catalogue readers of previous centuries would have heartily approved. The impact of the internet on high streets is still playing out. Some argue that it has dealt a fundamental blow to fixed shops, forcing many out of business, and therefore affecting the areas where they were located. It certainly impacted on services, as the banks which had been a reassuringly grand presence on high streets since the nineteenth century closed hundreds of branches. Online businesses aren't subject to the same punishingly high rates regime, which many retail experts – and shop owners – have blamed for shop closures over any other single factor.[30] Others have pointed out that it's just another way to shop, and that, like big shops or multiples or telephone ordering, it's up to shopkeepers to innovate and adapt, whether that's through selling online themselves, or through offering a personal service with which online retailers cannot compete.[31]

Also impactful for the range and number of retailers on the high street was the 2008 economic crash. The reduction of council budgets and decade of government-led austerity that followed hampered regeneration schemes and, of course, reduced the buying power of individual shoppers. Finally, a tipping point was reached that combined multiple factors, and brought debates over the state of the high street into the mainstream. Reports such as that of Mary Portas (2011) and John Timpson (2021) highlighted the complexity of the issues and the lack of one-size-fits-all solutions – but also pointed out that the majority of people cared deeply about the future of the high street.[32]

Debates were heightened by what looked like carnage in the most clone-like of towns. In 2009, only months short of its centenary, Woolworth's collapsed after decades of decline and poor decision-making. A generation weaned on pic 'n' mix mourned. Smaller chains followed. Some were specialists who had failed to adapt to new technology. Others, including the likes of Athena (posters), Blockbuster (video/DVD hire) and Virgin megastores (records and DVDs) struggled to retain their youth audiences as they aged. Lost, too, were more established retailers such as C&A, BHS and Austin Reed.[33]

By 2019 even the most occasional of high street frequenters could not have failed to notice the gaps where once familiar names had been. The first six months of that year saw the closure of 2,868 shops, including twenty-two Debenhams. Local newspapers joyously leapt on the possibility for cheap content generated through pictures of local shops that had gone, spurred by the nostalgia of their readers for childhoods spent buying nylon dresses in C&A and combing the racks at HMV for sale items before heading to Wimpy for a burger. Those chains that had weathered the storms of the previous decades by rebranding and remaining agile were ignored (or sometimes wrongly listed as having disappeared). Chelsea Girl was now River Island, while Hepworths had ventured into womenswear and become so successful it changed its name to Next. As Next, it took over some of the vacant stores left by those ventures that had done less well. In York, the draper-turned department store Leak & Thorp closed in 1987. By the early 1990s the building was shared between Next, River Island and women's clothing retailer Etam. On the top floor the former café, with its enviable river views, became a stock room.

Closures and conversions were as much a part of the changing high street as different styles of window and door, and the boarding-up of shops did help put an end to clone towns. Premises didn't stay empty for long; even in 2019 there were openings, 1,634 of them. Many of these were independent stores or small chains, along with higher-end brands whose customers wanted the physical experiences of a shop and the potential for personal service offered within.[34] The nadir for closures came in 2020 when the Arcadia group collapsed, followed by the final demise of Debenhams, who'd been hoping to be rescued by the group.

The year 2020 was a bad one. Not only did retailers have to contend with a confused and badly managed exit from the

EU – another area whose repercussions are still reverberating – but the global coronavirus pandemic saw the imposition of lockdowns and forced shop closures. As arguments raged over what counted as an essential item (yes to booze, no to books), a nation now addicted to supermarkets panic-bought pasta and caused a nationwide shortage of small bags of flour. Demand rocketed for online delivery services, which had been introduced by supermarkets in the 1990s after the phasing out of home delivery just twenty years before. When the dust started to settle in 2022, online spending stood at 26.6 per cent of total retail sales, versus 19.7 per cent two years before.[35] However, we were also buying fewer things; a mixture of a new credit crunch, changing consumer patterns after two years of turmoil, and the growing emphasis on reducing consumption to alleviate pressure on the planet.

Charity shops

One obvious beneficiary of all those empty premises was charity shops, especially in smaller towns or areas of economic depression. They weren't new – the first shops selling goods in aid of charity opened in the late nineteenth century, selling female-oriented products such as flowers and tea, the latter in support of the suffrage movement. Then came the Salvation Army, selling second-hand goods to the poor at as low a cost as possible. Other charities employed disabled people or otherwise disadvantaged members of society as workers and sold what they produced as a way of supporting them financially and mentally. The more modern iteration – essentially a jumble sale stall in a fixed premises – came about after the Second World War.[36] By the 1960s people were already complaining that there were too many charity shops. They are particularly problematic for other second-hand sellers, especially bookshops.

Charities get 80 per cent relief from business rates, and so escape one of the big burdens faced by other retailers.[37] But they are popular, and, in an age where environmental and ethical concerns are an increasingly important part of the decisions people make about their shopping habits, they may help keep items out of landfill – though the prevalence of poor-quality fast fashion or damaged donations means that much of what they receive is shipped abroad to become somebody else's problem. On the other hand, they do help fill empty shops, stopping town centres looking completely derelict and unloved. And, while the form may be fairly new, the buying and selling of second-hand goods is as old as selling itself.[38]

There are new types of trader too. We've lost the toyshops of the eighteenth century, the drapery warehouses of the nineteenth century and the mass market tailors of the twentieth, all rendered irrelevant by changing social norms. Tobacconists are now rare, but vape shops are everywhere. You can have your mobile phone mended in a brightly lit store full of garish accessories, or nip into a betting shop (present since a law change in 1961). You can grab a coffee to go, pick up a flaccid wrap, or a fish free sushi entombed in a commercially compostable box (other, more palatable options are also available).

And so we come to the present. You know what your local high street looks like – and plenty of others that are less local. Maybe you regularly use the shops and other facilities it has to offer, or consider yourself an occasional passer-by, content to shop online or in a supermarket or a mall. Perhaps you experience it from the vantage point of a pub window or as you grab a coffee to go to work.

You may only recently have rediscovered your closest high street, thanks to working more regularly from home. Or you may be lamenting the closure of your favourite sandwich shop, unable to survive, with offices on average currently occupied only three days a week. For some of you the only interaction you have with the high street is when you're return-ing a parcel via a drop-off point. Maybe you love it, and just maybe you're one of the small number of people who wouldn't care if all the shops disappeared completely. Either way, our shopping is done, and all that's left to do is wend our way home.

Conclusion

Reimagining our town centres should not be seen as a central programme dictated by government. It is a series of locally inspired and led initiatives that are supported by a government that offers information and helps to clear obstacles out of the way . . . providing help on a town by town basis, enabling local leaders to design future town centres that recreate a community hub.[1]

– John Timpson, *The High Street Report* (2021)

Go, step out of your door, and find yourself a reasonable-sized high street.

What'll you see? Your gaze will probably fall on the shops and shopfronts first. Some have signs which protrude into the street, others are flat-fronted. Some have regularly changing window displays, others opt for a view into the shop, enlivened with a few posters. You'll find a mixture of established names and newer, smaller brands aiming at carefully researched market segments. Clothing and footwear dominate, but there will be lots of food as well. Assuming they haven't decamped to a mall, the central part of the street will be dominated by multiples, though away from them you'll also find lots of independent shops, including bookshops, the number of which has been growing since 2016.[2]

And, yes, some shops will be shuttered. At the beginning of 2024 vacancy rates stood at around 14 per cent.[3] Perhaps your high street has a former department store with its blank windows full of dust and the occasional discarded shopfitting. Read the local newspapers, and you'll find arguments in favour of redeveloping it into housing or a food hall, or maybe it is already operating as an NHS walk-in clinic, yoga centre or axe-throwing venue. Others might say it should be ripped down, despite the environmental impact, to provide space for flats, or a hotel, or even a public open space. Around it, without the store to attract people to this part of the street, you'll doubtless see a few smaller outlets advertising space to let – or maybe they've already been refitted, open now for phone repairs, take-away cake, or gin.

It's easy to paint a picture of doom on British high streets, but that's not completely fair. In any case, if closures outnumber openings – so what? The number of shops has been steadily decreasing since the 1920s. In the 1970s Britain had around 400,000 shops, predicted then to fall to 220,000 by 2018. But despite the upheavals of the last few decades, in 2022 shop numbers still stood at 257,252.[4] And, once again, while shops define the high street, the high street – as we've repeatedly seen – is about so much more than shopping. In 2022, 60 per cent of the people surveyed by Mintel agreed that visiting a 'shopping destination' (admittedly not necessarily the high street) was a good way to socialise with family or friends. Nearly 80 per cent believed high streets were important to the local community.[5]

*

One of the reasons we've focused on the period up to 1965 is that today you won't find any shops which truly evoke the high street in its pre-1960s form (except in museum settings). The vast majority are now self-service, with digital tills and card machines and sophisticated stock-taking procedures – the adoption of tills hastened by decimalisation in 1971. That doesn't stop some people harking back to the high streets of their youth, kept fresh and frequently sanitised by time. It's often unhelpful, ignoring all that trudging and the burden on (mainly female) shoppers doing the weekly grocery run. But looking back is an intrinsic part of the high street, and, even while we consider the future, it is vital to gain perspective from the past.

Nostalgia can be a powerful thing. Take the ironmonger and hardware store probably lurking somewhere on the fringe of your street. They are often the most loved shops in a town, curiously romanticised, despite being generally peripheral to the high street proper. A good example is Barnitts in York, a veritable mecca whose unofficial catchphrase is along the lines of 'if you can't get it at Barnitts you can't get it anywhere' – you probably know a similar shop somewhere else. Barnitts was founded in 1896 as a general ironmonger and agricultural implement agent, expanding over the next half-century until it owned most of the block, along with a former Drill Hall which became its furniture emporium. In the 1960s the owners took advantage of the boom in DIY to expand still further, including an experimental second, suburban, branch. Over the years it sold everything from fireplaces to firearms and thermos flasks.[6] People who've lived in York tend to get misty-eyed over Barnitts, and it's true that the shop, with its varying floor levels and mishmash of interconnected rooms, feels comfortingly timeless. Nothing is actually timeless though. Few of its products would be recognisable to our great-grandparents, and the relentlessly cheery infomercials which play in the background are very much of the now. Despite the nostalgia that surrounds it and others like it, Barnitts, like its peers in other places, survived by having responsive owners who knew how to run a shop.

The past – or, at least, someone's rendition of it – is omnipresent on the modern high street. See how many high streets you can walk down before you find a café or tea rooms called the Copper Kettle. It's not new. In Arthur Ransome's *Coot Club* (1934), the central characters do a bit of shopping in Beccles (Suffolk) – the butcher, the greengrocer, and 'a big new shop with enormous plate glass windows'. Then they have coffee and biscuits in 'Ye Olde Cake Shoppe'. In 1953 Leominster had the remarkably awfully named Ye Olde Ducking Stool Shoppe, selling fancy goods and children's books.[7]

More significantly, the genuine heritage of the high street has been recognised as a crucial way to regenerate forlorn shopping areas, with funds available for heritage-led projects and a recognition that maintaining older buildings and shopfronts alongside more recent retail styles is key. There's rightly debate over whether imposing visually pleasing faux-historical fronts on swathes of the street invalidates locally distinct responses to an individual town's customer base and imposes a middle-class view of what's desirable on towns with a working-class population (though this itself can be reductive). When it works, though, it can be very successful.[8]

You won't have to look far to see the heritage of your chosen high street. All it takes is looking up. Shopping streets are still, by and large, a glorious cacophony of architectural styles, and while the upper windows are now more likely to be blocked by boxes and stock pertaining to the shops below, many still have flats or offices above the shops. You'll see datestones, and long-lost shop names, either carved in stone or in the form of ghost signs on walls.[9] You also can't miss the statement architecture of the banks. Most of the better ones have been snapped up, as the corner sites they occupy are still the most sought-after positions, and the decor which was designed to impress and reassure savers also works to wow hungry shoppers looking for a place to buy a burger or some spicy chicken. Once you know what to look for, you'll see the regular frontages and resplendent stonework of Woolies and Burton's in every town centre. Many of the shops you pass will have been selling stuff for a century or more, their occupants changing through time, along with their internal layout, external design and stock. Some may now be restaurants rather than retail, services rather than shops, while others may have been converted back to residential use, but you can still admire the buildings, breathe in the smells of cooking and watch other people all doing the same thing.

*

For all the change, we should not forget the continuities. From the point where there were enough fixed shops to form a focus for leisure and pleasure in the mid-seventeenth century, to the democratisation of shopping from the middle of the nineteenth century, the high street has attracted all sorts of people. When shops first appeared, the vast majority couldn't afford to buy things in them, though they might look at those who could. Shops meant shoppers, of course, but also voyeurs, thieves, street sellers and performers, beggars – and gently promenading ladies and gents, all enjoying the atmosphere of a bustling town centre. High streets were and are a focus for a town, not just for those who feel part of a community but also for those who are merely passing through.

The type of shop, the products on offer, and the way in which they are experienced by those who interact with them has changed shops a lot. But some things stay the same. Some people will come to the high street armed with information about what they want, or the ethics of consumption, and others will drift in seeking only to enjoy the experience in the moment. Some will spend to be seen to spend, others will seek only to buy the bare necessities. And shopkeepers will always adapt, or not, and shops will close and streets will contract or expand. Ultimately, the blend of continuity and change is a part of what makes the high street an interesting place to be.

On average, I walk along my local high street about once a week. In the twenty years I've lived here, we've lost two butchers, two interior design shops, a knitting shop, a terribly old-fashioned jewellers, and several chains, including Millets,

Blockbuster, Dorothy Perkins, Woolworth's and, in 2023, the last remaining bastion of emergency screw buying at 3.40 pm on a Sunday, Wilko. In their place we've gained a chocolate shop, a bakery, an exuberant cake shop, a deli, two refill outlets, a tattoo parlour, a salad 'n' sushi seller and a nail bar (or three). Few of the shops I know from when I moved here remain. And yet, the high street (and market) caters to its population, as it must, in order to survive.

In the course of writing this book, I've rethought my own relationship with the high street. I try to make time for it, often just mooching, but also making an effort to look for goods I might once have purchased elsewhere. Sometimes I succeed, other times I don't. I shop more than ever beyond the super-market, both to support my local shops and because I am more aware of the underlying issues with the concentration of power into the hands of just a few, big, buyers. When I shop online, I look for sites linked to bricks-and-mortar retail, and those that prioritise sustainability. After all, they may not be on my high street, but they're on someone's. I think very carefully and much more consciously, about what I need, and where the balance of price, convenience and ethics sits for me, depending on what exactly I am after. I've rediscovered the library (though I still have that pesky bookshop habit).

And I've become, more than ever, an inveterate high street noser. In strange cities, I'll deliberately walk to my destination via the commercial hub of a town. I'll annoy my colleagues, intent upon getting to our destination, by pointing out the architecture above the shops, or insisting that we stop to admire a particularly fine arcaded entryway, or the ghost of a once beloved town icon, now deserted, but still so full of memories and dreams.

Three hundred years ago, the high street barely existed. Its development has both been influenced by and in turn influenced the society in which we live. Whatever the future holds, we're part of it – we might not be able to predict it, or even (much) influence it, but I'm convinced that shouldn't stop us being conscious of what we like, and what we don't, and above all cognisant of what we might choose to do about it.

Selected Bibliography

If you want to read more on the history of the high street, this is a select list of the main works I consulted (or things I thought were pretty crucial). There are very few works that cover the entire period, and James Jeffreys (1954), along with Dorothy Davis (1966), remains key. Rachel Bowlby and Jon Stobart have written more modern, essay-based books. Carolyn Steel's *Hungry City* is a must-read on the way in which food has shaped the cityscape, from markets to shambles. However, if you want just one book, with lots of lovely pictures and architectural detail to swoon for, then Kathryn Morrison's *English Shops and Shopping* cannot be bettered. Her blog, Building Our Past, is great too. For full references, see the notes.

Adburgham, Alison, *Shopping in Style: London from the Restoration to Edwardian Elegance* (London, Thames & Hudson, 1979).

Allies & Morrison Urban Practitioners, *The Changing Face of the High Street: Decline and Revival* (Swindon, Historic England, 2015).

Benson, John, and Ugolini, Laura (eds.), *A Nation of Shopkeepers: Five Centuries of British Retailing* (London, Tauris, 2003).

Bowlby, Rachel, *Carried Away: The Invention of Modern Shopping* (London, Faber & Faber, 2000).

Bowlby, Rachel, *Back to the Shops: The High Street, its History and its Future* (Oxford, OUP, 2022).

Brett, Vanessa, *Bertrand's Toyshop in Bath: Luxury Retailing, 1685–1765* (Wetherby, Oblong, 2014).

Brewer, John, *The Pleasures of the Imagination: English Culture in the Eighteenth Century* (London, HarperCollins, 1997).

Burnett, John, *Plenty and Want: A Social History of diet in England from 1815 to the present day* (London, Routledge, 1989).

Burnett, John, *England Eats Out: A Social History of Eating Out in England from 1830 to the Present* (Harlow, Pearson Longman, 2004).

Cox, Nancy, *The Complete Tradesman: A Study of Retailing, 1550–1820* (London, Routledge, 2000).

Cox, Pamela, and Hobley, Annabel, *Shopgirls: True Stories of Friendship, Hardship and Triumph from Behind the Counter* (London, Arrow, 2015).

Davis, Dorothy, *A History of Shopping* (London, Routledge & Kegan Paul, 1966).

Dyer, Serena, *Shopping and the Senses, 1800–1970: A Sensory History of Retail and Consumption* (London, Palgrave Macmillan, 2022).

Gardiner, Marjorie, *The Other Side of the Counter: The Life of a Shop Girl, 1925–1945* (Brighton, Queenspark, 1985).

Hann, Andrew, 'Modernity and the Marketplace', in Margaret Whalley, Dave Postles and Sylvia Pinches, (ed.) *The Market Place and the Place of the Market* (Leicester, Friends of the Centre for English Local History, University of Leicester, 2004), pp. 65–86.

Horn, Pamela, *Behind the Counter: Shop Lives from Market Stall to Supermarket* (Stroud, Amberley, 2015).

Hosgood, Christopher, '"Doing the Shops" at Christmas: women, men and the department store in England, c. 1880–1914', in Geoffrey Croissick and Serge Jaumain, *Cathedrals of Consumption: the European Department Store, 1850–1939* (Farnham, Ashgate, 1999), pp. 97–115.

Hubbard, Phil, *The Battle for the High Street: Retail Gentrification, Class and Disgust* (London, Palgrave Macmillan, 2017).

Jeffreys, James, *Retail Trading in Britain, 1850–1950*. Cambridge, CUP, 1954).

Lancaster, Bill, *The Department Store: A Social History* (Leicester, Leicester University Press, 1995).

Michaelis-Jena, Ruth and Merson, Willy, *A Lady Travels: Journeys in England and Scotland from the Diaries of Johanna Schopenhauer* (London, Routledge, 1988).

Mitchell, Ian, *Tradition and Innovation in English Retailing, 1700–1850* (Farnham, Ashgate, 2014).

Morrison, Kathryn, *English Shops and Shopping: An Architectural History* (New Haven, Yale University Press, 2003).

Morrison, Kathryn, *Woolworth's: 125 Years on the High Street* (Swindon, Historic England, 2015).

Mui, Hoh-Cheung and Mui, Lorna, *Shops and Shopkeeping in Eighteenth Century England* (Kingston, Ontario, McGill-Queens University Press, 1989).

Palliser, David and Clark, Peter, *The Cambridge Urban History of Britain Vol 1: 600–1540* (Cambridge, Cambridge University Press, 2000).

Pearson, Lynn, *Street Furniture* (Stroud, Amberley, 2022).

Anon., *The Book of English Trades* (London, 1818).

Rappaport, Erika, *Shopping for Pleasure: Women in the Making of London's West End* (Princeton, PUP, 2000).

Richards, James Maude and Ravilious, Eric, *High Street* (Country Life, 1938; this facsimile Thames & Hudson, 2022).

Roberts, Cheryl, *Consuming Mass Fashion in 1930s England: Design, Manufacture and Retailing for Young Working-Class Women* (Basingstoke, Palgrave Macmillan, 2022).

Shapiro Saunders, Lise, *Consuming Fantasies: Labor, Leisure and the London Shopgirl, 1880–1920* (Columbus, Ohio State University Press, 2006).

Steel, Carolyn, *Hungry City* (London, Random House, 2009).

Stobart, Jon, *Spend! Spend! Spend! A History of Shopping* (Stroud, The History Press, 2008).

Stobart, Jon, *Sugar & Spice: Grocers and Groceries in Provincial England, 1630–1830* (Oxford, OUP, 2012).

Stobart, Jon, (2014), 'The shopping streets of provincial England (1650-1840)', in Furnée, Jan Hein, and Lesger, Clé (eds.), *The Landscape of Consumption : Shopping Streets and Cultures in Western Europe, 1600–1900* (Basingstoke, Palgrave Macmillan, 2014), pp. 16–36.

Stobart, Jon, Hann, Andrew and Morgan, Victoria, *Spaces of Consumption: Leisure and Shopping in the English Town, c. 1680–1830* (London, Routledge, 2007).

Vickery, Amanda, *Behind Closed Doors: At Home in Georgian England* (New Haven, Yale University Press, 2009).

Walsh, Claire, 'Stalls, bulks, shops and long-term change in seventeenth and eighteenth century England', in Furnée, Jan Hein, and Lesger, Clé (eds.), *The Landscape of Consumption: Shopping Streets and Cultures in Western Europe, 1600–1900* (Basingstoke, Palgrave Macmillan, 2014), pp. 37–57.

Winstanley, Michael, *The Shopkeeper's World, 1830–1914* (Manchester, MUP, 1986).

Notes

Introduction

1 Cowan, Rob, Editorial, in *Context: The Bulletin of the Institute of Historic Building Conservation*, 171 (2022), p. 13; Steel, Carolyn, *Hungry City* (London, Random House, 2009), p. 144; Cox, Nancy (2000), *The Complete Tradesman: A Study of Retailing, 1550–1820* (London, Routledge, 2000), p. 41.

2 Hubbard, Phil, *The Battle for the High Street: Retail Gentrification, Class and Disgust* (London, Palgrave Macmillan, 2017); Statista (2022), 'How much would you care if your local high street disappeared?' via https://www.statista.com/statistics/1302691/consumers-care-if-uk-high-street-disappeared/.

3 Burnett, John, *England Eats Out: A Social History of Eating Out in England from 1830 to the Present* (Harlow, Pearson Longman, 2004).

4 For a broader discussion of this, see chapter 1, and also Davis, Dorothy, *A History of Shopping* (London, Routledge & Kegan Paul, 1966); Cox, *The Complete Tradesman: A Study of Retailing, 1550–1820*; Stobart, Jon, 'The Shopping Streets of Provincial England, 1650–1840', in Jan Hein Furnée and Clé Lesger (eds.), *The Landscape of Consumption : Shopping Streets and Cultures in Western Europe, 1600–1900* (Basingstoke, Palgrave Macmillan, 2014), pp. 16–36.

Chapter One

1 Langland, William, *The Vision of Piers Plowman: Prologue* (late c.14th), accessed via https://chaucer.fas.harvard.edu/pages/piers-plowman-prologue.

2 Morrison, Kathryn, *English Shops and Shopping: An Architectural History* (New Haven, Yale University Press, 2003), p. 10.

3 Cox, *The Complete Tradesman: A Study of Retailing, 1550–1820*, p. 23.

4 Richardson, Harold, *The Medieval Fairs and Markets of York* (York, St Anthony's Press, 1961), pp. 16–17.

5 Davis, *A History of Shopping*, p. 33.

6 ibid., pp. 20–21.

Notes

7   Steel, *Hungry City*, p. 121.

8   Picard, Liza, *Elizabeth's London* (London, Phoenix, 2003), p. 166.

9   Cox, *The Complete Tradesman: A Study of Retailing, 1550–1820*, p. 45.

10 Palliser, David and Clark, Peter, *The Cambridge Urban History of Britain. Vol 1: 600–1540* (Cambridge, Cambridge University Press, 2000), p. 169.

11 Clark, David, 'The Shop Within?: An Analysis of the Architectural Evidence for Medieval Shops', *Architectural History*, 43 (2000), pp. 58–87.

12 City of York Council, building record MYO1458 – Our Lady's Row, accessed at https://her.york.gov.uk/Monument/MYO1458.

13 Keene, Derek, 'Shops and Shopping in Medieval London', in Lindy Grant (ed.), *Mediaeval Art, Architecture and Archaeology in London* (London, Routledge, 1990), pp. 29–46.

14 Walsh, Claire, 'Shops, shopping and the art of decision making in eighteenth century England', in John Styles and Amanda Vickery (eds.), *Gender, Taste and Material Culture in Britain and North America, 1700–1830* (New Haven, Yale Center for British Art & The Paul Mellon Centre for Studies in British Art (distributed by Yale University Press), 2006), pp. 151–78, 154.

15 Cox, *The Complete Tradesman: A Study of Retailing, 1550–1820*, p. 18.

16 Keene, 'Shops and Shopping in Medieval London'; Stobart, Jon, *Spend! Spend! Spend! A History of Shopping* (Stroud, The History Press, 2008), p. 34.

17 Stobart, Jon, *Spend! Spend! Spend! A History of Shopping* (Stroud, The History Press, 2008), pp. 36–7; Keene, 'Shops and Shopping in Medieval London'.

18 Hayward, Maria, '"Outlandish superfluities": luxury and clothing in Scottish and English sumptuary law from the fourteenth to the seventeenth century', in Giorgio Riello and Ulinka Rublack, *The Right to Dress: Sumptuary Laws in a Global Perspective, c.1200–1800* (Cambridge, CUP, 2019), pp. 96–121, 98.

19 Blondé, Bruno and Van Damme, Ilja, 'From Consumer Revolution to Mass Market', in Jon Stobart and Vicki Howard, *The Routledge Companion to the History of Retailing* (London, Routledge, 2019).

20 Vickery, Amanda, *Behind Closed Doors: At Home in Georgian England* (New Haven, Yale University Press, 2009), p. 167.

21 Bernard Mandeville, *The Fable of the Bees: or, private vices, publick benefits* (London, 1714), p. 62.

22 Cox, *The Complete Tradesman: A Study of Retailing, 1550–1820*, p. 55.

23 Baer, William, 'Early retailing: London's shopping exchanges, 1550–1700', *Business History*, 49(1) (2007), pp. 29–51, 36.

24 Morrison, Kathryn, *English Shops and Shopping: An Architectural History*, p. 31; Baer, 'Early retailing: London's shopping exchanges, 1550–1700', pp. 29–51, 40.

25 Ward, Ned, *The London Spy* (1703), quoted in Stobart, *Spend! Spend! Spend! A History of Shopping*, 64.

26 Baer, 'Early retailing: London's shopping exchanges, 1550–1700', pp. 29–51, 36.

27 Davis, *A History of Shopping*, p. 109.

28 Drake, Francis, *Eboracum or, the History and Antiquities of the City of York* (1736), facsimile from EP Publishing, 1978, p. 238.

29 Defoe, Daniel, 'Letter 9: Eastern Yorkshire, Durham and Northumberland', in *A Tour thro' the Whole Island of Great Britain, divided into circuits or journeys* (1724), accessed at https://www.visionofbritain. org.uk/travellers/Defoe/33; Boermans, Mary-Anne, 'Ouse Bridge Cakes' (2023), at https://dejafood.uk/2023/01/30/ouse-bridge-cake.

30 Wilson, Van, *York's Golden Half Mile: The Story of Coney Street* (York, York Archaeological Trust, 2013), p. 4.

31 I'm indebted to the York Streetlife team for help with this section: see https://streetlifeyork.uk/ for details of their work. Also vital was the Coney Street Heritage Project – http://coneystreetheritageproject.org. uk/; plus Drake, *Eboracum or, the History and Antiquities of the City of York*; Wilson, *York's Golden Half Mile: The Story of Coney Street*. See also Scott, Margaret, 'Coney Street' (2022) at https://yorkcivictrust.co.uk/coney-street/. Thanks also to the archivists of York City Archives for their help with maps and lists of aldermen and mayors. The list of shops in St Helen's Square is from Jenkins, Matthew, *The View from the Street: Housing and Shopping in York during the Long Eighteenth Century*, PhD, University of York (2013), p. 128.

Chapter Two

1 Dryden, John, *The Medal: A Satyre Against Sedition* (Edinburgh, 1682), p. 9.

2 Anon, *Trade of England Revived* (London, 1681), pp. 1–2; Mitchell, Ian, 'The development of urban retailing, 1700–1815', in Peter Clark, *The Transformation of English Provincial Towns* (London, Hutchinson, 1984), pp. 228–58, 259.

3 See, for example, Leyland, Adam, 'The scandal of supermarket egg pricing and rationing will soon tarnish their reputations' (2022), in *The Grocer*, accessed via https://www.thegrocer.co.uk/leader/the-

scandal-of-supermarket-egg-pricing-and-rationing-will-soon-tarnish-their-reputations/673918.article. Supermarkets are particularly problematic, but the balance between consumer desire for cheapness, shareholder or owner desire for profit and the producer needing to not starve had always been an issue: see Bowlby, Rachel, *Carried Away: The Invention of Modern Shopping* (London, Faber & Faber, 2000); Blythman, Joanna, *Shopped: The Shocking Power of Britsh Supermarkets* (London, Fourth Estate, 2004); Steel, *Hungry City*; Rioux, Sébastien, *The Social Cost of Cheap Food: Labour and the Political Economy of Food Distribution in Britain, 1830–1914* (Montréal, McGill-Queens University Press, 2019).

4 Cox, *The Complete Tradesman: A Study of Retailing, 1550–1820*, p. 29.

5 Anon, *Trade of England Revived*, pp. 4, 16.

6 Glasse, Hannah, *The Art of Cookery Made Plain and Easy* (London, 1747), p. 161.

7 Stobart, Jon, Hann, Andrew and Morgan, Victoria, *Spaces of Consumption: Leisure and Shopping in the English Town, c.1680–1830* (London, Routledge, 2007), p. 14.

8 Stobart, *Spend! Spend! Spend! A History of Shopping*, p. 77.

9 Fiennes, Celia and Morris, Christopher, *The Illustrated Journeys of Celia Fiennes, 1685–c.1712* (Stroud, Sutton, 1995), pp. 176–7.

10 Marshall and Stout, *The Autobiography of William Stout of Lancaster, 1665–1752*, p. 220.

11 Stobart, *Spend! Spend! Spend! A History of Shopping*, p. 76.

12 Marshall and Stout, *The Autobiography of William Stout of Lancaster, 1665–1752*, p. 90.

13 Defoe, Daniel. *The Complete English Tradesman* (London, 1726), p. 99.

14 Scott, Margaret, 'Pavement' (2022) at https://yorkcivictrust.wpengine.com/heritage/civic-trust-plaques/pavement/.

15 Davis, *A History of Shopping*, pp. 189–90; Meadows, Cecil, *Trade Signs and their Origin* (London, Routledge & Kegan Paul, 1957), p. 4.

16 British Museum Heal & Johnson Collection (henceforth Heal) 18.5.2735 (dated 1735); Heal 54.4 (1727); Heal 54.5 (1750–60).

17 Heal 52.64 (1670); Heal 52.22 (1750).

18 Marshall and Stout, *The Autobiography of William Stout of Lancaster, 1665–1752*, p. 171.

19 Mui, Hoh-Cheung and Mui, Lorna, *Shops and Shopkeeping in Eighteenth Century England* (Kingston, Ontario, McGill-Queens University Press, 1989), p. 177.

20 Picard, Liza, *Restoration London* (London, Phoenix, 1997), p. 139.

21 Stobart, Jon, *Sugar & Spice: Grocers and Groceries in Provincial England, 1630–1830* (Oxford, OUP, 2012), p. 19.

22 Stobart, Jon and Bailey, Lucy, 'Retail Revolution and the Village Shop', *Economic History Review*, 71(2) (2018), pp. 393–417.

23 Marshall and Stout, *The Autobiography of William Stout of Lancaster, 1665–1752*, p. 90.

24 Turner, Thomas and Jennings, G., *The Diary of a Georgian Shopkeeper, 1754–1765* (Oxford, OUP, 1979), pp. 22–3, 23 February 1758 (he writes that it is the 25th, but this is presumably because he was a bit drunk).

25 Cox, *The Complete Tradesman: A Study of Retailing, 1550–1820*, p. 77.

26 Marshall and Stout, *The Autobiography of William Stout of Lancaster, 1665–1752*, p. 165; Hannah Barker pers. comm.

27 ibid., pp. 79–80.

28 Mui and Mui, *Shops and Shopkeeping in Eighteenth Century England*, p. 9.

29 Marshall and Stout, *The Autobiography of William Stout of Lancaster, 1665–1752*, p. 118.

30 ibid., p. 190.

31 Stobart, *Sugar & Spice: Grocers and Groceries in Provincial England, 1630–1830*, pp. 159–60.

32 Davis, *A History of Shopping*, p. 185.

33 Stobart, *Sugar & Spice: Grocers and Groceries in Provincial England, 1630–1830*, p. 162.

34 Lowe, Roger and Sachse, William, *The Diary of Roger Lowe* (London, Longmans, Green & Co., 1938), p. 53.

35 Hilton Price, F. G., 'Signs of Old London', *London Topographical Record*, 4 (1906), pp. 27–112, 86 (available via https://archive.org/details/londontopograph09socigoog/page/n64/mode/2up).

36 Burnett, *England Eats Out: A Social History of Eating Out in England from 1830 to the Present*, p. 2.

37 *The Spectator*, 4 (1713), p. 338.

38 Jones, Erasmus, *The Man of Manners* (London, 1737), p. 35.

39 Misson, Henri, *M. Misson's Memoirs and Observations in his Travels over England*, trans. Mr Ozell (London, 1719), p. 146.

40 Old Bailey Online, 'Currency, Coinage and the Cost of Living' (2018), via https://www.oldbaileyonline.org/static/Coinage.jsp.

41 Burnett, *England Eats Out: A Social History of Eating Out in England from 1830 to the Present*, p. 3.

42 Meadows, *Trade Signs and their Origin*, pp. 56–7.

43 Stobart, Hann and Morgan, *Spaces of Consumption: Leisure and Shopping in the English Town, c. 1680–1830*, p. 35.

44 Waller, Maureen, *1700: Scenes from London Life* (London, Hachette, 2001), p. 247.

45 Anon, *The Fifteen Plagues of a Lawyer . . .* (London, 1711?), p. 6.

46 Heal 70.39 (1720s) V&A E.2299-1987 (the Martha Cole version); Erickson, Amy, 'Wealthy businesswomen, marriage and succession in eighteenth-century London', Business History, 66 (1) 2024, 29-58. Published online 2022.

47 Stobart, 'The Shopping Streets of Provincial England, 1650–1840'.

48 Cox, *The Complete Tradesman: A Study of Retailing, 1550–1820*, p. 132.

49 ibid., p. 92.

50 Walsh, Claire, 'Shop Design and the Display of Goods in Eighteenth-Century London', *Journal of Design History*, 8(3) (1995), pp. 157–76, 171.

51 Stobart, *Spend! Spend! Spend! A History of Shopping*, p. 90; Walsh, 'Shops, shopping and the art of decision making in eighteenth century England', pp. 151–78, 163.

52 ibid., p. 164.

53 ibid., p. 115.

54 Waller, Maureen, *1700: Scenes from London Life*.

55 Davis, *A History of Shopping*, p. 230.

56 Harrold, Edmund and Horner, Craig (eds.), *The Diary of Edmund Harrold, Wigmaker of Manchester, 1712–1715* (Aldershot, Ashgate, 2008), 20 (18 July 1712).

57 Brett, Vanessa, *Bertrand's Toyshop in Bath: Luxury Retailing, 1685–1765* (Wetherby, Oblong, 2014), p. 168. It's often stated that Twinings ran a tea shop alongside the coffee house off the Strand, but this is based on a Victorian comment, backed up by absolutely nothing.

58 Shapiro, Barbara, *Political Communication and Political Culture in England, 1558–1688* (Stanford, Stanford University Press, 2012), p. 51.

59 I would like to point out I've tried this, starting with green beans, and the result was pretty unpleasant. However, I fed it to a group of people and they all agreed that it was only as bad as most of the chain coffee shops in the average town in *c.*2010 (specific brands were mentioned as a comparison).

60 'The Women's Petition' and 'The Men's Answer' (1674) are both available online and definitely worth a read. Other good sources on coffee houses include Ellis, Markman, *The Coffee-House: A Cultural History* (London, Phoenix, 2004) and Brown, Peter, *In Praise of Hot Liquors: The Study of Chocolate, Coffee and Tea-Drinking 1600–1850* (York, York Civic Trust, 1995); Cowan, Barry, *The Social Life of Coffee: The Emergence of the British Coffee House* (New Haven, Yale University Press, 2005).

61 Dixon, Jenni, 'The toyshop, the cabinet, and eighteenth-century curiosity', *History of Retailing and Consumption*, 5(3) (2019), pp. 205–27, 206.

62 ibid.

63   Meadows, Cecil, *Trade Signs and their Origin* (London, Routledge & Kegan Paul, 1957), p. 71.

64   Cox, Nancy, *The Complete Tradesman: A Study of Retailing, 1550–1820* (London, Routledge, 2000), p. 71.

65   Stobart, Jon, Hann, Andrew and Morgan, Victoria, *Spaces of Consumption: Leisure and Shopping in the English Town, c.1680–1830* (London, Routledge, 2007), p. 162.

66   Borsay, Peter, 'Sounding the Town', *Urban History*, 20(1) (2002), pp. 92–102. See also the Official List Entry via Historic England's website at https://historicengland.org.uk/listing/the-list/list-entry/1084437.

67   Stobart, Jon, Hann, Andrew and Morgan, Victoria, *Spaces of Consumption: Leisure and Shopping in the English Town, c.1680–1830* (London, Routledge, 2007), p. 105.

68   Vickery, Amanda, *The Gentleman's Daughter: Women's Lives in Georgian England* (New Haven, Yale University Press, 1998), p. 250.

69   Morrison, Kathryn, *English Shops and Shopping: An Architectural History* (New Haven, Yale University Press, 2003), p. 43.

70   Walsh, Claire, 'Stalls, Bulks, Shops and Long-Term Change in Seventeenth and Eighteenth-Century England', in Jan Hein Furnée and Clé Lesger (eds.), *The Landscape of Consumption : Shopping Streets and Cultures in Western Europe, 1600–1900* (London, Palgrave Macmillan, 2014), pp. 37–56, 51.

71   Defoe, Daniel, *The Complete English Tradesman*, pp. 312–19.

72   Stobart, Jon, Hann, Andrew and Morgan, Victoria, *Spaces of Consumption: Leisure and Shopping in the English Town, c.1680–1830* (London, Routledge, 2007), pp. 87–8.

73   Dixon, 'The toyshop, the cabinet, and eighteenth-century curiosity', pp. 205–27, 208.

74   Brett, *Bertrand's Toyshop in Bath: Luxury Retailing, 1685–1765*, p. 40.

75   Brett, Vanessa, 'Derided and enjoyed: what was a toy – what was a toyshop?', *History of Retailing and Consumption*, 1(2) (2015), pp. 83–8.

76   Borsay, Peter, *The Image of Georgian Bath, 1700–2000* (Oxford, OUP, 2000), p. 30.

77   Pevsner, Nikolaus, *North Somerset & Bristol* (London, Penguin, 1990); Forsyth, Michael, (2003) *Bath (Pevsner Architectural Guides)* (New Haven, Yale, 2003).

78   Mason, Cai, and Mepham, Lorraine, 'Industry, Commerce and the Urban Poor: Illuminating Bath's lost quayside district', *Current Archaeology* (2020), 363, accessed via https://archaeology.co.uk/articles/features/industry-commerce-and-the-urban-poor.htm.

79 Stobart, Hann and Morgan, *Spaces of Consumption: Leisure and Shopping in the English Town, c.1680–1830*, p. 105.

80 Fawcett, Trevor, 'Bath's Eighteenth Century Coaching Inns', *The Survey of Bath and District*, 26 (2011), pp. 21–7, 21.

81 Historic England Official List Entry (last updated 2010), accessible at https://historicengland.org.uk/listing/the-list/list-entry/1396027?section=official-list-entry.

82 Fawcett, Trevor, *Bath Commercialis'd: Shops, Trades and Market and the 18th Century Spa* (Bath, Ruton, 2002), p. 87.

83 This whole section draws on the *Bath Chronicle* for 1792 (accessible via the British Newspaper Archive), the images available from the Bath In Time website, plus Fawcett, Trevor, 'Eighteenth Century Shops and the Luxury Trade', *Bath History*, 3 (1990), pp. 49–75; and Fawcett, *Bath Commercialis'd: Shops, Trades and Market and the 18th Century Spa*. I am also grateful to Amy Frost of No. 1 Royal Crescent, Bath, for advice on sources and for sending me maps.

Chapter Three

1 Michaelis-Jena, Ruth and Merson, Willy, *A Lady Travels: Journeys in England and Scotland from the Diaries of Johanna Schopenhauer* (London, Routledge, 1988), p. 152.

2 Mitchell, Ian, *Tradition and Innovation in English Retailing, 1700–1850* (Farnham, Ashgate, 2014), p. 5.

3 Pennell, Sara, 'Bargain hunt? Selling second-hand, c.1600 to the present', in Stobart and Howard (eds.), *The Routledge Companion to the History of Retailing*, pp. 80–98.

4 Mitchell, *Tradition and Innovation in English Retailing, 1700–1850*, p. 33.

5 Hann, 'Modernity and the Marketplace', in Margaret Whalley, Dave Postles and Sylvia Pinches, *The Market Place and The Place of the Market* (Leicester, Friends of the Centre for English Local History, University of Leicester, 2004), pp. 65–86, 74.

6 ibid.

7 Mitchell, *Tradition and Innovation in English Retailing, 1700–1850*, pp. 30–33.

8 Stobart, Hann and Morgan, *Spaces of Consumption: Leisure and Shopping in the English Town, c.1680–1830*, p. 73.

9 Place, Francis and Thrale, Mary (eds.), *The Autobiography of Francis Place (1771–1854)* (Cambridge, CUP, 1972), p. 215.

10 Stobart, Hann and Morgan, *Spaces of Consumption: Leisure and Shopping in the English Town, c.1680–1830*, p. 89.

Notes

11 Fawcett, 'Eighteenth Century Shops and the Luxury Trade', p. 69.

12 Cruickshank, Dan and Burton, Neil, *Life in the Georgian City* (London, Penguin, 1990), p. 14.

13 Michaelis-Jena and Merson, *A Lady Travels: Journeys in England and Scotland from the Diaries of Johanna Schopenhauer*, p. 140.

14 Cruickshank and Burton, *Life in the Georgian City*, p. 25.

15 Malcolm, James Peller, *Anecdotes of the Manners and Customs of London, during the Eighteenth Century* (London, 1810), p. 336.

16 Michaelis-Jena and Merson, *A Lady Travels: Journeys in England and Scotland from the Diaries of Johanna Schopenhauer*, pp. 131-3.

17 Vickery, Amanda and Grieg, Hannah, 'Shopping, Fashion, Sociability', lecture given on 9 May 2022, https://embodiedsociabilities.wordpress.com/.

18 Hanway, Jonas, *An Essay On Tea* (London, 1757), p. 17.

19 Vickery, Amanda, 'His and Hers: Gender, Consumption and Household Accounting in Eighteenth-Century England', *Past & Present*, Supplement 1 (2006), pp. 12-38.

20 Goss, Steve, *British Teapots and Coffee Pots* (Princes Risborough, Shire, 2005).

21 Stobart, Hann and Morgan, *Spaces of Consumption: Leisure and Shopping in the English Town, c.1680–1830*, p. 36.

22 Mitchell, *Tradition and Innovation in English Retailing, 1700–1850*, p. 107.

23 Vickery, *The Gentleman's Daughter: Women's Lives in Georgian England*, p. 165.

24 Stobart, *Spend! Spend! Spend! A History of Shopping*, p. 92.

25 Stobart, Hann and Morgan, *Spaces of Consumption: Leisure and Shopping in the English Town, c.1680–1830*, p. 66.

26 Place and Thrale (eds.), *The Autobiography of Francis Place (1771–1854)*, p. 69.

27 Mitchell, *Tradition and Innovation in English Retailing, 1700–1850*, p. 91.

28 Place and Thrale (eds.), *The Autobiography of Francis Place (1771–1854)*, p. 216.

29 Malcolm, *Anecdotes of the Manners and Customs of London, during the Eighteenth Century*, p. 357.

30 Davis, *A History of Shopping*, p. 201.

31 McKendrick, Neil, 'Josiah Wedgwood: An Eighteenth-Century Entrepreneur in Salesmanship and Marketing Techniques', *Economic History Review*, 12(3) (1960), pp. 408-33, 412.

32 Mui and Mui, *Shops and Shopkeeping in Eighteenth Century England*, p. 18.

33 McKendrick, 'Josiah Wedgwood: An Eighteenth-Century Entrepreneur in Salesmanship and Marketing Techniques', pp. 408-33, 419.

34 Cox, *The Complete Tradesman: A Study of Retailing, 1550–1820*, p. 105.

35 Turner, Thomas and Jennings, G., *The Diary of a Georgian Shopkeeper, 1754–1765* (Oxford, OUP, 1979), p. 67, 6 July 1764.

36 Mui and Mui, *Shops and Shopkeeping in Eighteenth Century England*, p. 15.

37 Berry, Helen, 'Polite Consumption: Shopping in Eighteenth-Century England', *Transactions of the Royal Historical Society*, 12 (2002), pp. 375–94; *Newcastle Courant*, 15 August 1752, p. 3.

38 Mui and Mui, *Shops and Shopkeeping in Eighteenth Century England*, p. 161.

39 Taverner, Charlie, *Street Food: Hawkers and the History of London* (Oxford, OUP, 2023), p. 57.

40 Place and Thrale (eds.), *The Autobiography of Francis Place (1771–1854)*, p. 229.

41 Davis, *A History of Shopping*, p. 204.

42 Clarkson, Janet, 'An Interesting Oriental Beverage in 1736' (2014), accessed at The Old Foodie: http://www.theoldfoodie.com/2014/11/an-interesting-oriental-beverage-in-1736.html.

43 Freya Purcell, 'Getting to the Root of It: Saloop in early modern London' (2022), via https://www.intoxicatingspaces.org/2022/02/08/getting-to-the-root-of-it-saloop-in-early-modern-london/; Old Bailey Proceedings Online (www.oldbaileyonline.org, version 8.0, 21 December 2022), October 1789, trial of William Cunningham (t17891028-18).

44 Anon., *The Book of English Trades* (1818), p.35

45 Jenkins, *The View from the Street: Housing and Shopping in York during the Long Eighteenth Century*.

46 Brewer, J., *The Pleasures of the Imagination: English Culture in the Eighteenth Century* (London, HarperCollins, 1997), p. 175.

47 Barker, Hannah, *The Business of Women: Female Enterprise and Urban Development in Northern England 1760–1830* (Oxford, OUP, 2006).

48 Stobart, Hann and Morgan, *Spaces of Consumption: Leisure and Shopping in the English Town, c.1680–1830*, p. 69.

49 Michaelis-Jena and Merson, *A Lady Travels: Journeys in England and Scotland from the Diaries of Johanna Schopenhauer*, pp. 36–7.

50 Barker, *The Business of Women: Female Enterprise and Urban Development in Northern England 1760–1830*.

51 Michelle Levy, 'Female Booksellers at the End of the Long Eighteenth Century', *Huntington Library Quarterly*, 84 (1) (2021), pp. 99–112.

52 The Coney Street Heritage Project (2022), via http://coneystreetheritageproject.org.uk/the-craftsmen-and-women/booksellers-and-printers.

53 Lackington, James, *The Memoirs of James Lackington* (New York, 1796).

54 Vickery, Amanda, 'His and Hers: Gender, Consumption and Household Accounting in Eighteenth-Century England', pp. 12–38, 34.

55 Brewer, *The Pleasures of the Imagination: English Culture in the Eighteenth Century*, p. 167.

56 Jenkins, *The View from the Street: Housing and Shopping in York during the Long Eighteenth Century*.

57 Willan, Thomas and Dent, Abraham, *Abraham Dent of Kirkby Stephen: An Eighteenth Century Shopkeeper* (New York, Augustus M. Kelley, 1970), p. 19.

58 Jenkins, *The View from the Street: Housing and Shopping in York during the Long Eighteenth Century*, p. 169.

59 Skelton-Foord, Christopher, 'To buy or to borrow? Circulating libraries and novel reading in Britain, 1778–1828', *Library Review*, 47(7) (1998), pp. 348–54.

60 Michaelis-Jena and Merson, *A Lady Travels: Journeys in England and Scotland from the Diaries of Johanna Schopenhauer*, p. 118.

61 Cox, *The Complete Tradesman: A Study of Retailing, 1550–1820*, p. 94.

62 Brewer, *The Pleasures of the Imagination: English Culture in the Eighteenth Century*, pp. 192–3.

63 Beattie, James, *Beauties Selected from the Writings of James Beattie* (London, 1809), pp. 148–9.

64 Brandwood, Geoff, Davison, Andrew and Slaughter, Michael, *Licensed to Sell: the History and Heritage of the Public House* (Swindon, English Heritage in association with CAMRA, 2004).

65 Lane, Christel, *From Taverns to Gastropubs: Food, Drink, and Sociality in England* (Oxford, OUP, 2018), ch. 1.

66 Briggs, Richard, *The English Art of Cookery* (London, 1791).

67 Freeman, Janet Ing and Rylance, Ralph, *The Epicure's Almanack: Eating and Drinking in Regency London* (London, British Library, 2012).

68 Phillips, Richard, *The Book of English Trades* (London, 1818).

69 Mui and Mui, *Shops and Shopkeeping in Eighteenth Century England*, pp. 167–8; *The Universal British Directory* (1790); *Silverthorne's Bath Directory* (1846). Trade directories are notoriously unreliable, but even such vague figures show a significant rise.

70 Defoe, *The Complete English Tradesman*, p. 314.

71 Michaelis-Jena and Merson, *A Lady Travels: Journeys in England and Scotland from the Diaries of Johanna Schopenhauer*, p. 138.

72 Stobart, Jon, 'The Shopping Streets of Provincial England, 1650–1840', p. 29.

73 Freeman and Rylance, *The Epicure's Almanack: Eating and Drinking in Regency London*, p. 17.

74 Levy, 'Female Booksellers at the End of the Long Eighteenth Century', pp. 99–112, 65.

75 Holcomb, Julie L., 'Blood-Stained Sugar: Gender, Commerce and the British Slave-Trade Debates', *Slavery & Abolition*, 35(4) (2014), pp. 611–28.

76 Cox, Nancy, 'Raffald [née Whitaker], Elizabeth', in *The Oxford Dictionary of National Biography* (2004).

77 Barker, *The Business of Women: Female Enterprise and Urban Development in Northern England 1760–1830*.

78 Cruickshank and Burton, *Life in the Georgian City*, p. 23.

79 Drawn together using Clive Lloyd's excellent website Colonel Unthank's Norwich, accessible at https://colonelunthanksnorwich.com/; Baynes, A. D., *A Comprehensive History of Norwich* (Norwich, Jarrold & Son, 1869); O'Donoghue, Rosemary, *Norwich, an expanding city, 1801–1900* (Dereham, Larks Press, 2014); *The Post Office Directory* for 1869; *Harrod's Directories* for 1869 and 1871; a trawl of the *Norfolk Chronicle* and *Norwich Mercury* for 1869; Pevsner on Norwich and the photographic collection accessible online via Norfolk County Council's library website accessible at https://norfolk.spydus.co.uk/cgi-bin/spydus.exe/MSGTRN/WPAC/HOME?HOMEPRMS=GENPARAMS. Thank you also to the staff at the Norfolk Heritage Centre for digging out various books and insurance maps so that I could check on street numbers.

Chapter Four

1 Anon., *The Book of English Trades*, p. 226.

2 Jerome, Jerome K., *Three Men in a Boat* (London, 1889).

3 Baynes, *A Comprehensive History of Norwich*, p. 315.

4 Mitchell, *Tradition and Innovation in English Retailing, 1700–1850*, p. 130.

5 ibid., p. 131; *Piggot & Co's National Commercial Directory for 1828–9*, pp. 146–7, accessed via https://specialcollections.le.ac.uk/digital/collection/p16445coll4/id/233467.

6 Stobart, *Spend! Spend! Spend! A History of Shopping*, p. 118.

7 Hann, 'Modernity and the Marketplace', pp. 65–86, 69.

8 Mitchell, *Tradition and Innovation in English Retailing, 1700–1850*, p. 163.

9 Hann, 'Modernity and the Marketplace', pp. 65–86, 75.

10 Mitchell, *Tradition and Innovation in English Retailing, 1700–1850*, p. 155; Morrison, *English Shops and Shopping: An Architectural History*, pp. 110–14.

11 Haskins, Ruth, 'The Guildhall Market in the Victorian Period', *The Survey of Bath and District*, no. 5 (1996), p. 23.

12 Hann, 'Modernity and the Marketplace', pp. 65–86, 78.

13 Ablett, William H., *Reminiscences of an Old Draper* (London, 1876), pp. 105-6.

14 Pearson, Lynn, *Street Furniture* (Stroud, Amberley, 2022).

15 Roe, Sue, *Gwen John: a life* (London, Random House, 2010), pp. 2–3.

16 White, William, *Directory of Leeds and the Clothing District* (Leeds, 1842), p. 13.

17 Winstanley, Michael, *The Shopkeeper's World* (Manchester, MUP, 1983), p. 146.

18 Morrison, Kathryn, 'A spotter's guide to historic butchers' shops' (2016), accessed via https://buildingourpast.com/2016/11/28/a-spotters-guide-to-historic-butchers-shops/.

19 Morrison, *English Shops and Shopping: An Architectural History* pp. 86–7.

20 Winstanley, *The Shopkeeper's World*, p. 149.

21 Anon, *Buckmaster's Cookery* (London, Routledge, *c.*1875), p. 101.

22 Philip, Robert Kemp (ed.), *Enquire Within Upon Everything* (London, Houlston & Stoneman, 1856), p. 4.

23 Dodd, George, *The Food of London* (1856), cited at The Dictionary of Victorian London (ed. Lee Jackson): http://www.victorianlondon.org/index.html.

24 Dillon, Patrick, *The Much Lamented Death of Madam Geneva: the Eighteenth Century Gin Craze* (London, Thistle, 2013), p. 260.

25 *Illustrated London News*, 6 May 1848.

26 Solmonson, Lesley Jacobs, *Gin: A Global History* (London, Reaktion, 2012).

27 Advert in *Harrod's Directory*, 1869.

28 Morrison, Kathryn, 'Bazaars and bazaar buildings in Regency and Victorian London', *The Georgian Group Journal*, XV (2006), pp. 281–308.

29 Harris, John, *A Visit to the Bazaar* (London, 1818).

30 Nightingale, Joseph, *The Bazaar* (London, 1816).

31 Stobart, *Spend! Spend! Spend! A History of Shopping*, p. 142.

32 Agg, John (writing as Humphrey Hedgehog), 'The London Bazaar or, where to get cheap things' (London, 1816).

33 Harris, *A Visit to the Bazaar*, p. 6.

34 Sala, George, *Twice Round The Clock, or The Hours of the Day and Night in London* (1859), accessed via https://www.victorianlondon.org/publications/sala-12.htm.

35 Stobart, *Spend! Spend! Spend! A History of Shopping*, p. 112.

36 Stobart, 'The Shopping Streets of Provincial England, 1650–1840', p. 3.

37 Morrison, 'Bazaars and bazaar buildings in Regency and Victorian London', pp. 281–308, 284.

38 Stobart, *Spend! Spend! Spend! A History of Shopping*, p. 108.

39 Horn, Pamela, *Behind the Counter: Shop Lives from Market Stall to Supermarket* (Stroud, Amberley, 2015), p. 170.

40 Booth, Charles, *Life and Labour of the People in London* (1903), via https://www.victorianlondon.org/entertainment/cocoa.htm.

Notes

41 Wright, Thomas, *Some Habits and Customs of the Working Classes* (1867), via https://www.victorianlondon.org/entertainment/temperanceopinion.htm.

42 Richards, Nick, 'Where were Norwich's temperance bars for alcohol free Victorians?', *Eastern Daily Press*, 26 January 2021, accessed at https://www.edp24.co.uk/news/where-were-norwich-s-temperance-bars-7069160.

43 *Loughborough Monitor*, Thursday 5 July 1860, p. 4.

44 *Banner of Ulster*, Thursday 2 July 1863, p. 2; *John O' Groats Journal*, Thursday 14 June 1860, p. 4.

45 Booth, *Life and Labour of the People in London*.

46 Thank you to Alex Hutchinson for providing a crib sheet on Lockharts.

47 Phillips, *The Book of English Trades*.

48 Gaskell, Elizabeth, *Cranford* (London, 1853), p. 97, accessed via https://www.gutenberg.org/files/394/394-h/394-h.htm.

49 Mitchell, *Tradition and Innovation in English Retailing, 1700–1850*, p. 129.

50 Toplis, Alison, *The Clothing Trade in Provincial England, 1800–1850* (London, Pickering & Chatto, 2011), pp. 25–6.

51 Horn, *Behind the Counter: Shop Lives from Market Stall to Supermarket*, p. 132.

52 Ablett, *Reminiscences of an Old Draper*, p. 166.

53 ibid., p. 103.

54 ibid., p. 10.

55 ibid., p. 38. Having done it myself, I apologise at this point to anyone who has worked a big ticket sale on the modern high street and is currently suffering flashbacks.

56 Horn, *Behind the Counter: Shop Lives from Market Stall to Supermarket*, p. 133.

57 Cox, Pamela, and Hobley, Annabel, *Shopgirls: True Stories of Friendship, Hardship and Triumph from Behind the Counter* (London, Arrow, 2015), pp. 11–12.

58 Hudson, Derek, *Munby: Man of Two Worlds: The Life and Diaries of Arthur J. Munby, 1828–1910* (London, Abacus, 1974), accessed via https://www.victorianlondon.org/professions/drapers.htm.

59 Horn, *Behind the Counter: Shop Lives from Market Stall to Supermarket*, pp. 140–41, 135.

60 Gaskell, *Cranford*, p. 199.

61 ibid., p. 131.

62 Bennett, Arnold, *The Old Wives' Tale* (London, Penguin, 1990, first published 1908), p. 510.

63 Dickens, Charles, *Sketches by Boz* (London, 1836), accessed at https://www.victorianlondon.org/books/boz-122.htm.

64 Jeune, Mary (writing as Lady Jeune), 'The Ethics of Shopping,' *Fortnightly Review*, 57 (Jan 1895), pp. 123–132.

65 Whitlock, Tammy, *Crime, Gender and Consumer Culture in Nineteenth Century England* (London, Routledge, 2016).

66 Stobart, *Spend! Spend! Spend! A History of Shopping*, p. 108.

67 Philip (ed.), *Enquire Within Upon Everything*, p. 327.

68 *A Directory for the City of Bath* (1852).

69 Mowat, Sue, 'Shopping for Clothes in Victorian Dunfermline' (nd), via https://dunfermlinehistsoc.org.uk/shopping-for-clothes-in-victorian-dunfermline/.

70 Mitchell, *Tradition and Innovation in English Retailing, 1700–1850*, p. 141.

71 Hood, T., 'Living and Dying by the Needle', *The English Domesticwoman's Magazine*, 40 (VII) (August 1863), pp. 180–86.

72 Dickens, Charles, *The Old Curiosity Shop* (London, 1841), via https://www.gutenberg.org/files/700/700-h/700-h.htm.

73 Barker, *The Business of Women: Female Enterprise and Urban Development in Northern England 1760–1830*.

74 *Leeds Mercury*, 15 December 1903.

75 ibid., 21 December 1903.

76 Chrystal, Paul, *Central Leeds History Tour* (Stroud, Amberley, 2021).

77 *Leeds Mercury*, 4 April 1903.

78 ibid., 22 October 1903.

79 ibid., 13 October 1903.

80 This section draws upon *Kelly's Directories* for 1903 and 1908; *The Commercial and Library Atlas of the British Isles (*1902); the various OS maps available at the National Library of Scotland website; the photographic collection of Leodis; plus Brears, Peter, *Images of Leeds* (Stoke-on-Trent, Breedon Books, 1992); Wrathmell, Susan, *Leeds (Pevsner Architectural Guides)* (London & New York, Yale University Press, 2005); Brears, Peter and Grady, Kevin, *Briggate Yards & Arcades* (Leeds, Leeds Civic Trust, 2007).

Chapter Five

1 *TitBits*, 12 August 1893, quoted in Hosgood, Christopher, '"Doing the Shops" at Christmas: women, men and the department store in England, c.1880–1914', in Geoffrey Croissick and Serge Jaumain, *Cathedrals of Consumption: the European Department Store, 1850–1939* (Farnham, Ashgate, 1999), pp. 97–115, 110.

2 ibid.

3 Wilkinson, Philip, *The High Street: 100 Years of British Life through the Shop Window* (Quercus, London, 2010), p. 70.

4 Hughes, Molly, *A London Family in the 1890s* (Oxford, OUP, 1979), pp. 146–7.

5 Bennett, *The Old Wives' Tale*, p. 511.

6 Bosomworth, Dorothy, *The Victorian Catalogue of Household Goods* (London, Studio, 1991).

7 Anon, *Yesterday's Shopping: Gamage's General Catalogue 1914* (Ware, Wordsworth Editions, 1994).

8 Winstanley, *The Shopkeeper's World 1830–1914*.

9 Keynes, John Maynard, *The Economic Consequences of the Peace* (New York, Harcourt, Brace & Howe, 1920), pp. 11–12.

10 Bowlby, Rachel, *Back to the Shops: The High Street, its History and its Future* (Oxford, OUP, 2022), pp. 46–7.

11 Stobart, *Spend! Spend! Spend! A History of Shopping*, pp. 116–17; Morrison, *English Shops and Shopping: An Architectural History*, p. 100.

12 Sala, George, *Twice Round the Clock, or the Hours of the Day and Night in London* (1859), accessed via https://www.victorianlondon.org/publications/sala-12.htm.

13 Warnaby, Gary, 'The Victorian Arcade as Contemporary Retail Form?', *History of Retailing and Consumption*, 5(2) (2019), pp. 150–68.

14 Morrison, *English Shops and Shopping: An Architectural History*; Warnaby, 'The Victorian Arcade as Contemporary Retail Form?', pp. 150–68, 104.

15 Morrison, *English Shops and Shopping: An Architectural History*, p. 100.

16 Morrison, Kathryn and Bond, Ann, *Built to Last? The Buildings of the Northamptonshire Boot and Shoe Industry* (Swindon, English Heritage, 2004), p. 16.

17 Baren, Maurice, *Victorian Shopping: How it All Began* (London, Michael O'Mara for Past Times, 1998), p. 98.

18 Jeffreys, James, *Retail Trading in Britain, 1850–1950* (Cambridge, CUP, 1954), p. 365.

19 'Olivia', *Olivia's Shopping and How She Does It: A Prejudiced Guide to the London Shops* (this edition ed. Charles Moseley, Stroud, Gunpowder, 2009, first published 1906), p. 52.

20 Morrison and Bond, *Built to Last? The Buildings of the Northamptonshire Boot and Shoe Industry*, p. 18.

21 'Olivia', *Olivia's Shopping and How She Does It: A Prejudiced Guide to the London Shops*, p. 56.

22 Morrison, Kathryn, 'The legacy of Freeman, Hardy & Willis on Building Our Past' (2016), accessed via https://buildingourpast.com/2016/02/26/the-legacy-of-freeman-hardy-willis/.

23 Morrison, Kathryn, 'Manfield & Sons: Shoes of Bespoke Character, on Building Our Past' (2016), accessed via https://buildingourpast. com/2016/09/04/manfield-sons-shoes-of-bespoke-character/; Stobart, *Spend! Spend! Spend! A History of Shopping*, p. 138; Thomas Farrell, 'Built to Last: Stead & Simpson' (2015), on Let's Look Again, accessed via http://letslookagain.com/tag/stead-simpson-history/.

24 'Olivia', *Olivia's Shopping and How She Does It: A Prejudiced Guide to the London Shops*, p. 53.

25 Morrison, *English Shops and Shopping: An Architectural History*, p. 80.

26 Adburgham, Alison, *Shopping in Style: London from the Restoration to Edwardian Elegance* (London, Thames & Hudson, 1979), p. 100.

27 Assael, Brenda, *The London Restaurant, 1840–1914* (Oxford, OUP, 2018), pp. 189–90.

28 Pascoe, Charles Eyre, *London of Today: an Illustrated Handbook for the Season* (Boston, Roberts, 1890).

29 Assael, *The London Restaurant, 1840–1914*, p. 194.

30 Anon, 'Lunch with the Linen-Drapers', *The Graphic*, 3 August 1872, pp. 98–9.

31 Burnett, *England Eats Out: A Social History of Eating Out in England from 1830 to the Present*, p. 125.

32 ibid., p. 150.

33 Penner, Barbara, 'A World of Unmentionable Suffering: Women's Public Conveniences in Victorian London', *Journal of Design History*, 14(1) (2001), pp. 35–51, 39.

34 Rappaport, Erika, *Shopping for Pleasure: Women in the Making of London's West End* (Princeton, PUP, 2000); Pearson, *Street Furniture*.

35 For example R. G. Hickling's advert in the *Eastern Daily Press*, 13 February 1888, p. 7.

36 Jeffreys, *Retail Trading in Britain, 1850–1950*, p. 417.

37 Morrison, *English Shops and Shopping: An Architectural History*, p. 68.

38 Since restored. http://www.racns.co.uk/public. asp?action=getsurvey&id=286.

39 Morrison, Kathryn, 'A spotter's guide to the high street: jewellers' clocks & time balls' (2017), via https://buildingourpast.com/2017/08/01/ a-spotters-guide-to-the-high-street-jewellers-clocks-time-balls/.

40 Jeffreys, *Retail Trading in Britain, 1850–1950*, p. 416; Morrison, Kathryn, 'The Story of H. Samuel: "Britain's Largest Jeweller" (2017), via https:// buildingourpast.com/2017/05/10/the-story-of-h-samuel-britains-largest-jeweller/.

41 Burnett, John, *Plenty and Want: A Social History of Diet in England from 1815 to the Present Day* (London, Nelson, 1989), p. 111; G. S. Layard, 'Family

Budgets, II – a lower middle-class budget', *The Cornhill Magazine*, 10 (59) (1901), pp. 656–66.

42 Jeune, 'The Ethics of Shopping', pp. 123–32.

43 Winstanley, Michael, *The Shopkeeper's World*, p. 127.

44 MacQueen-Pope, Walter, *Twenty Shillings in the Pound* (London, Hutchinson, 1949).

45 Morrison, *English Shops and Shopping: An Architectural History*, p. 81.

46 'Piccadilly, South Side', in *Survey of London: Volumes 29 and 30, St James Westminster, Part 1*, ed. F. H. W. Sheppard (London, 1960), pp. 251–70. British History Online http://www.british-history.ac.uk/survey-london/vols29-30/pt1/pp251-270 [accessed 10 November 2022].

47 Winstanley, *The Shopkeeper's World*, p. 132.

48 MacQueen-Pope, *Twenty Shillings in the Pound*, p. 219.

49 Winstanley, *The Shopkeeper's World*, p. 130.

50 Leonard, A., *The History of Misselbrook & Weston 1848–1997* (Salisbury, Brookton, 2001).

51 See Kathryn Morrison's Building Our Past blog, which includes spotter's guides to all of these and more.

52 Jeffreys, *Retail Trading in Britain, 1850–1950*, p. 139; Kathryn Morrison, '"Shop-Coolness and Counter-Cleanliness": The Legacy of the Maypole Dairy Co' (2016), at https://buildingourpast.com/2016/03/25/shop-coolness-and-counter-cleanliness-the-legacy-of-the-maypole-dairy-co/.

53 Information from the website of the Sainsbury Archive at https://www.sainsburyarchive.org.uk/timeline/152.

54 https://www.sainsburyarchive.org.uk/timeline/150, accessed July 2020.

55 Arthur, Max, *Lost Voices of the Edwardians* (London, HarperCollins, 2006), pp. 191–2.

56 Winstanley, *The Shopkeeper's World 1830–1914*, p. 135.

57 Horn, *Behind the Counter: Shop Lives from Market Stall to Supermarket*, pp. 114–15.

58 *Glasgow Evening Citizen*, 14 December 1881.

59 Cox and Hobley, *Shopgirls: True Stories of Friendship, Hardship and Triumph from Behind the Counter*, p. 142.

60 Davis, *A History of Shopping*, p. 282.

61 Horn, *Behind the Counter: Shop Lives from Market Stall to Supermarket*, pp. 93–7.

62 Hosgood, Christopher, 'A "Brave and Daring Folk"? Shopkeepers and Trade Associational Life in Victorian and Edwardian England', *Journal of Social History*, 26(2) (1992), pp. 285–308; Horn, *Behind the Counter: Shop Lives from Market Stall to Supermarket*, p. 115.

63 'Olivia', *Olivia's Shopping and How She Does It: A Prejudiced Guide to the London Shops*, p. 66.

64 Wells, H. G., *Tono-Bungay* (1909, Book 1, chapter 3 (no page number), this edition https://www.gutenberg.org/files/718/718-h/718-h.htm.

65 Burnett, *England Eats Out: A Social History of Eating Out in England from 1830 to the Present*, p. 123.

66 ibid., p. 157.

67 Pettigrew, Jane, *A Social History of Tea* (London, National Trust, 2001), pp. 134–5.

68 Rappaport, *Shopping for Pleasure: Women in the Making of London's West End*, p. 215.

69 Adburgham, *Shopping in Style: London from the Restoration to Edwardian Elegance*, p. 116; 'The Harding Family' at https://www.bellhouse.co.uk/harding-family.

70 Briggs, Asa, *Friends of the People: The Centenary History of Lewis's* (London, Batsford, 1956), p. 86.

71 Hughes, Mary, *A London Child of the 1870s* (Oxford, OUP, 1977), p. 21.

72 Morrison, *English Shops and Shopping: An Architectural History*, p.137.

73 'Another American Invasion', *St Andrews Citizen*, 20 March 1909, p. 3 (syndicated, so also in others).

74 'Is the Shopwalker Doomed?', *Oxford Chronicle and Reading Gazette*, 26 March 1909, p. 4.

75 Nava, Mica, *Visceral Cosmopolitanism: Gender, Culture and the Normalisation of Difference* (London, Bloomsbury, 2007), p. 50.

76 Morrison, *English Shops and Shopping: An Architectural History*, p. 139; Briggs, *Friends of the People: The Centenary History of Lewis's*, pp. 71, 86.

77 Lancaster, Bill, *The Department Store: A Social History* (Leicester, Leicester University Press, 1995), pp. 48–9.

78 Costello, Peter and Farmar, Tony, *The Very Heart of the City: The Story of Denis Guiney and Clerys* (Dublin, A&A Farmar, 1992), p. 28.

79 Horn, *Behind the Counter: Shop Lives from Market Stall to Supermarket*, p. 150.

80 Shapiro Saunders, Lise, *Consuming Fantasies: Labor, Leisure and The London Shopgirl, 1880–1920* (Columbus, Ohio State University Press, 2006), p. 28.

81 Will Anderson, 'The Counter Exposed' (1895), cited in Horn, *Behind the Counter: Shop Lives from Market Stall to Supermarket*, p. 142.

82 Shapiro Saunders, *Consuming Fantasies: Labor, Leisure and The London Shopgirl, 1880–1920*, p. 45.

83 ibid., pp. 98–110.

84 Cox and Hobley, *Shopgirls: True Stories of Friendship, Hardship and Triumph from Behind the Counter*, p. 47.

85 Anon, 'Straws in the Wind', *Lynn News & County Press*, 9 May 1933.

86 Letter from 'The Tyke', *Lynn News & County Press*, 10 January 1933.

87 The 'huge pile' is from their advert in 1910. See https://kingslynn-history.uk/shops/no-95/.

88 King's Lynn Archive KL/SE/2/2/2 #73-4, letter dated 11 April 1929.

89 This section draws upon material kindly provided by King's Lynn Archive, especially documents in KL/TC/10/2/12/1 (Electoral Register, 1925), KL/SE/2/2/2 (building control plans), KL/SE/2/2/1 (Jermyn's plans) and KL/TC/11/1 (slum clearance files). The website King's Lynn – High Street History, run by Martin Scott, is a fantastic resource and can be accessed at https://kingslynn-history.uk/. See also Booth, Bob, *King's Lynn: An Illustrated Street Directory, 1933* (King's Lynn, Tricky Sam, 2013).

Chapter Six

1 Stevenson, D. E. (Dorothy Emily), *Miss Buncle's Book* (London, 1934, this edition Persephone Books, 2009), p. 161.

2 https://www.statista.com/statistics/1208625/first-world-war-fatalities-per-country/.

3 Cox and Hobley, *Shopgirls: True Stories of Friendship, Hardship and Triumph from Behind the Counter,* p. 143.

4 Horn, *Behind the Counter: Shop Lives from Market Stall to Supermarket,* p. 228.

5 Cox and Hobley, *Shopgirls: True Stories of Friendship, Hardship and Triumph from Behind the Counter,* p. 149.

6 Horn, *Behind the Counter: Shop Lives from Market Stall to* Supermarket, p. 230.

7 ibid., p. 229.

8 These can be found under the heading 'The Passing of the Grocer', in *The Times,* 18 August 1902, p. 13; 21 August 1903, p. 9; and 29 August 1902, p. 6.

9 Winstanley, *The Shopkeeper's World,* p. 39.

10 ibid., p. 121.

11 Bentall, Rowan, *My Store of Memories* (London, W. H. Allen, 1974), pp. 67-71.

12 '1958: our first supermarket', at https://www.tescoplc.com/about/our-history/, accessed March 2023.

13 Winstanley, *The Shopkeeper's World,* p. 41; Cox and Hobley, *Shopgirls: True Stories of Friendship, Hardship and Triumph from Behind the Counter,* p. 233.

14 Jeffreys, *Retail Trading in Britain, 1850–1950,* pp. 62-5.

15 Davis, *A History of Shopping,* p. 277.

16 ibid., p. 277.

17 Front elevation of Hepworths, in King's Lynn Archive, KL/SE/2/2/2/569.

18 Richards, James Maude and Ravilious, Eric, *High Street* (Country Life, 1938; this facsimile Thames & Hudson, 2022), p. 8.

19 Morrison, *English Shops and Shopping: An Architectural History*, p. 230.

20 It is no longer a Boots, but keen shop nerds might like to know that it is two doors away from the ex-Burton's (on the corner with Market Street). In Lynn Boots has also moved, but the shopfront remains. (Here the ex-Burton's is about eight doors away, on the corner of Purfleet Street.)

21 Bowlby, *Carried Away: The Invention of Modern Shopping*, p. 43.

22 Alexander, Andrew, Shaw, Gareth and Hodson, Deborah, 'Regional variations in the development of multiple retailing in England, 1890–1939', in John Benson and Laura Ugolini (eds.), *A Nation of Shopkeepers: Five Centuries of British Retailing* (London, Tauris, 2003), pp. 127–54, 142.

23 Hammond, A. Edward, *Multiple Shop Organisation* (London, Pitman, 1930), p. v.

24 Peel, Derek, *A Garden in the Sky: The Story of Barkers of Kensington, 1870–1957* (London, W. H. Allen, 1960), p. 80.

25 Alexander, Andrew, Benson, John and Shaw, Gareth, 'Action and reaction: competition and the multiple retailer in 1930s Britain', *International Review of Retail, Distribution and Consumer Research*, 9(3) (1999), pp. 245–59, 248.

26 Diarist 5431 (Yvonne Stukey), diary for 29 November, Mass Observation Archive, University of Sussex Special Collections.

27 Bridgland, Albert Stanford, *The Modern Tailor, Outfitter & Clothier, Vol. II* (London, Caxton, 1928), p. 137.

28 Beeching, Charles Lemuel Thomas, *The Modern Grocer & Provision Dealer, Vol II* (London, Caxton, c.1920), p. 212.

29 Kirkland, John, *The Modern Baker, Confectioner and Caterer, Vol. III* (London, Gresham, 1924), p. 258.

30 ibid., pp. 269, 248.

31 ibid., p. 261.

32 ibid., p. 264.

33 *Derby Daily Telegraph*, 24 April 1930, p. 4.

34 Newmains & Cambusnethan Co-op advert, in the *The Wishaw Press*, 3 February 1939, p. 8.

35 Bowlby, *Carried Away: The Invention of Modern Shopping*, p. 114.

36 Hey, Kathleen, Malcomson, Patricia and Malcomson, Robert, *The View From the Corner Shop: The Diary of a Yorkshire Shop Assistant in Wartime* (2016), 142 (4 April 1942); 146 (16 April 1942).

37 Cox and Hobley, *Shopgirls: True Stories of Friendship, Hardship and Triumph from Behind the Counter*, p. 185.

38 Horn, *Behind the Counter: Shop Lives from Market Stall to Supermarket*, p. 264.

39 ibid., p. 269.

40 Cox and Hobley, *Shopgirls: True Stories of Friendship, Hardship and Triumph from Behind the Counter*, p. 191.

41 The origins and meanings of pharmacy symbols, at https://wellcomecollection.org/articles/We9Wqx4AAA5amD91, accessed March 2023.

42 Hunt, John, 'Pharmacy in the modern world, 1841–1886', in Stuart Anderson, *Making Medicines: A Brief History of Pharmacy and Pharmaceuticals* (London, Pharmaceutical Press, 2005), pp. 77–93, 88.

43 Homan, Peter, 'The development of community pharmacy', in Anderson, *Making Medicines: A Brief History of Pharmacy and Pharmaceuticals*, pp. 115–34.

44 Chapman, Stanley, *Jesse Boot of Boots the Chemist: A Study in Business History* (London, Hodder & Stoughton, 1974), p. 95.

45 Shields, E. H., 'Pharmacy in Britain from 1859', *The Chemist and Druggist*, Centenary Edition, November 1959, pp. 171–80.

46 Jones, Claire, 'Under the Covers? Commerce, Contraceptives and Consumers in England and Wales, 1880-1960', *Social History of Medicine*, 29(4) (2016), pp. 734–56.

47 Stobart, Jon, 'Cathedrals of Consumption? Provincial Department Stores in England, c.1880-1930', *Enterprise & Society*, 18(4) (2017), pp. 810–45; the Wells quote is from Mr Polly, cited in ibid., p. 813.

48 Peel, *A Garden in the Sky: The Story of Barkers of Kensington, 1870–1957*, p. 27.

49 Survey of London, 'Shopping in Style – D. H. Evans in 1937' (2016), at https://blogs.ucl.ac.uk/survey-of-london/2016/03/, accessed January 2023.

50 *Hendon & Finchley Times*, 2 December 1932, p. 23; *Daily Mirror*, 23 March 1936, p. 28.

51 Morrison, *English Shops and Shopping: An Architectural History*, p. 180.

52 Lancaster, *The Department Store: A Social History*, p. 182.

53 Bentall, *My Store of Memories*, p. 165.

54 ibid., p. 166, and 'Bentalls Summer Fair' in the *Dorking & Leatherhead Advertiser*, 18 August 1939, p. 4.

55 Peel, *A Garden in the Sky: The Story of Barkers of Kensington, 1870–1957*, p. 154.

56 Roberts, Cheryl, *Consuming Mass Fashion in 1930s England: Design, Manufacture and Retailing for Young Working-Class Women* (Basingstoke, Palgrave Macmillan, 2022), p. 247.

57 Ugolini, Laura, 'Ready-to-wear or Made-to-measure? Consumer Choice in the British Menswear Trade, 1900–1939', *Textile History*, 34(2) (2003), pp. 192–213, 201.

58 ibid., p. 199.

59 Bridgland, *The Modern Tailor, Outfitter & Clothier, Vol. II*, p. 123.

60 ibid., p. 112.

61 Honeyman, Katrina, *Well-Suited: A History of the Leeds Clothing Industry, 1850–1990* (Oxford, OUP, 2000); Ugolini, 'Ready-to-wear or Made-to-measure? Consumer Choice in the British Menswear Trade, 1900–1939', pp. 192–213, 204.

62 Kershen, Anne (ed.), *Off the Peg* (London, The London Museum of Jewish Life, 1988), p. 34.

63 Honeyman, *Well-Suited: A History of the Leeds Clothing Industry, 1850–1990*, p. 53.

64 Morrison, Kathryn, 'The Fifty Shilling Tailors and John Collier' (2022), at https://buildingourpast.com/2022/04/12/the-fifty-shilling-tailor-and-john-collier/, accessed Feb 2023.

65 Bridgland, *The Modern Tailor, Outfitter & Clothier, Vol. II*, p. 124.

66 Morrison, Kathryn, 'Burton's "Modern Temples of Commerce"' (2017), at https://buildingourpast.com/2017/01/28/burtons-modern-temples-of-commerce/, accessed Dec 2022; Stobart, *Spend! Spend! Spend! A History of Shopping*, pp. 156–9; Alexander, Andrew, 'Burton, Sir Montague Maurice', *ODNB* (2004), accessed September 2023.

67 Morrison, *English Shops and Shopping: An Architectural History*, p. 196; Baren, Maurice, *Up the High Street: How it All Began* (London, Michael O'Mara for Past Times, 1996), p. 80.

68 Roberts, *Consuming Mass Fashion in 1930s England: Design, Manufacture and Retailing for Young Working-Class Women*, p. 261.

69 ibid., p. 217.

70 Beatties advert, in *The Staffordshire Advertiser*, 17 February 1934, p. 10.

71 Gardiner, Marjorie, *The Other Side of the Counter: The Life of a Shop Girl, 1925–1945* (Brighton, Queenspark, 1985), p. 5.

72 ibid., p. 14.

73 Roberts, *Consuming Mass Fashion in 1930s England: Design, Manufacture and Retailing for Young Working-Class Women*, p. 230.

74 Kershen (ed.), *Off the Peg*, p. 8.

75 Stevenson, *Miss Buncle's Book*, pp. 157–62.

76 Corina, Maurice, *Fine Silks and Oak Counters: Debenhams 1778–1978* (London, Hutchinson Benham, 1978), p. 132.

77 Lomas, Clare, '"Men Don't Wear Velvet You Know!" Fashionable Gay Masculinity and the Shopping Experience, London, 1950–Early 1970s', *Oral History*, 35(1) (2007), pp. 82–90.

78 Bide, Bethan, 'Be My Baby: Sensory Difference and Youth Identity in British Fashion Retail, 1945–1970', in Serena Dyer, *Shopping and the Senses, 1800–1970: A Sensory History of Retail and Consumption* (London, Palgrave Macmillan, 2022).

79 Pimlott, Mark, 'The boutique and the mass market', in David Vernet and Leontine de Wit, *Boutiques and Other Retail Spaces: The Architecture of Seduction* (London, Routledge, 2007), pp. 1–15.

80 Sedacca, Matthew, 'The Rise and Fall of the Milk Bar' at https://www.myrecipes.com/extracrispy/the-rise-and-fall-of-the-milk-bar (2018), accessed Mar 2023; 'Ideal Home Opens', *Belfast Telegraph*, 4 September 1957, p.6.

81 *Diss Express*, 24 August 1951.

82 Horn, Adrian, *Juke Box Britain: Americanisation and Youth Culture, 1945–1960* (Manchester, MUP, 2009), p. 176.

83 *Belfast Telegraph*, 14 September 1959, p. 5.

84 *Kington Times*, 2 October 1953, p. 5.

85 Burnett, *England Eats Out: A Social History of Eating Out in England from 1830 to the Present*, p. 218.

86 Horn, *Juke Box Britain: Americanisation and Youth Culture, 1945–1960*, p. 178.

87 *Arbroath Guide*, 17 May 1958, p. 4.

88 Jeffreys, *Retail Trading in Britain, 1850–1950*, p. 149.

89 Morrison, Kathryn, *Woolworth's: 125 Years on the High Street* (Swindon, Historic England, 2015), p. 13; Morrison, Kathryn, 'British Home Stores part 1: 1928–1930', at https://buildingourpast.com/2016/04/10/british-home-stores-part-1-1928-39/ (2016), accessed March 2023.

90 Roberts, *Consuming Mass Fashion in 1930s England: Design, Manufacture and Retailing for Young Working-Class Women*, p. 257.

91 Morrison, *Woolworth's: 125 Years on the High Street*, p. 64.

92 Shute, Nevil, *Ruined City* (London, Pan, 1965, first published 1938), p. 65.

93 See, for example, the *Western Daily Press*, 3 May 1932, p. 5.

94 Morrison, *Woolworth's: 125 Years on the High Street*, p. 110.

95 *Derby Daily Telegraph*, cited in ibid., p. 22.

96 ibid., p. 23.

97 Bowlby, *Carried Away: The Invention of Modern Shopping*, p. 191.

98 Morrison, *Woolworth's: 125 Years on the High Street*, p. 112.

99 Alexander, Benson and Shaw, 'Action and reaction: competition and the multiple retailer in 1930s Britain', pp. 245–59, 257.

100 Morrison, Kathryn, 'The Centenary of Britain's First Self-Service Store', at https://buildingourpast.com/2023/01/09/the-centenary-of-britains-first-self-service-grocery-shop/ (2023), accessed February 2023.

101 Bentall, *My Store of Memories*, p. 152. For a good debunking of a bit of self-service mythology see Morrison, Kathryn, 'Debunking "Britain's first supermarket": the myth of Manor Park' (2023), at https://buildingourpast.com/2023/01/16/debunking-britains-first-supermarket-the-myth-of-manor-park/.

102 Morrison, *Woolworth's: 125 Years on the High Street*, p. 145.

103 Christie, Agatha, *The Mirror Crack'd From Side to Side* (London, HarperCollins, 2010, first published 1962), p. 4.

104 Horn, *Behind the Counter: Shop Lives from Market Stall to Supermarket*, p. 294.

105 Hamacher, Adriana, 'The unpopular rise of self-checkouts (and how to fix them)', at https://www.bbc.com/future/article/20170509-the-unpopular-rise-of-self-checkouts-and-how-to-fix-them (2017); Houlton, Cara, 'Supermarket jobs take a hit amid rise of self-checkout', at https://www.grocerygazette.co.uk/2023/10/30/supermarket-jobs-self-checkout/ (2023)(both accessed November 2023).

106 This section draws upon Antram, Nicholas and Morrice, Richard, *Brighton and Hove (Pevsner Architectural Guides)* (New Haven & London, Yale University Press, 2008); *Kelly's Directory of Brighton, Hove & Neighbourhood* (London, Kelly's, 1971); Collis, Rose, *The New Encyclopedia of Brighton* (Brighton, Brighton & Hove Libraries, 2010); plus the excellent resources at the My Brighton and Hove website (https://www.mybrightonandhove.org.uk/category/places/placestree/westernroad), and Simon Carey's detailed research on Western Road (2016), available via Geograph at https://www.geograph.org.uk/photo/4883862. Additional information from the Waitrose Memory Store (https://waitrosememorystore.org.uk/content/branches-3/branches-a-b/brighton-114/waitrose-brighton) and Sainsbury Archive (https://www.sainsburyarchive.org.uk/catalogue/search/branch/ref/p977-brighton-1416-churchill-square-1969-1988-sainsburys-branch/view_as/list). Photographs of numbers 1–28 prior to demolition may be found at the James Gray Collection, online at http://regencysociety-jamesgray.com/volume19/index10.html.

107 Cook, Matt, 'Queer Scenes in 1960s Manchester, Plymouth, and Brighton', *Journal of British Studies*, 59 (2020), pp. 32–56, 54.

108 Antram and Morrice, *Brighton and Hove (Pevsner Architectural Guides)*, p. 102.
109 Davies, Gareth, 'How Brighton's Churchill Square made the news' (2013), at https://www.theargus.co.uk/news/10752549.how-brightons-churchill-square-has-made-the-news/.

Chapter Seven

 1 Burns, Wilfred, *British Shopping Centres* (1959), cited in Bowlby, *Carried Away: The Invention of Modern Shopping*, p. 224.
 2 UK population trends based on World Bank statistics and definitions, at https://www.macrotrends.net/countries/GBR/united-kingdom/population.
 3 See https://theoceancleanup.com/.
 4 Mintel, Fashion and Sustainability Report (executive summary) (2023), p. 3.
 5 Woods, Hannah Rose, *Rule Nostalgia: a Backwards History of Britain* (London, W. H. Allen, 2022), p. 75.
 6 ibid., p. 76.
 7 Morrison, *English Shops and Shopping: An Architectural History*, p. 260.
 8 Horn, *Behind the Counter: Shop Lives from Market Stall to Supermarket*, p. 293.
 9 The Sainsbury Archive – timeline, via https://www.sainsburyarchive.org.uk/timeline/over-150, accessed 2022.
10 Premier Supermarkets, *Time for Leisure* (film, 1957), accessed via the Yorkshire Film Archive at https://www.yfanefa.com/record/19427.
11 Wilkinson, *The High Street: 100 Years of British Life through the Shop Window*, p. 231.
12 Rayner, Jay, *A Greedy Man in a Hungry World* (London, William Collins, 2013), p. 18.
13 Gallup Shopping Basket (London, Gallup, 1968, in conjunction with the association of point of sale advertising).
14 Hardyment, Christina, *Slice of Life: The British Way of Eating since 1945* (London, BBC Books, 1995), p. 44; Gwynn, Mary, *Back in Time for Dinner* (London, Bantam Press, 2015), p. 66.
15 Steel, *Hungry City*, p. 112.
16 Seth, Andrew and Randall, Geoffrey, *The Grocers: The Rise and Rise of Supermarket Chains* (London, Kogan Page, 2011), p. 80.
17 Steel, *Hungry City*, p. 113.

18 Burnett, *Plenty and Want: A Social History of Diet in England from 1815 to the Present Day*, p. 302; DEFRA, Family Food 2019/20 (2022), via https://www.gov.uk/government/statistics/family-food-201920/family-food-201920.

19 Rayner, *A Greedy Man in a Hungry World*, p. 18.

20 Simms, Andrew, Kjell, Petra and Potts, Ruth, *Clone Town Britain* (London, New Economics Foundation, 2005), p. 6.

21 Steel, *Hungry City*, p. 138.

22 Morrison, *English Shops and Shopping: An Architectural History*, pp. 256–7.

23 'Vos', contributor to discussion on Churchill Square (2013), via https://www.mybrightonandhove.org.uk/places/placeshop/churchill-square/churchill-square-8, accessed 2022.

24 Wilkinson, *The High Street: 100 Years of British Life through the Shop Window*, p. 240.

25 Morrison, *English Shops and Shopping: An Architectural History*, p. 262.

26 Gosseye, Janina, 'Milton Keynes' Centre: the apotheosis of the British post-war consensus or the apostle of neo-liberalism?', *History of Retailing and Consumption*, 1:3 (2015), pp. 209–29, 213.

27 Armstrong, Martin, 'The erosion of UK pub culture' (2022), at Statista.com.

28 On The Day, 28 August 1994 at http://news.bbc.co.uk/onthisday/hi/dates/stories/august/28/newsid_2536000/2536115.stm; 'Pubs enjoy taste of all day Sunday opening' (1995), *The Independent* via https://www.independent.co.uk/news/pubs-enjoy-taste-of-allday-sunday-opening-leaves-pubs-1595141.html.

29 Simms, Kjell and Potts, *Clone Town Britain*.

30 Iqbal, Nosheen, 'Don't save the high street – change it completely, says retail guru Mary Portas': *Guardian*, 6 December 2020, via https://www.theguardian.com/business/2020/dec/06/dont-save-the-high-street-change-it-completely-says-retail-guru-mary-portas.

31 Hill, Abigail, *The Vibrancy and Resilience of British High Streets* (London, UCL, 2022), p. 33; Allies & Morrison Urban Practitioners, *The Changing Face of the High Street: Decline and Revival* (Swindon, Historic England, 2015), p. 15.

32 Portas, Mary, *The Portas Review* (London, 2011, commissioned by DEFRA); Timpson, John and the high street experts panel, *The High Street Report* (2021). Both accessible via https://www.highstreetstaskforce.org.uk/resources/?q=&category=.

33 C&A left Britain but thrived elsewhere. By 2020 it had over 1,400 stores across Europe.

34 PwC, 'Store Openings and Closures: H1 2019', https://www.pwc.co.uk/industries/retail-consumer/insights/store-openings-and-closures-h1-2019.html.

35 ONS, 'How our spending has changed since the end of coronavirus (COVID-19) restrictions' (2022), via www.ons.gov.uk/businessindustryandtrade/retailindustry.

36 Gosling, George and Brewis, Georgina, 'What can we learn from the history of charity and charity shops' (2020), British Academy blog, available at https://www.thebritishacademy.ac.uk/blog/what-can-we-learn-history-charity-shops/.

37 Portas, *The Portas Review*, p. 26.

38 Some do sell new goods, which is more of an issue, though they risk losing the rate relief if the proportion gets too high. See https://squidex.mkmapps.com/api/assets/ipm/future-of-high-street-debate-pack.pdf for more on this.

Conclusion

1 Timpson, *The High Street Report*, p. 3. Accessed via https://www.highstreetstaskforce.org.uk/resources where you can find lots of different contemporary reports on aspects of the high street and its regeneration.

2 Wood, Zoe, 'Indie bookshop numbers hit 10-year high in 2022 defying brutal UK retail year' (2023), https://www.theguardian.com/books/2023/jan/06/indie-bookshop-numbers-hit-10-year-high-in-2022-defying-brutal-uk-retail-year.

3 Retail Week: 'Vacancies rise as 6,000 UK stores close in five years' (2023) at https://www.retail-week.com/stores/vacancies-rise-as-6000-uk-stores-close-in-five-years/7044261.article.

4 Cox and Hobley, *Shopgirls: True Stories of Friendship, Hardship and Triumph from Behind the Counter*, p. 233, and see https://www.retailgazette.co.uk/blog/2022/01/the-number-of-high-street-shops-rise-despite-covid-lockdowns-last-year for 2022 figures.

5 'UK the changing face of the high street report 2022', at https://store.mintel.com/report/uk-changing-face-of-the-high-street-market-report

6 Falsea, John, *Barnitts – through the years. The one about the shop in York* (Little Gem, 2019).

7 Ransome, Arthur, *Coot Club* (London, Puffin, 1973, originally published 1934), p. 271; Ye Olde Ducking Stool Shoppe, advert in the *Kingston Times*, 2 October 1953, p. 5.

8　Derby is the poster-child for heritage-led regeneration (though many of the carefully restored shops on The Wardwick are currently empty). Elsewhere the approach hasn't been as successful. See Hubbard, *The Battle for the High Street: Retail Gentrification, Class and Disgust* for the counter-argument.

9　Nerd alert! If you get really into it, head to the National Heritage List for England at https://historicengland.org.uk/listing/the-list/ and lose a few happy hours.

List of Illustrations

Colour plates

1 *An Eating House* by Thomas Rowlandson, *c*.1815 © SJArt / Alamy Stock Photo
2 Pellatt & Green, 1809 © Heritage Image Partnership Ltd / Alamy Stock Photo
3 *Sandwich-carrots* by James Gillray, 1796 © RKive / Alamy Stock Photo
4 *Black Charley of Norwich* by John Dempsey, 1823 via Tasmanian Museum and Art Gallery
5 John Burgess's Italian Warehouse, *c*.1830 © Westminster Archives/ Bridgeman Images
6 The Royal Bazaar, *c*.1828. Courtesy of Westminster City Archives
7 St John's Market, *c*.1822. Courtesy National Museums Liverpool, Walker Art Gallery
8 Colwyn Bay tinned good receipt © Amoret Tanner / Alamy Stock Photo
9 The Gainsborough advert, 1911 © Amoret Tanner / Alamy Stock Photo
10 Hepworths tailors, Kings Lynn, 1923. Courtesy of King's Lynn Borough Archive, KL/SE 2/2/2/569
11 John Williams & Sons Ltd interior © World History Archive / Alamy Stock Photo
12 Bettys fancy goods, courtesy of the Bettys and Taylors Group Archive
13 *Baker and Confectioner* by Eric Ravilious, 1938 © Bridgeman Images
14 Escalator halls at D.H. Evans, London © CCI Archives / Science Photo Library
15 Interior of Manchester Arndale Centre, *c*.1980 © Paul White 20th Century Britain / Alamy Stock Photo
16 Manchester Arndale Centre, from the Manchester School of Art Slide Library at Manchester Metropolitan University Special Collections Museum

List of Illustrations

Black-and-white illustrations

3.3 Bull in a china shop, 1808 © Heritage Image Partnership Ltd / Alamy Stock Photo

3.4 *Saloop seller* by Thomas Rowlandson, 1820 © Penta Springs Limited / Alamy Stock Photo

3.5 Todd's Warehouse, York. Courtesy of York Museums Trust/ Public Domain

3.6 *The Library* by Thomas Rowlandson © Penta Springs Limited / Alamy Stock Photo

3.7 *Billing and Cooing at the Jelly Shop*, 1798 © The Trustees of the British Museum. All rights reserved

3.8 *The Confectioner*, 1818 © Science Museum/SSPL/Getty Images

3.9 Birch's confectioner, London © DigitalVision Vectors/ Getty Images

Chapter Four

4.1 *Northgate, Chester* by Thomas Picken, *c.*1840. Courtesy Steve Howe

4.2 *London poor at Christmas*, 1872 © DigitalVision Vectors /Getty Images

4.3 *The Poulterer* by Francis Donkin Bedford, 1899 © Historica Graphica Collection/Heritage Images/Getty Images

4.4 *The Drunkard's Children* by George Cruishank, 1848 © WBC ART / Alamy Stock Photo

4.5 Chamberlins, Norwich, 1869. Courtesy of Project Gutenberg

4.6 Postcard of Briggate, 1904 in public domain

Chapter Five

5.1 The Royal Arcade, Norwich, 1978 courtesy of Newsquest

5.2 The Royal Arcade interior courtesy of Newsquest/Archant Archive

5.3 Receipt from J. Neal, London in 1876 © SSPL/Getty Images

5.4 Jones & Davis of Church Street, Malvern © Amoret Tanner / Alamy Stock Photo

5.5 ABC tearooms, London © Mary Evans Picture Library

5.6 Lyons in Brighton, *c.*1910 © Royal Pavilion & Museums, Brighton & Hove

5.7 Bon Marché, Brixton and reproduced produced by kind permission of London Borough of Lambeth, Archives Department

5.8 Whiteleys, Bayswater in 1961 © Edwin Smith / RIBA Collections

5.9 Umbrella department in Selfridges, London © Chronicle / Alamy Stock Photo

5.10 Clery & Co, Dublin, *c.*1885 courtesy of the British Library's Flickr Collection

5.11 Derry & Toms tea rooms, Kensington, London in 1893 via Historic England Archive

List of Illustrations

Acknowledgements

A book like this is never a solo activity. I've had a lot of research support from archivists and academics, and I'd like to thank: Julie-Anne Lambert at the Bodleian Library; Megan McCooley from the Yorkshire and North East Film Archive; Amy Frost from No 1 Royal Crescent in Bath and Anne Buchanan at the Bath Record Office; Luke Shackell from King's Lynn Archives; the staff of York Archives and the Map Room at the Cambridge University Library; Gavin Henderson of the John Lewis Partnership Heritage Centre; and the archivists of Norfolk Record Office and Leeds Local and Family History centre.

I'd also like to thank Kate Giles, Louise Hampson, Matthew Jenkins and the rest of the StreetLife York team for sitting down with me to go through Coney Street's history, and Richard Pollitt for filling in gaps related to Mansion House. Alex Hutchinson provided a lot of good information on topics as diverse as temperance and twentieth-century confectionery, while Ian Chipperfield and Serena Dyer pointed me in the direction of dressmakers and staymakers. Andrew Hann of English Heritage was his usual tremendous self in sharing detail on the early modern high street, as well as market halls, Mardi Jacobs gave me access to the inner sanctum of the Bettys & Taylors archive, and I had a lovely couple of hours with Kathryn Morrison, whose work on the high street was the kicking-off point for this book (and remained key throughout). Esther Wilson interned with me and helped define the scope of the book in its early stages.

I've relied on friends and family to read drafts of the vignettes, and walk down the various high streets detailed in them, as well as sharing their own views and memories of the changing street. They've also propped me up when the part of me which hates shopping and crowds and rampant consumerism threatened to take over: Marion Howling, Laura Gale, Katharine and Rich Boardman-Hims, Richard and Jess Gray, Alex Hutchinson (again), Mardi Jacobs (also again, and I'm sorry I made you walk up and down in the rain for so long); Kathy Hipperson, Lucy Worsley, Adam Howling and Hannah Carty, and Rebecca Lane. Thank you especially to Regula Ysewijn for taking me round Antwerp's shopping streets so I could ponder the parallels (and for being more generally fab).

Many of those people I owe professional debts as well as personal ones, especially Rebecca Lane, who freely allowed me to pillage her bookshelves, and pointed me to the resources held by Historic England as part of the High Street Action Zone scheme. I don't think this book would exist without her (and Melin).

Research and writing is, of course, only one part of making a book, so I'd also like to thank my publishers, Profile Books, in particular Zara Sehr Ashraf for sterling work on pictures, and Rebecca Gray for commissioning and championing the book, as well as gently steering it into much better shape than was originally envisioned. My editor, Grace Pengelly, was instrumental in wrestling it into its final form. Thank you as well to Annie Lee, my copy-editor, for having an eye for detail which totally escapes me, and to Emily Frisella and all of the behind the scenes team who've worked to make it all really real. Thank you also to Sarah McMenemy for the beautiful illustrations. My agent, Tim Bates, has been as brilliant as usual, plying me with beer and wine and not laughing (much) when I waved my arms around and made him stop to look at buildings on a crowded New Oxford Street.

Finally, and as ever, my partner, Matt Howling, has been a sounding board, a reader, a personal chef, reliable tea bitch and a patient high street crawler at my side throughout the whole thing. Thank you so much.

Index

Index

Index

Brighton, Thomas 147
Bristol 301
  chocolate 67–8
  market 104, 158–9
British Home Stores (BHS) 300, 303, 312, 313, 337
British Museum 75
Broadbent's, Leeds 192
Brotherton, Jessie 191
Brown, Henry 148
Brydges, Egerton 130
Buchanan Street, Glasgow 277
Buck Inn, Leeds 193
bulk buying 16
bulks 63–4, *106*, 163
'bull in a china shop' 113, *114*
Bull, John 164
Bull Ring, Birmingham 330, *331*
bull-baiting 113
Bullen's 217
bullock hunting 113
Buntings 149–50
Burlington Arcade, London 204, 205
Burns, Wilfred 315
Burslem 104
Burtol's 251
Burton, Montague 250, 283, 285
Burton's 250, 262, 283–5, *284*, 294, 311, 334–5, 344
butchers 18, 19–20, 54, 104, 161–6, *165*, 247–8, 259, 328
Butler, Richard 76
butter sellers 13–14

C&A 286, 312, 337
C. & J. Clark 210
Cadena Cafés 267
Caesar Ward's bookshop 44
Café Royale, Leeds 191
cafés 195, 213, 215, 266–7, 276–80, 333–4
Cambridge 86
Canterbury 14
Carlyle, Jane 213
Carnaby Street, London 293

Cash Clothing Company 195
cash payment 5, 30, 69–70, 118, 164, 181, 239, 325
cash registers 239, 268–9
catalogues 124, 126, 130, 202–3, 335
caterers 142–3, 266
Catherine the Great 116
Ceylon Café, Leeds 195
chain stores 201, 212, 228, 260–4, 294, 306, 333, 337
  cocoa rooms 178
  see also individual stores
Chamberlin, Sons & Co 146–7
Chamberlins 144, 145, *186*
Chapter coffee house 82
Charing Cross, London 108
charity shops 338–9
Charles II, King 82
Chatham 160
Cheapside, London 19, *24*, 25, 38, 57
Chelsea Girl 294, 337
Cheltenham *186*
The Chemist and Druggist 274
chemists 95, 272–3
Chester 87, 104, 107, 115
Chester Rows 25, *155*
Chesterton, G. K. 238
children
  clothes 232, 247, 249, 278
  'Junior Miss' departments 278
  shoes 210
chillies 29, 67
china warehouse 109–18
chocolate 29, 65, 67–8, 109
chophouses 71–3, 213
Chorleywood process 270
Christie, Agatha 305–6
Christmas cheese 227
Church Street, Malvern *221*
Churchill, Clementine 228
Churchill Square, Brighton 313, 330
Churchill, Winston 228
churchyards 11–12
Clarendon, Earl of 82

Index

Index

Index